EMOTIONAL INTELLIGENCE FOR SCHOOL LEADERS

Janet Patti

Robin Stern

HARVARD EDUCATION PRESS

Cambridge, MA

Paperback ISBN 978-1-68253-864-7

Library of Congress Cataloging-in-Publication Data is on file.

Published by Harvard Education Press,
an imprint of the Harvard Education Publishing Group
Harvard Education Press
8 Story Street
Cambridge, MA 02138

Cover Design: Ciano Design
Cover Image: 10'000 Hours/DigitalVision via Getty Images

The typefaces in this book are Candide and Neue Haas Unica Pro.

Contents

Foreword

Daniel Goleman

Some years ago, I was intrigued by the results of a study done for the British Ministry of Education. Researchers from the Hay Group analyzed the impact of positive leadership styles by head teachers (as they call principals in Britain). Their analysis found that positive leadership predicted that students in those schools would have higher achievement test scores than those in comparable schools where the head teacher's leadership style was not so positive.

That finding, and similar ones from the business world, got me to pursue the notion that an emotionally intelligent leader sets the emotional tone of an organization, and that in turn drives the performance of people there, for better or worse. The concept of emotional intelligence (EI) was new at the time, having been proposed in 1990 in an article by Peter Salovey and his then–graduate student, John Mayer.

Over the decades since that article appeared, strong evidence has been building; my hunch was right. Companies around the world have embraced EI as essential for effective leadership. And more recently, as the basics of emotional intelligence have become a more widespread component of preK–16 education, we have learned the critical role that

EI plays in the development of school leaders' competencies and in its implementation and sustainability.

Both Janet and Robin were promoting EI-based leadership development early on. I met Janet at a Fetzer Institute meeting when we were finding solutions for bringing EI education into schools. That group we now know as CASEL, the Collaborative for Academic, Social, and Emotional Learning. At that time, Janet was an assistant principal who was implementing such programs in her California middle school. Later, she would coordinate the educational leadership university program at Hunter College, where she infused emotional intelligence into the curriculum. Now, a professor emeritus, she continues to grow the EI leadership-based training and coaching in her role as CEO of STAR Factor.

I met Robin through her work at the Woodhull Institute for Women, where she taught EI skills at retreats for upward-bound women. She was also working at Teachers College, Columbia University, running workshops to advance this kind of education, coaching teachers for the School at Columbia University, and teaching a course for the Summer Principals Academy. Later she went on to cofound the Yale Center for Emotional Intelligence, where she is now senior advisor to the director while continuing her private practice as a psychoanalyst. At the time, I was working in the corporate arena collecting research on how emotional intelligence improved a leader's performance.

Both Janet and Robin were passionate about how we were missing a critical group who needed to learn about emotional intelligence: school superintendents and principals. When I was in town, we occasionally met for coffee, sharing my latest discoveries and brainstorming how to bring this learning to aspiring and seasoned school administrators. Toward that end, we organized a speaking engagement at Hunter College that was well attended by school leaders from across New York City.

Janet and Robin became active members of the Consortium for Research in EI, which I started with Cary Cherniss. They created a coaching model based on the emotional intelligence competence inventory (the Emotional and Social Competence Inventory, or ESCI) developed jointly by the Hay Group (now part of Korn Ferry), Richard Boyatzis, and me. They named their coaching program the STAR Factor, based on findings that I often spoke about: those who became star performers surpassed average performers because they demonstrated emotional intelligence. STAR Factor soon became well known throughout New York City schools, where they have coached more than five hundred principals and superintendents to date. Each time we met, Janet and Robin talked about what they were finding in their work with school leaders. I told them that they needed to write a book about their work with school leaders—and here it is!

The book opens with an overview of the real world of school leadership: school leaders' dedication to service, the challenges they meet, and the impact that stressors have on their well-being. The chapters take us on a journey through the EI framework: self-awareness, self-management, social awareness, and relationship management, all necessary for successful leadership. The school leaders' stories throughout the chapters give us historical and factual accounts of their experiences. The final chapter puts it all together with a systems view of successful leaders who have embraced emotional intelligence in themselves and in the organizations they lead.

This book describes EI in action. It will broadly inform any school leaders looking to embrace EI in their leadership and the culture of their schools. I recommend Janet and Robin's advice to anyone who cares about the fate of our schools and our children.

Introduction

Our humanity is at stake. Our increasingly individualistic way of life has sadly moved us further away from connecting with others. Our social norms of caring for and honoring one another are too often replaced by greed, competition, and even hate. As humans, we thrive by being collaborative and socially connected with one another. Despite an archaic structure that often still prevails today, school is where young people come together. And in that one place, there are windows of opportunity for cultivating the human dimension. Schools have the opportunity to help students build and be their best selves, both to negotiate their growing-up years and also to prepare them to go out into the world and ultimately contribute to society—not only because of what they know but also because of who they have become.

Our dream over the past several decades has been that children's social, emotional, and academic development would be part of every US classroom. As we write this book, in the year 2023, this dream is becoming a reality. We recognize the importance of outstanding teachers in making this possible, but we know that while an outstanding teacher can ensure that an individual child learns, the principal leads the building of a school culture that promotes the learning of every student in the school. The principal's values, mindsets, and behaviors can determine the health of the school culture and the vibrancy of the climate in which learning takes place. An outstanding superintendent ensures that all principals are effectively encouraging everyone's cultural responsiveness and academic, social, and emotional development. We are not saying that doing so is easy; in fact, it can be hard. But when school leaders have the tools they need both in their preparation and on the job, their schools' teachers, children, and young people thrive.

This book tells the stories of what the real world is like inside schools for school leaders who are upskilling themselves by developing their proficiency with emotionally intelligent leadership. These principals understand that they must create their own pathways to resilience by working with their emotions. Principals lead the charge for teachers to develop their skills in emotional intelligence before they integrate social and emotional learning (SEL) into their teaching repertoire. We hope that this book will provide an avenue for school leaders to be inspired by the colleagues they meet on its pages. The more school leaders come on board, the greater the potential of impacting the course of humanity's future.

A BRIEF HISTORICAL CONTEXT

This book represents more than forty years of our combined research and practice in working with schools to help them build essential social and emotional skills and competencies. We recognized early on that bringing SEL into schools would require a different kind of leadership, one in which leaders embody self-awareness, social awareness, self-management, and relationship management. We recognized that skillful leaders who value well-being, self-care, and relationships in their own lives would be those whose school vision encourages adults and children to take responsibility for their affective development as well as their cognitive learning.

In the paragraphs that follow, each of us describes the personal and professional experiences that brought us together in our work and served as a backdrop for the writing of this book.

I (Janet) am a former teacher, school counselor, school administrator, and professor of educational leadership at Hunter College for more than forty years. I became interested in the emotional well-being of children in my early years as a preschool through eighth grade teacher. I began my teaching at Public School 171 in East Harlem and continued teaching in San Ysidro, California, where I worked as a bilingual elementary and middle school teacher and a bilingual coordinator of a Title 7 literacy program. My journey then took me to the north of San Diego County, where I was hired as one of two assistant principals at the Roosevelt Middle School. The school was composed of 1,700 students and more than one hundred staff members. It was located in a White middle-income neighborhood in Vista, California. Black and Brown students were bused to the school from downtown Vista. With the support of a friend and colleague, Linda Lantieri, and my fellow administrators, teachers, and student leaders, we successfully implemented the Resolving Conflict Creatively Program (RCCP), a before-its-time SEL program.

By year two we saw an amazing positive shift in the school's climate and eventually in the culture. When I had begun working at Roosevelt, two years earlier, I spent the bulk of my time disciplining and suspending young people. After two years of RCCP implementation, at most two or three students were sent to my office daily. Over the next few years, the work spread throughout the district, reaching twenty-eight thousand students.

My pursuit of a doctoral degree in educational leadership at Northern Arizona University sparked my love of school leadership, especially thinking about schools as systems. I completed my doctoral dissertation by studying RCCP's impact at four sites nationwide. I watched school leaders, teachers, and students totally engrossed in the lessons and ways of being that they were learning. At Roosevelt, as a result of this collaborative work with Linda and with Roosevelt's staff, I witnessed the improvement that happened in our students' behavior and the school's climate and watched as the common language of the peaceful resolution of conflict spread throughout the school district. All this work led to my coauthoring with Linda a book, titled *Waging Peace in Our Schools* (1994), in which we discussed what we had been learning about the implementation of what was then called conflict resolution and diversity work in schools and classrooms, which we now know as cultural responsiveness and academic, social, and emotional learning. The more I learned, the more passionate I became about the power of this work to successfully turn a school around so conflict is minimized and students of all backgrounds learn skills to collaborate with one another in a safe and caring environment. This learning led me to become a founding member of the leadership team of the Collaborative for Academic, Social, and Emotional Learning (CASEL), the leading organization in SEL research and practices.

A move back to New York City in 1997 brought me to Hunter College, where, as program coordinator and professor of the educational leadership program, I developed courses and taught aspiring school leaders about emotional intelligence in leadership—how to create climates and cultures that support school-based SEL. During those twenty-three years, I was fortunate to reach hundreds of bright future administrators, many of whom hold leadership positions today in New York City schools.

In 2006, with my colleague Jim Tobin, I copublished the revised edition of our book *Smart School Leaders: Leading with Emotional Intelligence*. This was one of the first books that taught school administrators about emotional intelligence. I continued to publish articles in journals throughout the years with like-minded colleagues.

Since then, as president of STAR Factor of NYC Inc., I continue to train and develop school leaders in emotional intelligence leadership. With

Robin Stern, I cofounded STAR Factor Coaching, a coaching approach for school leaders widely used in New York City.

In addition to my "day job" at the Yale Center for Emotional Intelligence, I (Robin) am a psychoanalyst trained in individual psychoanalysis and group psychotherapy and psychoanalysis; and have had a private practice in New York City for thirty years. I have always been interested in "how people work"—why they feel the way they do in a particular instance or interaction, how they make decisions, how their emotions impact their relationships—and what they can do about it. I studied psychology in college and pursued first a master's in personality and social development at the Graduate Faculty, New School for Social Research, and then a doctorate at New York University, with a focus on developing social intelligence, under the guidance of the late Philip Merrifield and intelligence researcher J. Theodore Repa, then the chair of the Educational Leadership Department—both friends and colleagues. My postdoctoral work at the Postgraduate Center for Mental Health at New York University focused on the "how-to" of individual and group work. As a practitioner in mental health, I knew that the challenges we face as "grown-ups" are rooted in childhood, and I also knew that insight alone was not enough to create the behavior change that most of my patients were seeking; education and skills were necessary, too. Thus, I began to look for practitioners working at the intersection of psychology and education.

In my personal life, my son and my daughter (now "launched" in their own lives!) were in their first years of school, and I wondered about the preparation their teachers had had. And just at that time in 1995, I read Dan Goleman's book *Emotional Intelligence* and thought, "This is it!" In his book, Dan talked about many existing programs that were not necessarily called SEL but were teaching the skills nonetheless, as well as some new and emerging SEL programs.

Shortly thereafter, I reached out to Dan and to colleagues who were mentioned in Dan's book, including Linda Lantieri, our dear friend, and Tom Roderick, pioneers in SEL work. I made my way to work with Jonathan Cohen at Columbia Continuing Education, and I became his associate director in a new collaborative on SEL that brought together leaders of these many programs each summer for a learning institute. That is where I met Janet.

Janet and I became fast friends and colleagues—like-minded in our positivity and belief in people, the power of emotions, and the power of leaders to move systems and influence teachers who impact students daily. I also began consulting at The School at Columbia University, an elementary school bringing together children of Columbia and neighborhood children to build a school community. I worked at The School as an emotional intelligence coach for faculty. I began directing more and more of my time and attention to education, and I taught a course in self-awareness, as founding faculty in the Summer Principals Academy at Teachers College. Janet also spent a few summers as guest faculty in my class.

In 2007, after listening to countless stories of relationship dysfunction in my work with educational leaders and stories of psychological abuse in my private practice, I wrote *The Gaslight Effect*. Gaslighting is sadly even more popular now; it is talked about regularly in the mainstream and, in fact, is the subject of my new book, *The Gaslight Effect Recovery Guide*—a practical tool for those struggling at home, at work, and in relationships with gaslighting dynamics.

One of the opportunities that came my way as faculty at Teachers College was a retreat at the Garrison Institute, where I met Marc Brackett. Marc's focus at that time was bringing his work first to the adults who touch children's lives: teachers, leaders, and parents. Marc's approach to bringing emotional intelligence to schools, RULER, included developing a nuanced emotion vocabulary and learning the discrete skills of emotional intelligence and the mindset that emotions matter. Meeting Marc opened an opportunity to pursue work with him that I felt, and still feel, called to do. I am currently the cofounder and associate director of the Yale Center for Emotional Intelligence.

Janet and I brought our work in developing leaders to the Yale Center for Emotional Intelligence—and, ultimately, Marc joined us in bringing the Yale-based SEL RULER approach to New York City. We led the school leaders' training and coaching, and Marc taught the science of emotions, the foundation of the RULER approach, in more than four hundred New York City schools.

To step back and trace our partnership, Janet and I recognized that our joint interest in creating professional development opportunities for educational leaders was anchored in emotional intelligence (EI), using Goleman's framework of self-awareness, self-management, social awareness, and relationship management. As a result of our collaboration as an educator and a psychoanalyst, we developed an individual and group coaching model for school leaders designed to provide them with a space to develop their own social and emotional skill sets. We consulted with an amazing cadre of former school leaders who helped us anchor this coaching model in the real world of school leadership. Realizing that leaders needed support for their well-being as well as positive development in EI competencies, we were committed to developing a model that would resonate with their needs and level of training, informed by the science of self-care and resilience, the framework of EI from Dan Goleman, the intentional change model of Richard Boyatzis, and the wisdom of experts in the field including Cary Cherniss, Maurice Elias, Linda Lantieri, Peter Senge, Marc Brackett, Lester Lenoff, and others. Our diverse backgrounds in psychology and education provided the foundation for our work. And the STAR Factor coaching model was born.

Today, cultural responsiveness and academic, social, and emotional learning are being integrated into the education of all New York City children. And many superintendents and more than five hundred principals have been coached in our model. We are humbled and gratified when school leaders tell us that our work is making a huge difference in their lives, both at home and at work. New knowledge and practices continually make their way to the school leader's door. None of these, we believe, will be as critical as the human skills that make leaders who they are and create the possibility of who they, and those whose lives they touch, can become.

We hope that this book will serve as a helpful tool for school superintendents, deputy superintendents, directors, school principals, assistant principals, aspiring school leaders, university faculties, and anyone who cares about schools today.

CHAPTER ONE

The Leader's Well-Being

We all have a story—a story about ourselves: What did our growing up years teach us? Who inspired us, challenged us? What influenced us, what values do we live by, whom do we care about? This story led us to be who we are. Over the course of a lifetime, we may tell that story differently—as if we were to follow a path that winds around a mountain and spirals upward, allowing us to look over and over again at the same spot on the ground, but each time from a different perspective. Our story is uniquely ours—a narrative written over time and writing itself even now. Our story is filled with voices, words, and images of how we acted on the world, how the world acted on us, how we see ourselves, and how we believe others see us. From each new perspective, looking back, we may see or feel it a bit differently. Sometimes we feel stuck in our story, mired in it, continually perpetuating the same patterns; sometimes we feel liberated in the telling of it, proud in the remembering, and bittersweet as we think of the people and places whose memory still inspires us. And as we take the time to reflect, see new possibilities in our story, and live with intention, we gain a hand in shaping it. We can write it forward, and our story can become the story we aspire to tell and the story we want others to tell about us.

Consider your leadership story. Think of how it twists and turns; think of some defining moments. Even some of our earliest memories can be cameos of our leadership abilities showing up early in life.

You may want to begin with a few questions:

- What is your first memory of taking charge of something?
- What led you to take charge? Was it self-confidence that emboldened you? Fear or necessity that chased you?
- Did others support or celebrate your courage to take charge, no matter what the motivation?
- What about this experience feels resonant even now?

Before you begin this book, tell your story. Write it down, memorialize it. Tell it to someone who will really listen. When you come to the end of this book, you will revisit your story once again, add to it, and change it up, reflecting on the leader you have become. As Mendemu Showry and K. V. L. Manasa write, "Successful leadership often surfaces when people become aware of critical personal experiences in their life, understand the driving forces, and respond by rethinking about self, redirect their moves and reshape their actions."[1]

This book is replete with the stories of courageous leaders who embrace their unique talents and their emotional intelligence to lead their schools and honor each young person.

Our relationships are a source of healing and well-being hiding in plain sight—one that can help us live healthier, more fulfilled, and more productive lives.

—U.S. SURGEON GENERAL DR. VIVEK MURTHY[2]

Early in her principalship, Brooke, a White high school principal, struggled internally with the fact that her dedication to her school, her teachers, her students, and their families had put her health at risk. She was not sleeping through the night and suffered from high anxiety. She was giving everything to her job, not enough to her family, and nothing to herself. Brooke had been coached before, and she knew the importance of self-reflection. By sitting quietly and talking things through with her coach, she realized that she was living significantly out of balance and set herself on a personal course of change.

All too often, school leaders feel the same way Brooke was feeling. The nature of the principalship invites high stress. At certain times, such as when a student is injured or a parent attempts to physically punish his child for misbehaving while in your office, or in even more grave situations like a suspected intruder in the building or a global pandemic on the rise, stress levels skyrocket. The adverse effects on job performance and well-being are well known: stress, anxiety, burnout, and eventually departure from the principalship. The good news is that leaders with high levels of social and emotional competence report greater well-being and feel more resilient in combating negative feelings and rampant moments of despair.[3] The more skillful you are in EI, the more able you are to pursue other pathways to well-being. Principals who can regulate their emotions in stressful situations are better able to handle crises that may arise.[4] Researchers Yamamoto, Gardiner, and Tenuto conducted a qualitative study with eight US secondary school principals in which the principals talked about themselves as leaders and shared negative critical incidents that provoked emotion. In their everyday jobs, they are the strong ones, often holding back their emotions, causing them to be in a state of emotional labor much of the time. They often lack the outlets to share their stories. In this study, sharing their stories helped the principals to self-reflect, clear up any questions that were lingering in their minds and take this reflection process with them into their leadership. Yamamoto shares, "Leadership begins with self-knowledge and a continual practice of reflection, in solitude, and in relationship."[5]

Brooke is an emotionally intelligent school leader. She has worked hard at integrating her emotions into her leadership and uses her skills for good and with authenticity; her actions match her words and are aligned with her values. She is trusted by her staff. She works to develop healthy relationships and establish family and community partnerships anchored in cultural responsiveness and emotional, social, and academic development. Emotionally intelligent leaders have the skills to create and pursue well-being in their lives. Well-being creates clarity of mind and settles the body. It is the foundation upon which you can reflect, learn skills, and practice them.

Unfortunately, many leaders feel very alone in pursuing and maintaining well-being. Administrative supports have typically been few, for the leaders too often struggle to keep themselves above water and in balance emotionally and physically—and the job pressures continue to intensify.

Even though leaders who have strategies to regulate themselves *can* handle their big and intense emotions and those of others, they may not want to live everyday doing so. A nationally representative survey conducted earlier this year by the RAND Corporation found that 85 percent of principals are experiencing job-related stress, compared with 73 percent of teachers and 35 percent of other working adults. Forty-eight percent of principals are dealing with burnout, while 28 percent report symptoms of depression.[6] The national average tenure of principals in US schools was about four to five years even before the pandemic. Highlights of a 2022 National Association of Secondary School Principals (NASSP) survey of America's school leaders and high school students gives us more context on the conditions principals are facing and the thoughts of students post pandemic.

- One out of two school leaders claims their stress level is so high they are considering a career change or retirement. While most principals shared that they are satisfied with their role, the survey revealed that 38 percent of school leaders are looking to leave within the next three years.
- One contributing factor for principals exiting the job is staffing shortages. Trying to hire competent, caring, smart, diverse teachers is difficult.

The profession is just not as attractive today to young graduates who can make a six-figure salary in the corporate world in a relatively short amount of time. And without teachers, the show is over!

- Principals indicated that a better work-life balance, a higher salary, and more societal respect for the profession would keep them on the job.
- The majority of school leaders claim they spend more than six hours a week on administrative paperwork (70 percent), spending time with students (64 percent) and administrative meetings (52 percent). They would rather be spending that time working with their teachers on instruction and helping their students.
- Three-quarters of school leaders (73 percent) and students (74 percent) report they needed help with their mental or emotional health last year.
- The majority of school leaders (70 percent) and students (51 percent) report they have personally been threatened or attacked, physically or verbally, during the past year. Fifteen percent of school leaders and 14 percent of students report having been physically attacked or assaulted this past year.

School leaders and students agree that more work needs to be done when it comes to meeting the needs of underserved students.[7]

Principal turnover leads to teacher turnover, which causes dissatisfaction and burnout. Turnover limits the possibility of sustaining satisfying, caring relationships. This significantly affects schools, even more so in high-poverty neighborhoods with greater student mobility and unequal expectations about what makes for success. It affects young people who may lose healthy relationships and consistent learning. Constant reshuffling of principals occurs in many school districts, adding to leadership inconsistency and limited relationship building.

Principals are not the only administrators with high stress levels. According to a survey of 149 Illinois superintendents, "forty-seven percent of superintendents have considered changing their career due to stress, and over 76 percent stated that the superintendency has affected their sleep patterns and has negatively impacted their health. Sixty-three percent of superintendents noted concern about how the job is negatively impacting their current lives while 46 percent are concerned about the long-term impact."[8] What we know about central office administrators, including school superintendents, is that they work too hard, push past their limits, and feel out of balance. As CEOs of their organizations, they employ high-level business skills, such as the ability to create a strategic plan, knowledge of legal obligations, and systems thinking. They also must have outstanding interpersonal skills, such as communication, empathy, and problem-solving. All these skill sets require accessing their emotional intelligence.

This chapter tells the backstories of the experiences shared with us by veteran, dedicated, and currently overtaxed school leaders. We learn how they continue to give to others while trying to take care of themselves. We learn their strategies for building and enhancing well-being and resilience. We share with you the struggles we have heard and witnessed during this time of unprecedented stress and uncertainty. We argue that our high-achieving leaders need to balance their drive with a deep commitment to well-being. Only in this way can they model effective leadership for teachers, who are models for children to do the same.

Daily practices of mindful living and self-care are a pathway to more resilience. We talk about the importance of self-care, including good nutrition and sleep habits, regular exercise, and other healthy habits. We explore the concepts of happiness, well-being, and contentment and ask the reader to consider relevant differences. We share stories from principals who bring well-being to their schools via mindfulness practices and other strategies. As we speak with and about these leaders, we are aware that each of them serves in a unique educational environment and context based on the community in which the leader's school is located and the resources available. Inequity exists everywhere. Despite the inequities they may face, school leaders strive to make a difference in the lives of the children and families they serve.

Kevin, a White male principal who leads the Manhattan Hunter Science High School, is one such leader. He takes his well-being seriously through a daily practice of mindfulness meditation. Kevin models the effects of that practice in his everyday leadership and brings that practice to his colleagues, teachers, families, and students. Kevin's school serves a diverse population of students, consisting of 29 percent Hispanic or Latinx, 28 percent Asian, 20 percent White, and 16 percent Black students; 16 percent are students with disabilities. Despite the fact that Manhattan Hunter Science High School serves a high-poverty population, Kevin's school ranked seventeenth in the nation with a graduation rate of 99 percent and a college readiness score of 87.4 percent. When asked how he reaches these numbers, Principal Kevin says, "We focus on giving every student the resources they need to learn and succeed, including a strong foundation in social-emotional learning. We then shine a light on every child and leave no one behind."[9]

Dawn, a Black former elementary school principal and now deputy superintendent, shares her thinking, process, and strategies to create her school's culture, climate, and student success. Dawn's elementary school is located in Harlem, and her students are predominantly Black. The school is an oasis of calm and smiling children. As you enter the building you "feel" the calm; you hear soft meditation music that immediately brings serenity. Every child in her school can tell you how he or she is feeling when asked—and we have asked! The children know how to calm themselves down and self-regulate when triggered. Throughout the school, there are constant reminders that children can express themselves in words, as well as sitting corners where children can go to meditate or take a few breaths. Every morning, Dawn begins the day with a town hall attended by all staff and students where they recite their school creed and participate in a student-led guided meditation. These children are learning from the earliest grades on that their well-being matters as much as academics.

You might be thinking, "So what's all this talk today about wellness and well-being? And what exactly does it mean?" Truthfully, *wellness* means different things to different people. Some talk of taking yoga classes or doing Pilates. Others go for a massage or to a spa for the weekend, while some practice meditation and mindfulness. For many, prayer is their healing salve. Others feel left out because they just can't seem to fit in any self-care to improve their life balance. But everyone knows that self-care is essential for negotiating our daily lives with equanimity and the ability to combat the high stress we live through.

A BRIEF HISTORY OF WELL-BEING IN THE US

The wellness movement's concern for well-being is not new; it had its beginnings some five thousand years ago. Early beliefs and practices about health, wellness, and prevention were passed down to us from various traditions; Indian, Chinese, African, Latin American, Native American, and numerous indigenous cultures informed and framed how we view wellness and well-being today.[10] Many people consider wellness to be health-oriented, including physical and mental health; others see it as a personal journey with time for reflection; still others lean toward a more philosophical view of well-being as consisting of a purposeful and happy life.

Jon Kabat-Zinn, a practicing Buddhist, brought mindfulness to mainstream American culture in 1973. Kabat-Zinn's science-based work resulted in an eight-week program to reduce stress called Mindfulness-Based Stress Reduction, which drew from his learning in both Eastern and Western traditions.

Many other Western wellness practices began much earlier, in the 1600s and 1700s, and they flourished during the nineteenth century. Homeopathy, herbalism, exercise and nutrition, osteopathy, and chiropractic took on importance in the eighteenth and nineteenth centuries. By the twentieth century, the Carnegie Foundation denounced alternative healing methods because they lacked scientific rigor and promoted an approach to medicine consisting of a disease-oriented treatment of symptoms, much of which still exists today.[11] By the 1950s, the wellness movement began inching back, and in the twentieth century, the first national university wellness institute was founded in the US.[12] Since then, the wellness movement has continued to grow. Businesses began bringing wellness alternatives into their organizations to promote work-life balance for healthy and happier employees. The 1980s and '90s saw an increase in yoga and calming mindfulness practices. And the twenty-first century has decidedly moved the marker on wellness. Fitness, healthy diet, healthy living, and well-being concepts and offerings have proliferated widely, promoting the benefits of self-care. A focus on wellness has become integrated into and is transforming industries from food and beverage to travel and corporate organizations.

An essential part of well-being is our mental health. With anxiety and depression on the increase in the US, in 1999 Martin Seligman, in his role as president of the American Psychological Association, brought the field of positive psychology to the forefront. He believed that too much mental health treatment drilled into the negative—pain, trauma, abnormalities, and aberrations—"while little attention was given to positive thinking that sparked happiness, well-being, exceptionalism, strengths, and good health."[13] This shift led to the widespread focus that we see today in methods such as coaching, cognitive behavioral therapy, and strength-based training. In more recent years, Seligman and others have incorporated into their practice *mindfulness* techniques. "Mindfulness can come in lots of different forms—it could be yoga practice, it might involve setting aside time for mindfulness meditation sessions, or prayer. It could include practicing mindfulness during everyday activities (such as washing the dishes, as Thich Nhat Hahn advocated)."[14]

Another link between mindfulness and positive psychology is that mindfulness increases well-being and positive mental qualities, including compassion. Mindfulness-based meditation has been used in compassion training, to increase sensitivity to one's own and others' needs. By being empathic, we are more motivated to help others. In return, helping others gives us feelings of joy and satisfaction.[15]

Think about the on-the-ground, real-time result of a half hour of meditation on one's emotional and mental well-being: calming down the arousal system, clearing the mind for greater focus, and often lifting one's spirits. While *wellness* has been the term predominantly used throughout history to describe health and fitness, including psychological health, the term *well-being*, which has entered the public health field more recently, expands this description. The Centers for Disease Control and Prevention describes well-being as "the presence of positive emotions and moods (e.g., contentment, happiness) and the absence of negative emotion (e.g., depression, anxiety), satisfaction with life, fulfillment and positive functioning."[16] Well-being includes physical, economic, social, emotional, and psychological aspects; life satisfaction; development and activity; domain-specific satisfaction; and engaging activities and work.

With all this talk about well-being, how is the human experience right now? Since 2012, the *World Happiness Report* led to the passage of Resolution 65/309 by the General Assembly of the United Nations, initiated by the prime minister of Bhutan, and happiness and well-being gained importance on the world stage. The annual report has reported different countries' emotional temperament, and much of the report examines well-being. This report seeks to inform us about people's life satisfaction. The 2023 report explains, "The ethos of a country matters—are people trustworthy, generous, and mutually supportive? The institutions also matter—are people free to make important life decisions? And the material conditions of life matter—both income and health." The report concludes that countries need to have virtuous citizens and supportive institutions. People need to cooperate and care about each other, and government needs to support this belief. Protecting the human rights of every individual is essential, and to that end, so is promoting their well-being. The 2023 *World Happiness Report* measures well-being by income, health, having someone to count on, having a sense of freedom to make key life decisions, generosity, and the absence of corruption. The report concludes that "the role of well-being in sustainable development is already present, but well-being should play a much more central role in global diplomacy and in international and national policies in the years to come."[17] Finland continues to be the world's happiest country based on its healthy life expectancy, gross domestic product per capita, social support, low corruption, generosity in a community where people look after each other, and freedom to make key life decisions. The US ranks fifteenth and, not surprisingly, Russia is No. 70 and Ukraine is No. 92.[18]

The pandemic increased loneliness for many in our country, but the loneliness crisis has been going on for much longer. Just in May 2023, "the United States Surgeon General Dr. Vivek Murthy released a new advisory calling attention to the public health crisis of loneliness, isolation, and lack of connection in our country."[19] The human need for social connection cannot be underestimated. James Floman, associate researcher at the Yale Child Study Center, says, "Loneliness is not about physical separateness; it is the perception that one has about the quality of the relationships with others—our social connectedness. Loneliness predicts morbidity, mortality, longevity, and the risk for heart attacks and other illnesses."[20]

Crises such as the pandemic put great stress on everyone. As a leader, you have the added stress of the responsibility for the lives of everyone in your organization or building. The day-to-day stress alone is enough to detract from your well-being. Burnout can be the result.

THE BURNOUT TREND: LEADERS ARE NO EXCEPTION

We have noted that "nationally, the average tenure of a principal is about four years (2019) and nearly one in five principals, approximately 18 percent, turn over annually. Often the schools that need the most capable principals, those serving students from low-income families, have even greater principal turnover."[21] More recently,

> the RAND Corporation conducted a study of 300 principals in both public and charter school networks. They found that teacher turnover in 2021–2022 was highest (around 12 to 14 percent) in urban districts, high-poverty districts, and districts serving predominately students of color. Meanwhile, principal turnover was highest (around 21 to 23 percent) in high-poverty districts and in rural

districts. By the beginning of the 2022–23 school year, principal turnover increased too, reaching 16 percent nationally.[22]

Even before the pandemic, more principals were leaving, at about the same rate. So let's make this personal. Before you read any further, take a few moments to answer the following questions:

- Do you drag yourself to work and have trouble getting started?
- Have you become irritable or impatient with coworkers, teachers, or clients?
- Do you lack the energy to be consistently productive?
- Do you find it hard to concentrate?
- Have you become cynical or critical at work?
- Do you lack satisfaction from your achievements?
- Do you feel disillusioned about your job?
- Have your sleep habits changed?
- Are you troubled by unexplained headaches, stomach problems, or other physical complaints?[23]

If you answered yes to even one of these questions posted on the Mayo Clinic's website, you are experiencing negative stress, which is pumping the hormone cortisol into your system when it is not needed. Burnout includes three dimensions: emotional exhaustion, cynicism or depersonalization, and reduced personal accomplishment.[24]

THINK ABOUT IT

Take a moment to reflect on your recent years as a school administrator. What are the top causes of your stress? In what ways does stress take its toll on you? Where do you experience it in your body? What do you do when you feel stress?

To be sure, under the right circumstances, cortisol is necessary to get you ready for fight or flight. But if you're constantly in a state of high stress, cortisol causes the adrenal glands to be overused, and they exude greater amounts of insulin into the body, causing the heart to pump faster; blood pressure rises, and a multitude of illnesses can result. Unfortunately, most of us probably answered yes to several, if not more, of the questions just listed.

Remember Principal Dawn, who was mentioned earlier in this chapter? She shared that the most significant drain on her well-being was checking her email and social media into the night to avoid missing anything important: "It's just hard to sleep. Once I get into it, it's hard to detach, and then I'm checking emails, and then somebody will email me something, and that'll take me down another rabbit hole."

We asked Principal Dawn many questions—among them what she wanted her legacy to be. She told us, "I want the children to know that I really gave everything that I had and that I cared about them deeply, loved and cared about the school, about my parents and the teachers, and really wanted to do everything that I could, and gave my whole self to do that." Dawn works day and night, driven by her commitment to "give of her whole self."

THINK ABOUT IT

What about you? Do you have a plan for reducing your stress? Do you value good health and long life? Perhaps, like Principal Dawn, you can't rest or take care of yourself until everything is off your daily plate. Or maybe you don't recognize stress when you're experiencing it. How have you managed stress during your leadership? What about right now? What causes you to be stressed?

We have heard so many of our principal colleagues share their frustration over a lack of control—one of the common issues leading to burnout. Especially during the pandemic, swift changes kept coming from the top, causing leaders to pivot quickly; communication was not always clear or timely, and site leaders had to ensure that their teachers could cooperate. Leaders' focus was placed on obtaining air filtration units, keeping students from contracting COVID, and meeting every child's needs. For many leaders, there was little time for implementing new initiatives, as educators strove to adapt to online instead of in-person classes and principals worked to support teachers struggling to create a totally online curriculum. Teachers and school administrators also had to respond to parental concerns that arose daily.

Leaders such as Brooke and Dawn made teacher well-being a priority. Brooke brought her staff of educators together every morning to check in—and she let all of them know that the essential part of their job at the time was to support the emotional well-being of their students. Student well-being was a priority, and teacher well-being was a necessary first step. Through Principal Brooke's supportive leadership, teachers were able to develop the self-compassion necessary to put on their own life vests first. Then they could focus on supporting their students' well-being, as Principal Brooke did for them. Dawn started every school day with the whole school coming together for mindfulness exercises, setting a positive tone for the school.

Many principals today are struggling with their emotions from the uncertainty, unpredictability, and ongoing stress they experienced from 2020 through 2022, during the pandemic. Principals have had to "hold it together" for all school stakeholders. During the pandemic, handling these needs was often secondary to addressing demands for ensuring proper air quality, testing for COVID, rearranging workable spaces for learning, and securing laptops for every child—basically, fixing everything that was broken in the school.

The literature confirms that the "two specific types of stress that many principals feel include emotional exhaustion and depersonalization, two constructs of burnout."[25] Burnout is especially insidious because emotional exhaustion leaves diminished energy for a job that demands so much. Our educators are depleted of resources, and feeling depleted interferes with performance and success on the job.[26] The nature of work-related stress is not unique to the principalship; research from the business and medical world informs educational leaders and analysts about how stress manifests and what can be done to prevent or mitigate its effects.[27]

COVID-19 and its variants, as well as outbreaks of monkeypox and respiratory syncytial virus (RSV), have taken their toll physically, cognitively, emotionally, and spiritually. The weight of the day-to-day demands of the principal's job—and the emotional exhaustion of being there for teachers to help them improve their craft, adapt to new demands, build bonds that unite the culture, and form a caring community—are simply too much. Nevertheless, school leaders we spoke to expressed a deep commitment to catch themselves when stress interferes with them becoming their best selves. They avoided possible blind spots that interrupted their authenticity. Noah, a Latinx male high school principal, speaks about his experience: "My energy gets zapped because I'm navigating people's energy. For example, if a teacher says she is overwhelmed, and I know she didn't do what I had asked her, I will tell her what she did and still hold her accountable but with empathy in a caring way." Principal Noah is skilled in active listening and other communication skills, so he knows how not to put anyone on the defense or offense. This makes all the difference to his loyal staff. He goes on, "I can usually stay above all the turmoil because I am consistent. Teachers know what to expect from me. They know I care, above all."

Principal Kevin, Noah's colleague and friend, struggles with his passion, which moves him to sometimes act quickly and push too hard. He started working with a trainer who shared five-minute workout routines that Kevin does throughout the day in addition to his ongoing mindfulness practice. These routines make a world of difference in his well-being.

Principal Dawn has created a virtual oasis in her school, which is in the middle of a low-income area with fewer resources and opportunities. The sound of the meditative music as you enter her school immediately restores your spirit and calms your arousal system. Still, Dawn is up at night, working overtime mentally, which prevents her from getting the sleep she needs to meet the high-stress demands that start at 6 a.m. the following day.

Work-life balance is almost impossible for many to achieve, yet increasingly school leaders know that they must find it. When we asked a group of fifteen principals who have been working with us if they were getting good sleep at night, only one said yes. The three most popular strategies these leaders engaged into de-stress are mindfulness, spending time with loved ones, and exercising. One key reason they all were using contemplative practices is that they were part of the Gray Fellowship, a collaboration of the Gray Foundation and Hunter College of the City of New York that focuses on teaching these practices to school leaders. Furthermore, these principals formed friendships and found support that met their need to connect with their peers and avoid loneliness. The need for belonging is a driver for us all.

THINK ABOUT IT

Take a moment and reflect: How is the need for belonging a driver of your behavior or the behaviors of your teachers? Reread that question and think about it!

Meena Srinivasan, a BIPOC (Black, Indigenous, People of Color) author and expert on contemplative practices, shared her thoughts about the work that she does as executive director of her organization, Transformative Educational Leaders (TEL). She communicates her understanding about bringing mindfulness into the schools: "Mindfulness is a way to elevate our consciousness and get back to our wholeness. We have been very mind-focused and yet our spirit is animated through the body. Mindfulness practices help us to embody that which lifts us up to resist all the ills we face in society and remain aligned with our bodies."[28]

As school leaders, the clearer we are and the more focused we are on what matters, the more regulated we become, and our best self emerges.

Bringing mindfulness into our everyday lives involves accessing our self-awareness and being intentional about our desired goal. Mindfulness roots us in the present moment and distances us from taking on too much and being placed into a state of high negative stress. For some, mindfulness can make us aware of the kind of food we consume—they would say that eating nutritious foods is the key to a long life. Yet even though we know so much more today about how to eat well, many of us grab fast food regularly or skip meals altogether. We tax our bodies with unhealthy foods, even though we know better.[29] Mindfulness can help us be aware of these patterns and choose differently.

Many leaders we spoke to embrace mindfulness as a way to address or cope with burnout. Leaders report despairing about burnout, as it has severe consequences—leaders' vision and energy for change and growth define their purpose to move a school forward—yet, it is challenging to be an energetic leader when one is feeling emotional exhaustion from the job. And, these days, leaders talk about being *beyond* burned out; they say they are hurting at the soul level and require more profound healing than can happen in thirty minutes of meditation or even in two weeks off. These leaders need a restoration of spirit and way more time for self-care and to make connections with others than is possible in our current education system.

The data supports what we hear from leaders. Christina Maslach and Michael Leiter reported that the dimensions of burnout included exhaustion, cynicism, and a reduced sense of efficacy on the job. People who score high on burnout dimensions feel emotionally exhausted instead of energized, a dimension that is the most widely reported in the literature; job overload contributes to the feeling of exhaustion and burnout.[30] By understanding how burnout contributes to stress and how stress fuels the constructs of burnout, we can plan programs to prevent, manage, and reduce the stress that school leaders encounter on the job.[31] It is essential to recognize the early signs of stress before it takes its toll physically and mentally. The stress levels that school leaders face are similar to what those in other high-service professions experience, including teachers, doctors and nurses, and nursing home attendants. Service fields such as education and health care won't allow us to close the door and shut the client out. School leaders and health-care professionals are always on. You are there the minute you are awake—taking phone calls, always serving, in the interest of protecting the child or the patient from any harm.

Unless resources for school leaders to improve well-being are placed front and center, we are at risk of losing many of these dedicated warriors who fight daily to provide the best for students. Unfortunately, not many supports are available to school leaders. The absence of external protective factors that can shield them from high stress and burnout is a sign of the unconscious message that leaders hear: *Do your job. The schools need you. Parents need you. Children need you.* School leaders' dedication to children and families keeps them pushing hard, no matter what. Peter DeWitt, former principal, coach, and author, said:

> The other day I was working remotely with some school principals and their administrative teams that I coach. Their faces showed the stress they feel. Some of the principals were in tears during our conversation, and many spoke about how tired they feel due to all of the present pressures of the job on top of the ones that they have been experiencing for years.
>
> Keep in mind it was only the second week of school.[32]

Consider also that many school leaders are parents of young children, as are the teachers who work for them. We all know the difficulties of raising a family while working. If parents do not buffer the responsibilities for each other, parenting becomes even more challenging. And when there is only one parent in the home, these responsibilities double. Today, one in four moms are single parents in the US, and this does not include data on single dads.[33]

Maven, a worldwide clinic for supporting women's health, conducted the largest-ever study of the best workplaces for women's health. The researchers who worked on the study reported that 65 percent of parents actively seek new work experiences and are 2.5 times less willing to work when previously burned-out. Maven explored the characteristics of positive environments that reduce burnout and make workplaces 4.5 percent more successful in retaining employees. The researchers found that what mattered most was "the quality of support working parents receive in meeting their unique stressors and when their work environment is empathetic, psychologically safe and accepting of who they are."[34] Yet, even with these improvements, it's too much; everyone struggles with the inability to do it all, and younger parents and BIPOC and Latinx parents still experience burnout more readily than older, White employees.[35]

"As a BIPOC person, lack of safety is something that we deal with on an everyday basis. Lack of resources is another," said Dr. Akua Boateng, a licensed psychotherapist who specializes in anxiety, depression, and mood disorders. "We are often living in survival mode. That has a cascading effect on our physiological health, our emotional health, and our ability to see our future in a way that is safe and sound."[36]

THE HAPPINESS FACTOR AND POSITIVE PSYCHOLOGY

"The premise of positive psychology is that well-being can be defined, measured, and taught. . . . Achieving it not only makes people more fulfilled but, when achieved in a collective, it makes corporations more productive, soldiers more resilient, students more engaged and marriages happier." What brings us the greatest well-being varies with each individual. What brings us joy?

With all that we have covered in this chapter, and all the leaders' voices confirming how challenged they are, what can we all do to make life happier and less stressful? A. Lees and David Barnard provided evidence that certain emotional intelligence competencies ultimately lead to greater job satisfaction (and higher student achievement): when people feel good, they work at their best.[37]

Dr. Martin Seligman points to five factors that lead to well-being: positive emotion, engagement, relationships, meaning and purpose, and accomplishment (PERMA). Seligman's PERMA+ model builds on Abraham Maslow's description of a self-actualized person who is in a state of well-being.

- **Positive emotions** refer to the experience of positive feelings and emotions, such as satisfaction, awe, joy, and contentment.
- **Engagement** relates to our experience of flow and being consumed in an activity and environment.
- **Relationships** refer to the quality and quantity of social connections inside and outside our immediate group.
- **Meaning** brings importance to having a sense of purpose or meaning in life.
- **Accomplishment** is based on the experience of achievement and progression toward goals.[38]

The PERMA model joins together the characteristics of a self-actualized person and well-being.[39]

THINK ABOUT IT

What parts of the PERMA model are fulfilled in your work? What parts would you like to experience more of?

Since Seligman's shift to positive psychology, much research has proved the impact that PERMA characteristics have on health, energy, and satisfaction in work and life.[40] Gallup's research has also found that social well-being is one of the foundational elements of a thriving overall life.[41] The more time we spend alone, the more we experience negative emotions such as sadness or loneliness. As humans, we are designed to be in a relationship with others; we are social beings. Being with positive people lifts our spirits. We become more positive about our situations, and with positivity comes happiness. Friendship matters.

LONELINESS

After twenty years, I (Janet) can remember how excited I was to move home from California to New York City. I searched for a one-bedroom apartment on the Upper East Side in the vicinity of Hunter College. Finally, I could walk back and forth to work! I had always wanted to live in the *big city*. Born and raised on Staten Island, I had previously commuted into the city daily.

At last, I no longer had to stress out about traveling to work. But after several months, the newness wore off. I was lonely. My family members lived in Staten Island and Brooklyn, and I had no friends in the city. I spent most of my time in my office at the university, at home, or in the gym. I never realized how lonely one could be, especially in one of the most populated, exciting cities in the world. A year later, I moved to Staten Island. I had never considered this a possibility, but it was the best thing I could do, despite again having a long commute! The feeling of loneliness was replaced by the contentment and joy of being close to family and friends, and my mom and dad were ecstatic to have me so near.

In her poem "Alone," genius poet and author Maya Angelou described loneliness so well:

> Lying, thinking
> Last night
> How to find my soul a home
> Where water is not thirsty
> And bread loaf is not stone
> I came up with one thing
> And I don't believe I'm wrong
> That nobody,

But nobody
Can make it out here alone.
Alone, all alone
Nobody, but nobody
Can make it out here alone.

There are some millionaires
With money they can't use
Their wives run round like banshees
Their children sing the blues
They've got expensive doctors
To cure their hearts of stone.
But nobody
No, nobody
Can make it out here alone.
Alone, all alone
Nobody, but nobody
Can make it out here alone.

Now if you listen closely
I'll tell you what I know
Storm clouds are gathering
The wind is gonna blow
The race of man is suffering
And I can hear the moan,
'Cause nobody,
But nobody
Can make it out here alone.

Alone, all alone
Nobody, but nobody
Can make it out here alone.

We need one another. With so many worrisome and negative life influences (many without an end date) that burden top educators, and with few opportunities for social support, it becomes more challenging to keep one's energy up and to remain positive. The job of the school leader—in particular, the principal—is more isolated than the work of other system leaders.

And given the nature of the position, the divide between teacher and assistant principal, principal, or superintendent often prohibits school leaders from befriending those with whom they work. Principal Dawn talked at length about this topic, sharing with us the need for peer support at the top, especially in times of crisis such as the pandemic. For Dawn, sharing her anxiety wasn't the right action, given that teachers had so much need. "You share ideas, commiserate, exchange innovations, and spark creativity together. Meetings can replace social isolation with support, hope, and a sense of belonging—and reinforce your commitment to the work. We feel blessed that all personnel are helping one another even though they are all feeling stressed."[42]

As the leader of your community, you are in a powerful yet lonely place. Building peer groups within districts or schools counters that loneliness by creating a community. Unless they are educators, our significant others may not be interested in rehashing the events of the day with us, even though we could benefit from releasing the tension and getting good feedback. And even when our significant others welcome our sharing, it's (of course) not the same as sharing with someone walking the same landscape. Even though I (Janet) had been an administrator at the building level and understood what my husband's days must have been like as a principal, when he came in the door after work, he had no desire to rehash the events of his day. I watched as he removed his work persona and donned his comfort clothes: shorts and a T-shirt. Only hours later would he share if he had something to get off his chest, such as the tough decisions that he had to make to let someone go after several corporal punishment charges or to not approve a new teacher's tenure. These are only two of the many hard calls someone may need to make as a school leader. To ensure that children get the best education, a school leader might have to take away someone's income, the source of a family's sustenance. Actions such as these can create anguish but must be done.

WHAT HURTS OUR SOULS

We think it's important to talk briefly about the emotional pain often felt by school leaders. Constant stress raises cortisol levels. So let's look first at an obvious factor that causes anguish. Although schools are still considered among the safest places in the US, the average American may not feel they are safe. Our records show that seven more people died in mass shootings at US schools between 2018 and 2022—for a total of fifty-two people—than in the previous eighteen years combined since the watershed 1999 Columbine High School massacre. As of the time we are writing this book, *Education Week* reports 23 school shootings that resulted in injuries or deaths so far in 2023. There have been 167 such shootings since 2018.[43] While gun violence is the leading cause of death of kids in America and school shootings have increased overall, schools are still considered safe places. There are many prevention methods used in schools to safeguard students, parents and educators and allay their fears. Increases in social workers and mental health practitioners provide psychological safety to students.[44]

I (Janet) remember when my husband came home from work after a grueling day preparing for actions he would take if there were an active shooter in the building. Barry shared with me photos of himself and his "A-Team" in hazmat suits.[45] He said somberly, painstakingly, "It was so real. I was genuinely scared. I pray that I will never have to don this suit." I thought, "What have we come to as a country when preparing for school includes taking steps to ensure that our children and educators are not shot?" Every day that we send our eighteen-year-old to school in Manhattan, we pray that she will be safe from harm. As never before, school leaders must protect everyone else, the school community, and themselves. Unfortunately, the school shooting scenarios we hear about most frequently end in fatalities, too often including children. While such occurrences are not constantly on leaders' minds, it hits close to home when a shooting occurs at the school down the block.

Uncertainty leads to anxiety, stress, burnout, and other unhealthy and unfulfilling pursuits, such as alcoholism, drug addiction, sex addiction, overeating, and neglect of our well-being and those closest to us. Other anxiety-producing events and conditions include tragic deaths of students, poverty, homelessness, gang violence, and institutional racism, to name a few. These conditions can lead to unconscious fears that impact administrators' leadership and teachers' and students' capacity to excel. Alongside these large events come the lesser events that the school leader must contend with, such as students who consistently fail, students with poor attendance, suspensions of students, investigations, teacher incompetence, and the need to manage up. Each of these takes its toll on the leader, teachers, and students.

For example, imagine that an emotionally unskilled and incompetent teacher manages to slip through the system for years and becomes a thorn in the side of a principal with a thriving school. The teacher is, of course, tenured, so the principal must go through a series of district and union protocols to meet the teacher's right to due process. Years pass before the teacher is removed, and during that time, children are deprived of their right to a sound education by a qualified teacher. In this scenario, the principal does her best to place the teacher in a class where he can do the least amount of harm. Should the principal place this teacher with the brightest students or the lower-performing students? The anguish felt by the principal is palpable when she realizes that there is little that she can do while she goes through the necessary protocols to have the incompetent teacher removed, other than have coaches and seasoned teachers work with the teacher so that the students are learning.

THINK ABOUT IT

Would you want your child in this class? What would you do?

At the superintendent level, one of the most painful aspects of leading happens when the school board is at odds with its leadership because
of differences in educational beliefs, partisanship, political point scoring,
or all of the above. Jerry Patterson interviewed twelve highly successful superintendents from across the country. He shares, "The message
delivered by most of the superintendents is consistent and clear: It's not
a question about whether board support will change. It's a question of
when. And keep in mind that this message is not delivered by a group
of mediocre, whining superintendents. These highly respected school
district leaders succeeded in the districts where board support started
strong but ultimately decayed."[46]

Each of these superintendents shared stories about the turmoil their
jobs inflicted on their careers, health, and family lives. One superintendent told the story of how he found out that he was being let go after
he decided to not hire a baseball coach wanted by the board: "At a routine board meeting, there was a motion to bring an attorney in to resolve
a personnel matter. When everybody started leaving, I turned to the
board president and asked if there was something I should know about.
The board member said, 'Yes, we want to negotiate a settlement to your
contract. We don't want you to talk to us. Talk to our attorney.'" We find it
hard to believe that such a lack of caring and empathy exists in a profession that should be the model for organizational emotional intelligence.
Candidates for boards of education should not be permitted to run for
membership on these boards unless they complete a course in EI! We
all need to learn ethics, caring communication, and empathic responses
in leadership. No one should be reduced to the kind of stress incurred
by these leaders because of another's ambitions or lack of compassion.
"The stress of the job caused me high blood pressure and it got to me
emotionally," shared another superintendent. Another suffered a heart
attack. Finally, the job took its toll on family members. One superintendent shared tearfully, "I got paid big bucks to take the abuse of this job.
My wife and children didn't get a penny for the abuse they endured."[47]

In the next chapter, we talk about ways to sustain our commitments to stay centered and nurture ourselves during these difficult moments. Sometimes, the best thing to do is to get up and leave when a win-win solution can't be worked out. No one should sacrifice his or her well-being for a job, even one with a powerful purpose. We are meant to lead in a wholesome way that doesn't compromise our lives, our families, and our communities.

CHAPTER TWO

What Sustains Us?

And once the storm is over you won't remember how you made it through, how you managed to survive. You won't even be sure, in fact, whether the storm is really over. But one thing is certain. When you come out of the storm you won't be the same person who walked in.

—HARUKI MURAKAMI

RESILIENCE KEEPS US MOVING FORWARD

What allows some school leaders to weather the storms and causes others to crumble? What can we learn from those who thrive no matter what the circumstances? What does it take to persevere in the face of emotionally, psychologically, or physically hurtful and painful odds? Is it just some leaders' DNA that makes this possible? Have they learned better self-regulation and organizational skills, or do they have faith and optimism that things will change? What these school leaders do have more of is the awareness of what they need, many pathways to build and strengthen resilience, more protective factors from childhood on, and the resources—including social support—to help get them through tough times.

What is resilience? "Psychologists define resilience as the process of adapting well in the face of adversity, trauma, tragedy, threats, or significant sources of stress—such as family and relationship problems, serious health problems, or workplace and financial stressors."[1] Resilient people bounce forward after stressful events. Their flexible and positive mindset—"I *will* move through this"; "I *will* find a way"—urges them to keep going and not give up. As educators, we always marvel at the students who come from challenging beginnings, including high-poverty, violent, or neglectful home environments, and continue to excel in school and forge healthy friendships.

When I (Janet) lived in San Diego, I taught in a middle school in the border city right across from Tijuana, Mexico. The school population was 99 percent Mexican American. The families held high regard for their child's *maestra*, and so did the children.

There was one sixth grader, Gloria Yvonne, whom I had the good fortune to teach for three years in a row. She was in my drama class in seventh and eighth grade. Aside from being "school" smart, she was extremely creative and talented. She took the starring role in two productions, *As You Like It* and *Annie*. Yet her good grades and lauded performances represented only half the picture. Gloria always seemed somewhat distracted, her mind off in the distance. Eventually, I discovered that she was being regularly abused by her mother. As she described her home, it was far from a happy place, far from a pretty scene. I decided to take this young person under my wing. Even Cinderella was treated with more care than Gloria Yvonne.

Gloria is fifty-one now, and we have remained very close. When she last visited me, we spent time reviewing the events of her past, trying to make sense of them. I learned that for the first four years of her life, she was raised by her grandmother, who loved Gloria and protected her from harm. At the age of four, she suddenly was returned to her mother, and the horrible physical, emotional, and psychological abuse began then. I continue to learn more about Gloria's early life. On her most recent visit to New York City, I learned that she doesn't like being called Yvonne because that's the name her mother used when she commanded Gloria to do chores and punished her if they weren't done to her mother's liking.

Fortunately, Gloria is now happily married, the mother of four beautiful children, the grandmother of one precious girl, and a successful businesswoman. She says that my presence in her life as a caring, consistent mentor is what gave her hope that there was a better life outside of her home. She had other protective factors, too. Those first four years of her life with her grandmother were a foundation and a true blessing. All her teachers recognized her strengths and brought out the best in her; she regularly scored in the highest percentiles on standardized tests, had a great sense of humor and a sparkling personality, and was well-liked by young people and adults. She was, in fact, skillful in social and emotional intelligence and continues to be. I tell her story because her inner strength and resilience and social supports helped her to break the cycle of oppression. She has been and continues to build resilience and has led a fulfilled life, whereas many others who grew up in the same conditions as she did, with less abusive situations than she had, did not thrive.

As an educator and a psychoanalyst, we—along with the many educators and counselors we have spoken to—have so many stories of resilience. I (Robin) was in New York City on September 11, 2001, when the Twin Towers fell, and I worked with many families of students at Columbia University in the months after the terrorist attack on our city. The devastation and heartbreak of students who lost their parents, boyfriends, girlfriends, sisters, and brothers were mind-numbing. These students' ability over time to move forward, filled with grief and carrying their love and memories with them, was a testament to their resilience. And, as it turns out, we are all much more resilient than we think. We somehow find that strength of spirit and make meaning from the ashes; surrounded by the loving support of others, we somehow use our ability to adapt to a new normal and rebuild. Ten years after 9/11, I had the privilege to meet and interview ten survivors of the tragedy, and I cowrote a book with journalist and author Courtney E. Martin, *Project Rebirth*, about their strength, their lives over the years since the attack, and the pathways to resilience they used to rebuild their lives.[2]

Resilience is key for all of us moving forward in a world that is filled with uncertainty and unpredictability. As we write this book, the worst of the pandemic and its variants is behind us. Many of our colleagues and friends lost homes, lost jobs, and tragically lost loved ones without even the opportunity to say goodbye in person. Many lost their social networks that were the backdrop of every day. Our youth lost celebrations of milestones they waited for and counted on for years. It touches our hearts to reflect on the strength and motivation of our educators—despite the Great Resignation, the isolation and burnout in leadership, the worse than ever mental health crisis for our youth, the school shootings and ongoing random gun violence on the streets, many of our colleagues arrive at school every day still moved by their calling to serve children and still flexibly finding their unique pathways to resilience.

EMOTIONAL INTELLIGENCE BUILDS RESILIENCE

Emotional intelligence skills and competencies help to build resilience. Learning and making meaning from adversity help to build resilience. Creating a positive narrative, even in the most challenging of times, helps to build resilience. Allowing yourself to feel all your feelings and not judge yourself is critical for strengthening resilience—so is believing in yourself despite what you hear from others and, sometimes, despite verbal and physical abuse. So many of us have tried to be there for our own Glorias, but not all Glorias have moved past surviving to thriving. Social support is a critical factor in strengthening resilience—as is asking for and accepting help when you need it and moving forward alone when necessary. While we work to serve our children and families, many of us carry baggage from our early years that still whispers in our ears and leaves us unable, ashamed, or too proud to ask for help. We have encouraged many—and we encourage you, too—to do the inner work necessary to free yourself from your whisper that inhibits you from seeking help when needed, and to count on friends and colleagues as they count on you.

RELATIONSHIPS ARE EVERYTHING

Remember Principal Brooke, whom we met at the beginning of chapter 1? She has found the support she needs to build her resilience at work. Experience has been her best mentor. She tells us:

> I know who I am, so I lean into it as a strength all the time. I have a support group in my AP [assistant principal], Christina, and my former AP Meagan, who is now a principal, to collaborate and get feedback. They are my moral compass. I often bounce things off other people to get more collaborative and honest feedback. When I am unclear, I'll go to one of them because I know that I need a trusted person and someone who will give me what I need for heavy things, mental illness, violence, etc. Having these two women who know me matters. It's so important to have people who will speak the truth.[3]

Beyond her own needs, Principal Brooke recognized that her teachers also needed the comfort, support, and strength of others to get them through the tough times. Early in the pandemic, when daily stress easily overwhelmed us and uncertainty and fear were our daily background music, Principal Brooke brought her teachers together every morning to start their day with a daily check-in, a community holding space for each other's thoughts and feelings before the day started.

More education systems would greatly benefit from an emphasis on building community and making more time for people to connect with each other. Some school districts, like Principal Brooke's, do encourage a social, emotional, and academic environment in which relationships can flourish. But not all. It's not that leaders and policymakers don't care;

it's just that many believe that the purpose of school is to solely support and develop academic achievement, and others are forced to behave as if they believe that as well. Further, it's not widely understood that an emotionally intelligent focus in a supportive environment begets high achievement.

And the lack of time is always a culprit, especially in view of the ongoing pressure to achieve. In many cases, there still exists a deeply ingrained culture that views education as a continuation of the early 1900s, when we were preparing students for a world transformed by the Industrial Revolution and mass production on assembly lines. Decades of research tell us that, even more vitally in today's technologically driven world, *relationships are everything*—including the ones that we have with ourselves. As leaders, our many social and emotional skills, especially empathy, are essential for knowing ourselves and others and forming generative teams who will carry out the work. To be resilient, we need to identify our strengths and challenges and lean on others to carry us when things are hard. Principal Brooke knew herself and the importance of people who would always be there for her, and she ensured that she included them in her life.

WHEN CRISIS HITS

But what do we do in a moment of crisis, such as the initial breakout of COVID and the beginning of the pandemic? What do we do when a school shooting happens, like the horror in Cobb County, Uvalde, where nineteen people were killed, all but two of them children; or when we see mass shootings such as the one that took place in a Buffalo supermarket, where those killed were shopping for their groceries, or the one that happened at a Fourth of July celebration in Highland Park? How do you get through these kinds of moments?

Principal Brooke described her response to the pandemic:

In the beginning, I had baseline fear. I didn't want to get sick or jeopardize my kids. I debated whether or not to go to school. Am I taking care of myself and my family or my school? The doctor told me to stay home, but I went in except when schools were closed. I kept asking myself, "What is best?" Once I was doing it and avoided the subways, it was OK. We talk about not making assumptions about what another family is going through. Simplistically, I compared my experience with the pandemic responses of my colleagues who worked in other districts with no food, shelter, etc. My kids felt horrible. It was a real crisis. I had a lot of feelings as to why the depth of need is always the case. Why are the resources not distributed equally? I had friends driving around the city delivering laptops. I saw this as we have inequitable jobs. My students had consistent high-level learning daily. Other principals were getting grief counseling. Kids in the shelters had no access to computers. I experienced a different kind of stress because I could not rely on proximity and communication to lead. I felt challenged, out of my element. I do the best work standing by the water fountain when everyone is at school. Where am I supposed to be, popping into Zoom?

I did Zoom yoga. It served me well. I scheduled my Zoom day and made sure I had an hour. It was about not being on the computer, being with my body, and breathing. I don't like working at home, but it did allow me to exercise in the mornings. I took a nap in the afternoon.[4]

Brooke talks about optimism and hope as critical to resilience and as the basis for a forward-looking mindset when moving through crises. And we can also hear her deep empathy for all and concern for the inequities in schools, families, and children. While she is a servant leader, she has learned the importance of self-compassion and self-care. She shared, "I finally grew up and learned how I have to take care of myself, as well as everybody else. I'm calmer; I don't need to make everybody feel good all the time. You don't have to be loved by all. I'm human, and I love my job."

Brooke's experiences remind us of the importance of social connection to avoid the loneliness we feel from being isolated from peers. We hear her reach out for support when needed. We hear about her deep empathy and how she does not micromanage and is not going to her staff when she is needy. We hear about her decision-making to make desired changes when push came to shove. We learned about her advocacy for what she believes in. Optimism gets her through many situations and, finally, so do self-compassion and care. All these paths have led to her resiliency and her fifteen years as a principal who is looking forward to many more.

STRATEGIES FOR BUILDING RESILIENCE

There are many strategies that we use to restore optimism, resilience, and general well-being. Brooke said that we build optimism by "trusting that you can create your joy." Optimism and positivity are certainly important mindsets for leaders of schools. The practice of creating joy for yourself and others is uplifting for a school climate and serves as a protective factor for both self and others. In fact, in the assessment we use when we coach people, a positive outlook is one of the essential competencies we build on. Seeing a situation for what it is and yet focusing on the positive should be basic training for all. Shifting from constantly thinking of the worst scenario to envisioning a good, positive outcome doesn't come easily. Cognitive strategies, such as reframing and positive self-talk, help. It turns out that activities such as meditation and mindfulness exercises can be very helpful—they stimulate and strengthen the part of our brain involved in activating positive thinking. We modified the activity in the mindfulness exercise from neuroscientist Richie Davidson: an exercise for developing the prefrontal lobes and allowing us to relax our thoughts and cultivate an openness to creativity and possibilities.

MINDFULNESS EXERCISE

Set the stopwatch on your phone for three to ten minutes, or even longer, if you wish, depending on how much time you have.

Start by getting comfortable in your seat and sit with a straight spine. You may simply close your eyes for this practice, or you may lower your gaze. Take a few deep breaths as you gather your attention.

Now begin to pay attention to the natural flow of your breathing—in and out, in and out. Focus on the unforced and natural cadence of your breath—in and out, in and out. Focus on the inhalation and exhalation of the breath—in and out.

Neuroscientists call this interoception, "your brain's perception of your body's state, transmitted from receptors on all your internal organs."[5]

As soon as you notice your mind has drifted off toward your thoughts or emotions, bring your focus to your breath. In fact, each time you find your mind wandering, just drop your thinking and bring your attention back to your breath. By engaging in this type of mind training, again and again, for meaningful periods of time, we increase the activity in the prefrontal area of our brain.[6]

The American Psychological Association describes factors that build resilience (we have combined ours with theirs).[7] All of the strategies and pathways can be helpful for all of us. Which ones do you use? Which ones would you like to add to your repertoire? As leaders, also consider which of the strategies below you can use at the organizational level to create new pathways to well-being and strengthening resilience.

- Prioritize relationships by creating opportunities for connection.
- Foster wellness by practicing good sleep habits, nutrition, and daily movement activities.
- Practice mindfulness by finding your own pacing.
- Accept that change happens by reframing the challenge to a learning opportunity.

- Keep things in perspective by asking yourself, "How important is this challenge in your life?"
- Learn from your past: How have you been resilient before?
- Ask for help when needed: Allow others to be there for you.
- Help others by listening to what they need.
- Avoid negative self-talk and negative talk about others. Say no to gossip.
- Move toward your goals be proactive, check in with your motivation.
- Maintain a hopeful outlook: Tell yourself a story about how you *can and will* move forward and list a few new things to do or people to see.

WHOSE RESPONSIBILITY IS IT?

Traditionally, in the education world, there has been little interest in developing adults' social and emotional skills. It's now more and more accepted that education and training in emotional intelligence leadership is one clear way to help school and district leaders grow and strengthen their resilience to persevere during stressful times—and to establish the best behaviors and practices for themselves and for their school communities. We envision schools and school districts as becoming more motivated to support the private inner life of school leaders as well as their outer lives (and eventually becoming such places for teachers and all staff). This can be done in so many ways—imagine:

- Senior leaders are interested in and curious about who their employees are. They look for opportunities to spend time with school-level administrators in the district. Creating time and spaces for connecting and activities for them to participate in helps them be seen and cared for.

- Leaders create special events—dinners and fun activities—to foster connection among staff.
- Superintendents of school districts also create avenues for themselves and their cabinet members to renew. The golf course is one place where many of these senior leaders socialize and talk shop.
- Senior management trusts in principals and other managers to accomplish what must be done, affirms their decisions, and offers guidance when needed.
- Leaders at the senior level recognize the importance of renewal and arrange for school managers to receive a discount at gyms or fitness centers near school locations that are open before and after school.
- Paid childcare is available for school leaders to call on when needed.
- Health clinics are either within the district radius or close by, so leaders who push themselves to get to work when ill can see a physician during the school day.
- Districts cover the costs of mentoring and coaching resources, and school leaders can sign up when they need a guiding hand.
- There is a ready and available coverage system for principals and assistant principals who have family emergencies.
- Twice-yearly community retreats are held for leaders across schools and districts as well as within schools for administrators and teachers.
- Short-term sabbaticals are available to administrative applicants to develop and implement research-based instructional or prosocial strategies for adults and school personnel or for teams of lead teachers and school leaders.
- Assistant principals are upskilled so they can take some tasks away from principals.
- The school district uses a progressive developmental lens with principals to avoid fear-based accountability.
- Built-in weekly time within the school day is available for self-care, exercise and meditation, or spiritual renewal.

- A coaching leadership style is used for managing down or up, versus an authoritative or peacemaking style.
- Professional development includes ongoing coaching based on Boyatzis's intentional change model.[8]
- Goals emanate from school leaders' reflection and aspirational strategies, rather than mandates from above.

Dedicated leadership retreats are a wonderful way to provide a pause, a holding environment, reflective time, and a sense of belonging to a like-minded community. In retreat settings, usually in nature or in purposeful isolation from the everyday crowds of people, leaders can slow down their pace and open their hearts to restore energy and commitment, vulnerability, and trust. When we build a trusting community, it can truly feel like a family—and, with some serious emotional intelligence work, a happy, healthy one! Trusting, caring relationships encourage the motivation to excel. Perhaps part of the reason is that people are more willing to be vulnerable together; they trust showing their challenges as well as their strengths. In showing their challenges, people allow for conversation that can take their understanding deeper and open themselves to feedback and thereby to growth and new learning.

PREPARING OUR LEADERS

We are certain that one needed change is the way we prepare and develop school leaders and the ongoing support they receive as they become masters of their trade.[9] Both of us have taught EI- based leadership at universities. Our classes are usually the first time that prospective school leaders learn about emotional intelligence. Few universities currently include EI or any form of soft skills as part of their leadership curriculum. Often, reflection may be included, but it is a mirror of others' responses rather than an intrapersonal approach in which we evaluate our mindsets and behaviors.

At one point in the early 2000s, when both of us were training leaders in emotional intelligence at Hunter College and Janet was teaching her courses there, the dean of the School of Education at that time referred to our work as unnecessary and not rigorous enough for future school principals. To him, the concept of EI was a sham—a clear example of what *not* to do as a leader. His approach would squash anyone's voice and passion. Fortunately, the president of the university saw Janet's teaching and our work in coaching leaders in EI as more important than the dean did. Emotional intelligence can enable individuals to be sensitive to nuances in others' emotions and detect what they are feeling, as well as respond to others in ways that promote interpersonal acceptance and liking.[10] Individuals with high EI have better interpersonal relationships.[11]

Each of us had the good fortune to integrate this work into our leadership courses at both Teachers College and Hunter College. At both universities, this course was part of the larger leadership program. Each course had its own syllabus, but both taught variations of emotionally intelligent leadership and included school-based social and emotional learning, too.

If we begin this work in preservice training, it will naturally extend into assistant principal practice and eventually the principalship and beyond. Of course, EI isn't everything. But by learning and practicing EI, we can start to change behaviors and attitudes so that they serve the goals we have for desired change. A self-proclaimed emotionally intelligent person—for example, someone with a Machiavellian approach to the world—can do more harm than good. Conversely, emotionally intelligent people who are ethical and compassionate leaders can move mountains in their schools and beyond.

Developing strong adult relationships adds to the possibility and probability of positive change. These are questions we often ask ourselves: "What can I do to support my teachers and the families they serve? What could our communities and larger society do to support the well-being of the people who most influence their children's education?" *Social wellness* refers to the relationships we have and how we interact with others. Social wellness involves building healthy, nurturing, and supportive relationships as well as fostering a genuine connection with those around you. Our relationships are what heal us during difficult times. Every school leader and school district leader will benefit from asking the stakeholders in the school or district what they need to be successful—especially in uncertain times, such as the present.

CREATE SPACE FOR LIVING OUR CORE VALUES

As we talk about resilience, we need to open doors for leaders to have the agency to speak about their deepest values and beliefs, to include them in their school's core values, and to take a stand for injustices that they see hurting young people and families in their communities. Long-held discriminatory mindsets and practices are alive in our institutions. We talk a lot about social justice, but how is the real work to make a difference happening? Schools are prime places for resilience to be nurtured. Unfortunately, as one principal recently said to me, "I have very strong beliefs about the injustices in our society and in my school caused by race and ethnicity. I want to be more proactive, but I am afraid of being targeted by the system in some way."

I (Janet) completed my master's degree in the 1980s in bilingual education. It was a new discipline back in the day, and many of my Latinx classmates were hopeful that the best education would finally be provided to bilingual children. But the field of bilingual education developed slowly due to a pervasive mental model that still permeates states' policymaking bodies: "In America, we speak English." The battle over bilingualism emerged then and is still being carried on today. The flawed thinking that bilingualism hurts children's acquisition of the English language, that transitional programs assure that children will learn English sooner, and that maintenance programs slow down the learning of English is still touted. Despite the strong evidence that bilingual education and especially dual immersion programs work, we have still not gotten it right, and many of our children and young adults continue to struggle to graduate from high school due to improper placement in bilingual programs or in English-only classes.

Americans have not had a strong propensity to learn a language other than English. Most Europeans, for example, speak two or more languages.[12] Our global economy depends on the advancement of bilingualism and biculturalism. We know that bilingualism has neurocognitive benefits. Code-switching from their home language to the target language, for example, increases students' abilities to deal with cognitive conflict. We have marveled at the skill that bilingual children have when they switch between Spanish and English often to translate for their parent.

We hope this chapter has posed some questions to think about for everyone who cares about education. Some of you who are reading this book may even be planning retirement. One principal told us that he was thinking of stepping back into the assistant principalship because he was so overwhelmed by the job. We ask: How can we support well-being and expand the resources that make public education viable, holistic, equitable, and just? What are we prepared to do to help our school leaders maintain well-being at the top of their game, work to their fullest potential, and communicate joy and inspiration to those they supervise? What can we do to help our leaders feel fulfilled and spread their wings as leaders, not just be effective managers? What can we do to help leaders transform those who work with our nation's children—the thousands of teachers who want to do their best for young people and their families? Resilience is built by creating protective factors.

THINK ABOUT IT

What can we as a society consider doing to shift the weight that we put on our school leaders and, in turn, our teachers?

We end this chapter by once again attending to Principal Brooke's inner struggle and her resilience as she advocated for changing the designation of her school from closed admission to open admissions, which would allow students from throughout the city to enter a lottery for entrance into her high-performing high school. Previously, only students in the zoned area for this school could attend, and most were White and middle-class. The following is excerpted from a longer story:

> We had been working on internal changes to make our school anti-racist. We got to a point where not only the teachers, but the students illuminated what was happening. There are so few people of color in this community. The absence of their presence was like a stalemate. When I read *White Fragility*, I felt like [the author] was talking to me. I was missing out on not having the perspective of a person of color. I wanted to give my students an understanding of the inequities caused by race and class. More of what my activist students raised was that the school was an example of racist practices. Some teachers were on the other side whenever we talked about changing our school population of students. A group of kids who visited other diversified schools saw vibrant communities and others struggling. They asked, "How can we be true to our mission of compassion, collaboration, and courage, and be a glaring example of exclusiveness?"
>
> I moved from defensiveness to saying, "I cannot do this anymore." I had in my head this idea of integrity. I pushed on the district to look at the screening process. It was the most glaring example of maintaining the status quo of those who already have the privilege. The next person who became superintendent shepherded me through. She said, "You have a stance, and it is my job to support you in your stance." I wrote an open letter, which was picked up by social media. The *Times* said it was an indictment of the mayor for not having exercised his agency for a better outcome. I said it is not OK to be the only Black kid in a literature class reading Toni Morrison, to be that much of a racial minority in a school. The letter was one part macro and one part micro. I took a lot of criticism because the district said, "You don't like our kids." "What will happen to my younger kid without priority?" Some criticism came from

a staff member: "If you want to teach those kids, you should go to another school." On the other hand, supporters flocked around me. When I asked, "How did you know about Lab [the New York City Lab School for Collaborative Studies]?" One teacher candidate said, "I saw your open letter and I wanted to work for someone like you."

The PA [Parents' Association] president gave me headaches. There was no response from the mayor or the chancellor. Some pseudo-political people were tasked to manage me. I did collaborate with the principals of Eleanor Roosevelt School, as they had a similar priority. Once we spoke to enrollment as a united front, it helped a lot because it was clear that the policy was retrograde.

The results? Mayor DeBlasio did end geographic screens. For the last three years, we have been a citywide open school. At the orientation it was amazing. It's not yet an accurate example of the cities' demographics. There are kids of color, Muslim and African, Latinx, and African American. A beautiful mix of youth. Now we have race equity. Rather than having kids come in from the local elite middle schools, they come in from everywhere.[13]

THINK ABOUT IT

Do you have the courage to stand up for what you believe in your role as a school leader? Is there support for you to have a voice? What can help you become more resilient?

CHAPTER THREE

The Self-Aware Leader

"Know thyself." The ancient Greek motto inscribed at the entrance of the Temple of Delphi, often ascribed to Socrates and visible in Plato's writings, was one of the earliest mentions of the importance of knowing your likes and dislikes, your strengths and challenges, what is in alignment with your values and what is not.

Emotional self-awareness is the capacity to tune into your feelings, sense inner signals, understand what you are feeling and recognize how your emotions impact your ability to focus, make decisions, build and maintain relationships, and negotiate your everyday ups and downs, as well as your performance. It is a competency for leadership at any level, as well as for many other aspects of life.[1]

LEADERS' SELF-AWARENESS: EI IN ACTION

Self-awareness is foundational to leading a healthy, happy, fulfilling personal and professional life. It is key to our ability to set a vision for ourselves, seek out the type of work we most desire, create and maintain fulfilling relationships, and perform to our highest potential. Self-aware school leaders are perceived as authentic. They know their values and their purpose and move consciously through life—and people who interact with authentic leaders feel that they live in congruence with the values they espouse and are aligned with who they say they are. They are aware of their impact on others and how others may see and experience them, and they use that awareness to inform their job performance. Self-awareness is the anchor of emotional intelligence. Self-aware leaders know themselves. When leaders do not, scenarios like the following told by a high school teacher may unfold:

> My assistant principal sometimes has a hard time "reading the room." The other day I went into his office to check in as I usually do every day. I was sharing how I felt mentally drained between balancing work and my graduate classes as the semester was ending. I expressed how I was finding it hard to find time for myself to relax and "shut off." While I was speaking, he was nodding his head as if he was listening. Right after my emotional "confession," he responded, "Well, speaking of having too much on your plate, I would like you to cover my senior class next Wednesday while I'm out of the building. I want you to create a lesson on college degrees." I was shocked at this insensitive response. I answered his request by saying I could not do this right now given my current workload and asked him if he had heard anything that I was just saying a few seconds before. His facial expression appeared as if he realized not to ask this favor at this time. He responded, "It's okay, I'll get someone else to do it." His lack of emotional attunement reminded me of his limitation in empathy—a serious concern for any educational leader. And beyond that, while his "realization" could be seen on his face, he made no effort to apologize. This assistant principal was all about his own agenda. When I finally said something to him, he realized how insensitive he had been. Still, no apology.

Unfortunately, stories like this one are all too common. Why does self-awareness (of our emotions *and* the impact of our emotions) matter to us as educational leaders? Think about it. Without self-awareness, we are out of touch with our feelings, our behaviors, and how we are impacting others. We may hurt others because we are unaware of how our behavior lands on our colleagues or teachers. We may not have a clue when our own facial expressions or body language or stress sets the tone for our faculty meeting. And when we are not aware, the cascading disconnected effect is felt in the response of our teachers and staff. While it may not be easy, we can improve our self-awareness through reflective strategies that enhance self-development, others' development, and ultimately the culture and climate of the school.

Self-awareness matters to educational leadership because it is the foundation of adult development. "Korn Ferry Hay Group, a global organizational strategy and talent consulting firm, found that among leaders with multiple strengths in Emotional Self-Awareness, 92% had teams with high energy and high performance. Conversely, leaders low in Emotional Self-Awareness created negative climates 78% of the time."[2] Emotionally intelligent school leaders can identify and understand their feelings and how they impact their day-to-day leadership. EI leaders use those data to make decisions and adjust their behaviors accordingly. The more self-aware we are, the more success we will have in making intentional changes in our thoughts and behaviors.[3] Self-awareness is the prerequisite for self-management, the subject of chapter 4.

Self-awareness is the necessary foundation for managing our own behaviors, engaging productively, working to our fullest potential, and developing mutually satisfying relationships.[4] Self-awareness allows leaders to check in on their feelings to be present for themselves and others—which is particularly critical in times of turmoil or crises. Leaders who are self-aware read others' emotions (using social awareness) more clearly, and they know when to ask questions to understand what someone is thinking or feeling. Self-awareness is the process that lets leaders know when an action or choice is aligned with values and when something feels "off." Ultimately, self-awareness is the anchor that deepens the way we engage others, build, and maintain positive relationships, co-regulate with others, and allow trust to grow.

THE LEADER'S IMPACT ON CLIMATE AND CULTURE

The school principal directly impacts the school's culture, teachers' commitment to the work, job satisfaction, student achievement, and well-being.[5] Over time, the principal's emotions, values, mindsets, and behaviors influence the climate in which learning takes place, the health of the school culture, and the quality of the relationships that principals build with their staff and that superintendents build with principals. These elements create or negate the support teachers need to be most effective in their classrooms.[6] With the trust and guidance of the school leader, teachers increase their motivation and willingness to perform their jobs to their highest ability. "Principals' social and emotional competencies (SECs), well-being, and leadership form the foundation that influences the school climate, teachers' commitment and well-being, family and community partnerships, and student outcomes."[7] A 2021 review of the relationship between a school leader's emotional intelligence and leadership revealed that the top three skills and competencies that mattered to a leader's effectiveness are self-awareness, self-management, and empathy. Communication skills were also important.[8]

Tracey, a former graduate student who had been an assistant principal for six years in East Harlem decided to become a principal at a local elementary school in her own city. In a meeting with her during the summer before the school year began, we asked, "What is the first change on your agenda?" Her immediate reply was, "The culture and climate." This school had the same leader for almost twenty years. "This former leader used top-down micromanagement. The teachers were so used to her telling them what to do that they can't think for themselves, make the right decisions for their children," she said wistfully. We responded, "Sounds like you are going to need professional development in EI."

She agreed, "Yeah, that's if I can get my staff to stay after dismissal at 2:35. The teachers at this school are out the door as soon as they dismiss their students!" Four years later, the school has become an authentic learning environment—a warm and caring, high-achieving, emotionally intelligent school. Teachers have agency, and students have a voice. Tracey accomplished this change slowly, methodically, and strategically with tons of emotional intelligence. Clearly, her self-awareness allowed her to stay optimistic and maintain patience as individual staff members came around. By the way, today, her teachers are also teaching a social and emotional learning curriculum, The Leader in Me, in every classroom. Mission accomplished.

SELF-AWARENESS AND SCHOOL CULTURE

It takes a smart school leader to "see and sense" the system.[9] Seeing and sensing a culture and climate requires leaders to use all their senses to see the connections between each system on both an organizational level and an intra- and interpersonal level. This self-aware, often intuitive process makes the difference between a manager and a leader and between a mediocre leader and a highly effective one.[10] Smart school leaders conduct analyses of the many factors that contribute to their success as leaders, whether they are leading a building or a district. Careful analysis leads to a strategic plan so that the leader and her team can plan, implement, and monitor the changes needed in the years ahead.

What many leaders forget to do is to explore the faculty and staff mental models that are often hidden in the system. The beliefs and values of others may remain dormant when avoided, but they still impact every decision that is made. And when threatened, these beliefs and values can rise to the surface, slowing down forward movement and disrupting the allegiance you thought you had. If we want a culture of honesty and clear values, we must address the elephant in the room and allow ourselves to be vulnerable. That means we must allow everyone's voice to be heard so that we know where everyone stands. This can happen only if you have spent time building trusting relationships. Don't get us wrong: there is a time and a place for everything. A toxic culture will take time to heal, so moving too fast can lead to failure. Take one step at a time. Build allegiances.

Remember what researchers say: for every negative comment you make, it takes five positive comments to clear the air!

THE LEADER'S SELF-AWARENESS

A LEADERSHIP CHALLENGE

Which part of me will come to the fore
with each situation that knocks at my door?
Which tape from my past will play in my ear
amplifying or muffling the words that I hear?
What scenes from my past do I see in your face?
Is the flashback pleasant . . . or one to erase?
For with each day's encounters seeming fresh
and so new,
There's probably some link to our lives in review.
—DEIDRE R. FARMBRY

What does an emotionally intelligent, highly self-aware school leader do that differs from what someone without high self-awareness might do? Emotionally intelligent, self-aware school leaders are reflective—of themselves and others. Like Farmbry's protagonist in the poem we just quoted, emotionally intelligent leaders, scan their bodies to ensure they are centered, clear-minded, and present in each moment, so as not to overlay any situation with their own experiences and traumas. The most outstanding characteristic of emotionally intelligent leaders is their ability to reflect on their own and others' emotions that drive behavior. These leaders' self-awareness may take into consideration factors of their identity and how perceptions may impact their capacity to lead. They are self-aware of the nuances of their behaviors and how context may challenge or support their leadership. This proactive thinking can ward off negativity and put a check on any personal biases that might impede positive outcomes.

In the following example, what does self-awareness look like in this leader's words and actions?

> Principal Solas found herself in a quandary when she learned that half of her staff were discontented with a new direction in teaching writing. They had been using their current writing program for more than five years, and they could not see the benefit of switching now. Principal Solas believed that this new approach would make a substantial difference in her students' writing skills. She had recently spent six months obtaining training and coaching in emotionally intelligent leadership. As a result of this professional development journey, she noticed that she was dealing with her emotions differently than she typically would have; she was actually managing them in the service of her goals—rather than venting, as she tended to do previously. Principal Solas shared, "Instead of being angry about the situation, I was able to reflect, identify what I was feeling and why, and put an effective plan of action in place, which allowed all voices to be heard as they were shaping and incorporating the new learning." As a result, she began the writing program at one grade level as a pilot instead of adopting the program schoolwide right away. This choice built trust with her staff, creating allies and ambassadors for the new program and resulting in a greater readiness to move forward.

This is a pretty clear example of a self-aware leader—but how do we get there?

There are several steps that we can take. These include regular reflection, 360-degree surveys, feedback conferences, regular journaling, and listening to our self-talk. Self-talk is the inner dialogue that we hold with ourselves in our minds. We listen to our thoughts and reflect on their meaning and relevance to situations in our lives.

THE PROCESS OF REFLECTION

Perhaps you are thinking now, "How do I become more self-aware, or even take the time, when every minute of my day is spent responding to a teacher, a parent, or a supervisor?" One key to enhancing self-awareness is to spend more time tuning in to yourself, engaging in self-reflection, meditation, or journaling. How much time? You may be thinking, "That's a commodity I don't have." But you can start by making the time for a check-in that takes as little as two minutes! Considering the clear and science-supported benefits of being self-aware, and the risks of *not* being self-aware, ask yourself, "Do I want to do this—can I commit?" And then, consider (because it's important to be a realist) what barriers may get in the way. Self-reflection requires dedicated time. Dedicating this time allows reflection to move from being a good idea to a practice to a habit. Reflection allows us to pause and look at our own feelings and those of others. It gives us the chance to see different perspectives and opens the opportunity for possible actions that were not previously evident. Reflection creates the space for us to understand our motivations and our impact, to see into the near future, and to envision other possibilities. The result? We can manage our emotions and then our actions, communicate more effectively, create more fulfilling relationships, and make better decisions. There are many apps that can help you, by pinging you to check in with your feelings; among them is How We Feel, developed by the Yale Center for Emotional Intelligence and Ben Silberman and the project team at How We Feel.[11]

Neuroscience is becoming more sophisticated in support of these leaps. When we move away from an overstimulated amygdala, the part of the brain that controls our emotions, to a more rational response from our prefrontal cortex, the thinking part of the brain, we calm down, and the outcome is always better than it is when we do not tune in to ourselves or the feelings of others.

THINK ABOUT IT

What type of self -reflection do you engage in? What type of reflection do you ask of others? How do some school leaders find the time to build the habit of self-reflection? What type of reflection seems possible: check-ins, journaling, increasing positive self-talk? How will this reflection enhance your practice?

FEEDBACK

How do we know that we are self-aware? The truth is that we are not necessarily the best observers of our skills in self-awareness. In fact, we are bad at it—most of us overestimate our ability. Large-scale studies found that "in ten distinct studies consisting of over 5,000 people they found that 10%–15% of the people studied were actually self-aware."[12] Across the studies, two broad categories of self-awareness kept emerging. The first, which researchers dubbed *internal self-awareness*, represents how clearly we see our own values, passions, aspirations, how we fit with our environment, reactions (including thoughts, feelings, behaviors, strengths, and weaknesses), and impact on others. We've found that internal self-awareness is associated with higher job and relationship satisfaction, personal and social control, and happiness; it is negatively related to anxiety, stress, and depression.

The second category, *external self-awareness*, means understanding how other people view us, in terms of the same factors listed above. Our research shows that people who know how others see them are more skilled at showing empathy and taking others' perspectives. Leaders who see themselves as their employees do tend to have a better relationship with them, feel more satisfied with them, and see them as more effective. "Successful leadership often surfaces when people become aware of critical personal experiences in their life, understand the driving forces, respond by rethinking about self, redirect their moves, and reshape their actions."[13]

To be more accurate about our self-awareness we need to understand what we are feeling and thinking on the inside. We need to ask ourselves, "How are we outwardly expressing this awareness? Do our outer behaviors match our inner thoughts and feelings? Are they OK to display or to talk about in the social context?" We administer the 360-degree Emotional and Social Competency Inventory (ESCI) survey to school leaders to assess their EI behavioral competencies. They take a self-assessment and send the assessment to raters. When the scores come back, each school leader works with a coach to determine their strength and challenge competencies. If the perceptions of others match the leaders' own perceptions about their self-awareness and other behavioral competencies, this match adds greater validity to the scores; the leaders' self-perceptions are probably accurate. Others see them as they see themselves. Each of these competencies relates to one or more leadership behaviors that encompass emotional intelligence. There are times when we use the Mayer-Salovey-Caruso Emotional Intelligence Test (MSCEIT).[14] This ability-based assessment gives a closer look at the actual emotional intelligence a person has, as opposed to perceptions. The MSCEIT can be very helpful in assessing the actual ability of the person in discrete emotion skills. However, just because we get high scores on an EI assessment—and demonstrate EI knowledge doesn't mean that we choose to *act* emotionally intelligent all the time! MSCEIT results help practitioners know what they are capable of feeling and doing emotionally. Then it is up to each person to manage his or her words and actions.

One way or another, honest feedback from people who work with you can make a world of difference in your willingness to take a hard look at yourself and think about your own experience. As professors and clinicians, we often have students and clients complete a self-rating in EI and then seek feedback from three others, including a boss or supervisor. When assessments are not accessible due to cost factors, we ask students and clients to select three people with whom they work and who see them regularly. They ask these three people to respond to the following questions, either face-to-face or in writing:

1. What do you believe are my greatest strengths as a person and professional, and how do you see these in my professional behaviors?
2. What do you believe is an area that is an opportunity for me to grow in (challenge area) as I pursue my professional goals?
3. Can you give me an example of how I demonstrate behaviors in this area, as I would genuinely appreciate the feedback. Can you tell me how improving in this area might help me to grow personally and professionally?

Most of our coaches who have completed the assessment are surprised at the honest feedback they receive. It's unusual for educators to ask for such feedback from a supervisor or even a coworker. The coachees take these responses to heart and sincerely set a course for improving an area that they feel needs improvement.

The higher up you are in your position, the less likely you are to seek and receive honest feedback. Who wants to take the chance of telling their boss what they think about their leadership? Who feels psychologically "safe" enough to give tough feedback to their leader? School leaders have commented on the usefulness of the ESCI tool for seeing themselves through both their own eyes and others'.

In our work with leaders, we use various assessments to look at personality, conflict style, empathy, and more. These assessments provide a person with a snapshot of who they are, which they reflect on to learn more about themselves. There are many vehicles available to know oneself better. One needs only the desire to look—and to bring this to faculty.

LISTEN TO YOUR INNER VOICE

When we take the time to tune into ourselves, to listen to our inner voice, we also become more familiar with our self-talk. Self-talk is the inner monologue or dialogue that we say to ourselves in our minds. Most of us have a long list of innermost thoughts and feelings—and, sadly, judgments: "I can't manage this level of stress—I am not strong enough." "I am way too caring to others." "I can't believe I opened the meeting that way—so ridiculous." Introspection involves consciously examining our thoughts, feelings, motives, and behaviors.[15]

Author Nir Eyal writes of self-talk, "it gives you access to understanding yourself, self-reflection lets you process what you learn, and insights are the answers you come up with and that you can act upon."[16] Through self-awareness, you become less likely to veer off track when difficult emotions surface. The goal is to have knowledge about ourselves to utilize in some action that creates movement away from the patterns that we long to escape. We refer to this as *actionable self-reflection*. Introspection by itself does not guarantee insight or improved self-awareness.

You may be surprised to know, or to become fully aware, that you are emotionally present only part of the time. For school leaders who feel unbearably stressed, their own residual feelings can impact how they show up emotionally. Deep-rooted abuses, as well as lesser yet intense immediate circumstances, can distract us or leave residual scars that can interfere with performance. In these cases, leaders need to allow themselves to feel their feelings and to work through these feelings and thoughts. In this way, leaders can recognize when a strong emotion may interfere with their sound judgment. As a profession, we pay too little attention to the inner life of school leaders. We need to engage with them more consistently; we need to know how they are feeling. We know they need the conversations, the suggestions on how to manage, how to cope in tough times. They need possible outlets for feelings so that they can manage their pain and suffering, balance the joys and challenges, ameliorate the sometimes unbearable stress, and change unwanted and unproductive behaviors. Leaders need to learn how to love themselves enough to take care of themselves, too. In developing new behaviors, new routes to self-awareness, school leaders may even find the fortitude to address situations that created pain and suffering. Powerful self-reflection can be a catalyst for positive change in problematic contexts. And you are the role model. When you are at the top of your game, others will follow you; others will walk the path you light for them and practice the skills and tools you model.

COACHING

Coaching (outside of sports) is an opportunity more recently engaged as a pathway to increase self-awareness and build emotional and relational skills for leaders in all fields. Like a therapist, the coach takes specific actions unique to each coachee or school leader—we will give you more detail in later chapters—to create a trusting relationship and a safe space to explore feelings. Unlike a therapy session, coaching is not a place to unearth past traumas or discuss troubled marital relationships. Coaches work to create a psychologically safe space where school leaders are encouraged to be vulnerable; where leaders can let down their guard and openly discuss stressors, challenges, and uncertainties, as well as mining their goals and strengths for ways to positively impact their performance. We hear from many that sharing uncomfortable feelings and challenges—or even being vulnerable enough to share goals—is a new, sometimes tough and yet a very welcome experience. Unlike a mentor, a coach is not likely to tell someone what to do. Instead, coaches look at the present, explore what is working or not working, and let their coachee lead the way, identifying actions that could be helpful to the school leaders' achieving a desired goal or outcome. Using powerful open-ended questioning and listening to their coachee with calm and positive presence, the coach guides the school leader to leverage strengths to enhance more challenging areas, characteristics, and skills. School leaders, when asked what they take away from this experience, share comments such as the following:

- I was able to take time to reflect, which I often don't give myself.
- My survey results led me to understand how I need to become more empathetic.
- My perception of a leadership model has shifted to include new ways to support others and encourage their best performance.
- I have gained confidence in my abilities to create a supportive environment.
- Thinking about my emotions and feelings factors into the decisions I make. I have increased my self-awareness, built more positive relationships, and am able to set goals personally and professionally.

Goal setting with aspirational thinking is an essential part of the coaching process. It moves the leader into action. School leaders are accustomed to being achievers and regularly setting goals. What is more difficult for them is dreaming big dreams or aspirational thinking, which creates a vision and a space for possibilities to happen. Working in such a high-accountability system can stifle creativity and the ability to envision things other than what is immediately expected or what others deem the norm. A seasoned coach helps school leaders expand their thinking and make the connections between their inner selves and their role as leaders. With this awareness, insights can be reached and steps toward desired change accomplished. Self-insight is understood as the clarity with which individuals can perceive and understand their thoughts, feelings, and behavior.[17]

There is a significant amount of empirical research indicating the existence of a positive correlation between self-insight and well-being.[18] Change is never easy. We need all the support we can get. We'll tell you more about coaching in chapter 8.

HONORING THE SACRED AND THE SPIRIT

For some, the belief in a higher power helps them put things in perspective. An expression of love for and thanks to their creator or teacher is central to their being. We hear from many that in challenging or frightening moments, prayer or conversations with a higher power can be comforting. The spiritual elements of one's identity sit at the core of one's being. Having regular prayer time, either alone or with others in the community and family, fortifies the spirit. Our life experiences have either rooted us in a deep faith or taken us to other ways of connecting with our deeper selves. Some may hold on to universal truths and values as guides to living a good life, caring for others, and the greater good. Religious beliefs are not the same as your relationship with your inner and outer worlds, though for many, such beliefs are central to their lives.

Transformational Educational Leadership (TEL) is a not-for-profit group that invites educational leaders to cocreate a beloved community that welcomes everyone's faith and spirituality.[19] Together, they engage in promoting well-being and fostering collective action for social justice by engaging in sacred activism, heart-centered practices, Indigenous ways of knowing, and embodied presence. Leaders realize their inner potential to lead from an awareness of the interconnection of all beings and a radical love that embraces all life. Your life experiences have either rooted you in a deep faith or taken you to other ways of connecting with your deeper self. For some, looking within has not been or is not a priority area, and such exploration is novel and awakening or fearful or simply undesirable. At Transformative Education Leadership, leaders realize their inner potential to lead from an awareness of the interconnection of all beings and a radical love that embraces all life, while calmly acknowledging and accepting one's own feelings, thoughts, and bodily sensations.[20]

Lisa Miller, author of *The Awakened Brain* and professor of clinical psychology at Columbia University, defines spirituality as both a transcendent relationship with something bigger than oneself and an understanding that this connection runs through each of us: "The belief in a higher power helps many people put things in perspective. Expressing love for and thanks to their creator or teacher is central to their being. In challenging or frightening moments, this relationship can be comforting. The spiritual elements of their identity sit at the core of their being. Having regular reflective time either alone or with others in the community and your family fortifies the spirit."[21]

JOURNAL WRITING

Another way to access your inner voice and increase your self-awareness is through focused writing. Taking the time to reflect on a situation or a strong feeling can help unravel the components of the problem, bringing you greater clarity for decision-making. This actionable self-reflection uses the wisdom gained from self-reflection to move us toward the best possible steps to take in that moment or situation. As we have noted, introspection may lead to insight, but unless it is followed by action it won't lead to change.

We strongly encourage journal writing for school leaders. Many school leader colleagues say that they can't journal because of the time it takes. Educational leaders are always concerned first with their constituents—students, teachers, and parents—and the expectations and mandates from above. Taking fifteen minutes to write down their thoughts and feelings seems impossible—an unrealistic ask. Some people, however, have used a journal for many years and have made it a daily endeavor. Using prompts can get you started. Write for five minutes at first and slowly increase the time. Work with a trusted colleague or a coach and tackle tough questions: "What keeps you up at night?" or "How did you come to embrace your personal values?" "What questions about your leadership are you living with right now?" "Who in your life is taking up most mind share? And is that OK with you?" Writing is a gateway into the healing process, a portal to thoughts and feelings. Writing can lead us to be open and curious about seeing other perspectives. Author James Pennebaker tells us, "Expressing painful emotions is hard—yet it can actually improve our mental and physical health"—one compelling reason to journal![22]

MINDFULNESS

Mindfulness was popularized in the US by Jon Kabat-Zinn, professor emeritus of medicine and creator of the Stress Reduction Clinic and the Center for Mindfulness in Medicine, Health Care, and Society at the University of Massachusetts Medical School. Kabat-Zinn adapted Buddhist teachings on mindfulness to develop the Stress Reduction and Relaxation Program, later renamed Mindfulness-Based Stress Reduction (MBSR). This limited possible connections between mindfulness and Buddhism, instead putting MBSR in a scientific context.[23]

Mindfulness is the psychological process of bringing one's attention to the internal and external experiences occurring in the present moment, which develops through the practice of meditation and other training. Many see mindfulness as stress reduction because of Kabat-Zin's work.[24] It is that and more.

Another perspective is that of Ellen Langer, a social psychologist and the author of the book *Mindfulness*, originally published in 1989, in which she defines the practice from a purely scientific perspective. For Langer, mindfulness is the simple act of actively noticing things.[25] Langer's ideas, once considered unconventional, are now more mainstream. For Langer, language and mindset are what make mindfulness so powerful. She speaks of context as the ability to reframe one's thinking in the moment, to see a negative event as a favorable possibility. One avoids judgment and negative thinking and replaces them with hope and positivity. Another component of Langer's understanding of mindfulness is variability, which means knowing that one can change any aspect of life depending on one's mindset. For example, a person could see specific symptoms of a cold as indicators of increased sickness (mindlessness) or instead notice small bodily changes as indicators of getting better (mindfulness). In this way, the person can feel more positive about the situation and get better.

A well-known giant in the Western field of mindfulness is Richard Davidson, William James and Vilas Professor of Psychology and Psychiatry at the University of Wisconsin–Madison and the founder and director of the Center for Healthy Minds. He is best known for his groundbreaking work studying emotion and the brain. *Time* Magazine named Davidson one of "the 100 most influential people in the world" in 2006.[26] Richard is a highly sought-after expert and speaker, leading conversations on well-being on international stages such as the World Economic Forum, where he serves on the Global Council on Mental Health.

Valerie Brown, ordained by Thich Nhat Hanh as a member of the Tiep Hien Order, is an educational consultant who specializes in leadership and mindfulness. In her book, *The Mindful Leader,* she talks about the positive effects of mindfulness, and even more helpful are the numerous examples she provides of mindfulness practices for the school or district leader. Several examples are the twenty-second breathing practice, the body scan, the beauty bath, mindful walking, half-breath practice, and more. We like the practice called RAIN, which is particularly helpful when you are very upset and about to "lose it": *Recognize* what is happening. *Allow* things to be as they are. *Investigate* the inner experience with kindness. Practice *non-identification* (don't identify yourself with the thoughts and emotion).[27]

If you would like to learn about some of the research and practice in mindfulness, the Mind & Life Institute is the site to visit. The Mind & Life Institute is a US-registered, not-for-profit 501(c) organization founded in 1987 to establish the field of contemplative sciences. Based in Charlottesville, Virginia, the institute "brings science and contemplative wisdom together to better understand the mind and create positive change in the world."[28]

CREATE A SELF-AWARE MINDFUL CULTURE

You may be asking yourself, "What does mindfulness have to do with me and my school?" Or if this speaks to you, there may be an existing program in your school as part of your SEL focus; or you may be interested but have decided there is no time. Over the past decade, mindfulness programs have become more common in schools. Research over decades (resting on hundreds of years of mindfulness practice) reveals, repeatedly, that mindfulness skills improve memory, organizational skills, and reading and math scores, as well as strategies to reduce stress. These practices are providing young people with strategies to reduce anxiety and to regulate anger and other strong emotions.[29]

Several of the star leaders we work with have built mindfulness practices into their own lives and into the school's culture. Like any other school change effort, building mindfulness doesn't happen overnight. These principals have experienced the positive effects that mindfulness practices had on them and desired to bring these practices to their staff and students. Principal Kevin Froner of the Manhattan Hunter Science High School (MHSHS) shared, "I wanted to give my students the strategies that I have acquired; they help me be a better person and leader. If my students could begin their practice early in life, they will have a greater chance at a successful life." Kevin spoke about the steps he has taken to bring this thinking into his schools:

> First, I provided the teachers with different opportunities for professional development. Two years ago, we brought mindfulness into our advisory period. Every teacher taught an advisory, but not all of them were supporters of teaching mindfulness. This year my support staff, counselors, etc., are teaching this component, and it's working much better. I am expanding their practice into three periods of the school day. I hope to slowly integrate mindfulness into the culture.

"Right now," he says, "our kids are using these strategies. They know how to use their breath before acting impulsively. There is a common language forming in which mindfulness practices make a difference in their lives. Teachers and students are mostly on board." The good news is that students at MHSHS are not just learning how to regulate their thoughts and behaviors; they are reducing the stress in their lives and academically scoring at the top of urban schools nationwide.[30]

Principal Kevin is a graduate of the Summer Principals Academy at Teachers College, Columbia University—affectionately known as SPA. The transformational program, founded by Dr. Craig Richards in 2005 and conducted over the course of two summers with an intervening year of a shadowing practicum, prepares aspiring leaders for taking on the role of a school leader. From the beginning, SPA offered a track named SAT—Self-Awareness Training.

I (Robin) was on the founding faculty and one of the instructors of SAT, which consisted of two parts: social and emotional learning and mindfulness training. At the time, we chose to name the course Self-Awareness Training because, in practice, students were asked to turn their attention to themselves—both to recognize and understand their emotional life, including the nuances of emotion vocabulary and the way they express and regulate emotions, and also to quiet the mind and learn the art and practice of focused attention in the present. In the first year of SPA, mindfulness training, which was held every morning in summer, was optional. Dr. Richards encouraged but did not require attendance. Many students were reluctant because the training was new, it added another hour to the day, and they had never made the connection before. Leadership and self-awareness training—*why?* But, as more people attended regularly with the ongoing support of Dr. Richards and a team of expert SAT practitioners, the course became required.

Principal Kevin wasn't the only graduate of SPA's course in self-awareness training who later brought emotional intelligence to his school. One outstanding star leader who has deeply infused mindfulness into her school's culture, Dawn DeCosta, was one of the students at SPA who initially questioned the requirement of SAT practice and leadership. Of course, even with her curiosity and questions, Dawn embraced the practice and immediately became an enthusiastic, passionate student of mindfulness. Years later, when she reflected on her initial skepticism, she told me that it wasn't until her first days in the role of leader that she really knew, experienced, and wholeheartedly embraced mindfulness as a daily practice. Dawn's recognition of the importance of settling and being present not only to herself but to the moment has translated into infusing mindfulness into school culture. This includes beginning each day with a student-led mindfulness moment in the cafeteria, interspersing mindfulness meditations throughout the school day, and training fifth-grade meditation leaders to teach mindfulness to the younger students. I (Robin) had the privilege of working with Dawn's fifth-grade meditation leaders; I was awed by the visit.

Deputy Superintendent Dawn has now taken her work to another level. She is implementing CRASEL (Culturally Responsive Affirmative and Social and Emotional Leadership) in her district. Its goals are to prepare leaders and teachers to meet the social, emotional, and cultural needs of Black and Brown students; protect the rights of Black and Brown students to receive an equitable education; and modernize curriculum, pedagogy, and assessment to support the positive academic ability of all learners.[31]

SELF-AWARENESS AND EQUITY

Self-awareness can help us recognize how our mental models impact how we see the world around us, others, and ourselves. It's impossible to be a leader today and not recognize the influence that these assumptions have over our decisions, the relationships we form, and how we promote equity for every student. First and foremost, we need to expand our consciousness of how race influences our self-awareness and how different cultures view the process of becoming more self-aware. Racial and ethnic identity development involves a sense of self that is shaped over time by experiences. Because we live in a society that stereotypes groups of people—most often people of color—in negative ways, it is important to have a foundational strength rooted in who you are that can effectively deal with society's "isms."

There is research that shows the more you see your racial and ethnic identity in positive ways and take pride in your group identity, the better your mental health. Racial and ethnic identity develops over time. It is not linear but circular, meaning that people can go in and out of stages of development, returning to an old way of thinking or remaining in one stage for a long time.

We are living during a time when emotions are heightened, and people have had enough. The Black Lives Matter movement that emerged from the unvindicated killing of Trayvon Martin by George Zimmerman in 2012 continues to push for changes in response to senseless murders that plague the lives of Black citizens and other people of color. The history of these vicious, senseless murders of mostly Black boys and men started long before Trayvon's murder. In the 1960s, Martin Luther King Jr.'s leadership allowed for a ray of hope in Black communities, but his death left the door wide open for White supremacy to reign with impunity. Between 2013 and 2019, 1,976 Black people were killed by police, and the numbers continue rising to this day. Trayvon Martin's death, followed by the guilty verdict for Derek Chauvin and other police officers in George Floyd's murder, has placed the conversation about race at every American's dinner table. Shortly after Floyd's death, twenty-five police officers were charged with murder. Still, in 2020 alone, 229 Black people were killed by police.[32] Furthermore, "the increase in murders of Black women comes as the overall US murder rate rose nearly 30% during the pandemic, the biggest jump in six decades." Some 2,077 Black women and girls were killed in 2021, a 51 percent increase over 2019 and the largest jump for any racial or gender group during that period, according to the Centers for Disease Control and Prevention. Overall, the number of killings nationwide increased 34 percent during that time frame.[33] The year 2021 also saw the highest number of trans and gender-nonconforming individuals killed to date, the majority of whom were Black.[34]

The Black Lives Matter movement, described by *National Geographic* as the fourth wave of US civil rights protests, is not new.[35] What is new is the presence of social media, which has brought the movement to men, women, and children of all ages. As always with social change, schools have become responsible for helping young people and families grapple with the repercussions of these tragedies. Educators answer the call to help young people claim their identities and self-worth, hold high expectations for their success, and acquire knowledge and agency to make a difference in their lives.

These atrocious acts of violence draw your attention, but what about the daily jeers and discriminating acts that are rarely talked about? As we think about racism, it's become common practice to encourage school leaders to first reflect deeply on and grapple with their own feelings and mental models concerning issues of social justice and difference. We reflect on our own views of the world and how these views may have developed into biases that influence organizational culture and climate. We are remiss if we do not do this work to prepare school leaders.

As hard as it is for many to talk about race, the omission invites assumptions to grow. Teachers and staff members cannot feel safe in their beliefs and points of view. When we don't openly create a platform to share our values around equity and social justice, we limit the opportunity to create an inclusive environment that promotes equity of opportunity for all. School leaders who lead inclusive schools willingly explore their cultural competence as a key component of becoming more self-aware. They provide opportunities for others to do the same. As school leaders develop an understanding of interpersonal, institutional, and system-wide racism, they make better decisions about students' needs, interests, and opportunities for success.

We can't ignore the fact that racism exists at the very core of our society. No child should be left out of the conversation. All children need to be seen and heard. As school leaders, we need to assure others about where we stand; we need to examine what message we project to others about what true equity looks like and what it requires of each of us in our pursuit to cultivate well-being. Leaders cannot arrive at this level of understanding without deep introspection that contributes to greater self-awareness. For White people, our words and actions must promote anti-racism. It is our responsibility to speak against racism, to learn its effects on adults and children, and to do everything we can to contribute to a transformative change in how Black people and people of color are seen by Whites and continuously kept down by systemic inequities. But first and foremost, the responsibility is to change ourselves.

Knowing ourselves is the work of a lifetime. It is more than pausing and tuning into our emotional life; it is doing so every day, with curiosity, not judgment. And in that process, we must improve our racial literacy. Yolanda Sealey-Ruiz of Colombia Teacher's College defines racial literacy in English classrooms as "the ability to read, discuss, and write about situations that involve race or racism."[36] There are so many avenues to having these discussions in safe places and ways in schools.

THINK ABOUT IT

What is your stance around these issues, and how do these conversations live at your school?

WHAT FACILITATES CHANGE?

When a school or district models its values strongly and clearly, most followers come along. A third of them will buy in completely, another third may mostly buy in, and the final third may be more resistant and need a lot of coddling and coaching to come along. Many may resist at some point in the process, and some will just refuse. It takes people time to adapt to change, to review and let go of the old, even in favor of something that feels right for now. The school leader's self-awareness must be heightened at this time, checking in on others' emotions and demonstrating calm support. Leaders' awareness of what others are feeling also must be heightened, to relate to them effectively. To have this heightened awareness, people need to be honest with themselves about what they know and don't know, the information they have and what they still need to learn.

That said, all new learning needs to move into practice to become part of our active repertoire. Mandy, an urban principal of eight years, shares with us an outcome that came about from working on enhancing her self-awareness: "My assistant principal did not follow a specific priority directive from me. Instead of 'flipping out,' I questioned him and sought to understand his perspective and rationale. I would have never approached him in this way before my training." Mandy effectively managed her emotions at this moment. She tuned in to her thoughts and feelings (self-awareness), took three deep breaths, and listened without interrupting, which allowed her to hear his perspective (social awareness). Self-awareness is always the first step, as it asks us to go within and check in with what we are feeling and thinking before we act.

Benjamin, a fifth-year principal, shared: "When dealing with a teacher who is having personal problems at home and work, I listened and helped her tune into her feelings to understand how they impacted her coping with problems in school—both with students and teachers." Benjamin had always been a caring person but never had the time to listen to his staff or tune in to their feelings. After noting lower scores on his empathy competency assessment, he worked hard to pay attention to his actions. In the moment described above, he empathized with the teacher and then helped her shift to thinking about how her feelings were also affecting her relationships with her students. He put his self-awareness into action by listening to the teacher's situation and feelings, asserting his concern and care, and helping her to adjust and seek the support she needed to get back on her feet.

These anecdotes are just two of many examples of the power of self-awareness. Perhaps the best way to close this chapter is with the saying by Gautama Buddha, "Peace comes from within. Do not seek it without." Self-awareness is the foundation for what comes next in this book. As school leaders, you make decisions all day long. Without self-awareness, there is no guarantee that you will make the right decisions and choices. Stay tuned to your feelings and allow yourself to learn from them. Your inner voice and the feelings you notice and acknowledge will open your mind and heart as you go through your days. Listening to your inner voices allows you to be true to yourself and those you lead.

CHAPTER FOUR

The Self-Managed School Leader

What if we told you that managing your emotions is the most important skill you will need as a school leader? Would you agree? Or would you tell us that we are overreaching the mark? Think about it. How many times during the day do you want to walk away, scream, or pull your own—or someone else's—hair out (figuratively)? Maybe you are skilled in self-management, for the most part; the thoughts and feelings do come up, but you have practiced through the years, managing your emotions in more skillful, more helpful ways. Or maybe you are masterful at self-management with *some* people, not others, and in *some* situations, not others.

We have all witnessed the wreckage that results when someone's big emotions were controlling the person's behavior in a moment of intense anger or frustration; we have all witnessed people being so depressed they would even refuse coffee with a friend; and some of us may have experienced this ourselves. Most of us have personally experienced the "I just can't get out of bed this morning" feeling—and the wish that we could keep the glow of positive emotions after a beautiful night or weekend. Emotion regulation or the lack of it helps calm us or it can make or break a friendship, a marriage, a career—sometimes in a few seconds. Regulating our emotions can help calm us when we need to focus, create initiative when we need it, and help us hold onto positive feelings that we want to last. In the pages ahead, we will explore the concept of self-management and its special significance for school leaders.

In chapter 3, we explored the construct of self-awareness—the foundation that anchors emotional intelligence. We shared stories from the field, as we will in this chapter and all chapters. We talked about the importance of achieving personal agency through developing—and sometimes rewriting—our narrative. We emphasized that self-awareness is the anchor without which self-management and management of others become nearly impossible. Think of self-management as the glue that keeps us from spilling over when the going gets tough. The result of managing our emotions (or not) is what we experience and what others see. And it's how reputations are made about us as people or leaders: "Wow—she can really keep it together." "She was so strong during that crisis—never saw a flicker of wavering." "It left the faculty very anxious to see him so frazzled—can't he just keep it together in front of people?" "She is great at inspiring energy in a totally exhausted faculty." Self-management is the key to small things (which, left undone, lead to big things) that we need to get done every day—such as creating and managing your schedule, booking doctor's visits, scheduling meetings, and creating time and space for getting things done. Self-management is also about knowing when to say something and when to hold one's tongue. Remember that well-known quotation from Aristotle: "Anybody can become angry. . . . That is easy. But to be angry with the right person, to the right degree, at the right time, for the right purpose, and in the right way—that is not easy."[1]

Emotion regulation, the skill of self-management with self-awareness, is key to building healthy relationships, knowing how to communicate what we intend to communicate in helpful ways, being able to listen to feedback without blowing up or shutting down, and being able to "code-switch" in different social or professional settings—for example, in school, at home or church, or with friends. Self-management is essential for everything we do and for every interaction we have each day.

Have you ever stopped to think about how many times a day you must manage your emotions, and how the strategies you use will differ from one emotion to another? Every minute of the school leader's day is filled with situations that require immediate attention. The immediacy and urgency require a tremendous amount of emotion regulation; student crises, parent needs, teacher comportment, community violence, and school bus driver incidents all depend on the leaders' response.

Think about the first hour of Principal Stone's day, just last week. Her alarm rings; she opens her eyes and suddenly has a sinking feeling in the pit of her stomach thinking about her son's high fever last night—she needs to check in on him—but, first a cup of coffee and breakfast with her fifteen-year-old daughter, who is already in the kitchen (she heard the cabinet door slam a few minutes ago): yogurt, berries, and toast. After a few questions on her part and a few exclamations of "Mom!" from her daughter—a typical exchange these days—Principal Stone gets into her car to drive to school and turns on the ignition. She feels a moment of relief thinking that she now has fifteen minutes of planning and thinking time between her parking spot at home and the school parking lot. As she is relaxing her shoulders and taking a breath (mindfulness classes *do* help), thoughts about her son and his fever begin to creep back in and, with them, anxiety and fear. She is worried because he was at a basketball game three days ago: "Was anyone masked? What if he gets that horrible flu thing going around? It's bad." Principal Stone is thinking about whom she can call before she starts her day. Scanning people in her mind, her phone starts ringing. Her assistant principal sounds uncharacteristically stressed: three teachers called out sick, and school planning is underway. "Breathe," she says to herself. "Breathe," she repeats as she pulls into her usual spot. A few more minutes and she is through the double doors—people are greeting her with smiles—she "catches" the good feeling and rides it until she sees the face of her AP. One of her teacher's husbands tested positive for COVID; the teacher is on the line. A parent is on hold and is livid about the unfairness with which her son is being treated by his chemistry teacher. Principal Stone passes the art supply closet on the way to her office and has a fleeting wish that she could sneak in there, shut the door, and leave all the problems outside.

We all have our own roller coaster of emotions every day. And, to state the obvious, we are not as practiced as we would like to be at using helpful strategies to regulate those emotions. While there is no one correct way to handle your emotions, you are likely to be more successful if you pay attention to the emotions you are looking to address (to tame, initiate, or maintain), their intensity, your context (school, home, somewhere else), and how you are expressing what you feel.

HOW SELF-MANAGEMENT AND EMOTION REGULATION IMPACT OUR LEADERSHIP

Working with our emotions skillfully, especially during times of crisis, helps us navigate complex challenges more successfully and ameliorate the psychological impact of extraordinary stress on those around us.[2] Further, using our emotions wisely is an expression of our skill in emotional intelligence. And our level of skill is obvious to others. No one wants to work for a leader who is always out of control or even just unpleasant. And no matter how much we know about managing our emotions, what we *do* is what defines us. Most of us can think of people we have worked with who often wear a scowl rather than a smile, put people down rather than lift them up, roll their eyes in meetings when they don't agree, blame others with an angry edge, or make an argument out of everything. Their emotions are contagious and can sap the energy out of an otherwise healthy organization.

Let's consider the perspective of a high school teacher named Mary:

One of the tyrannical assistant principals at our school often projects his emotions outwards when he is angry or frustrated. He is notoriously known for publicly arguing with other assistant principals and yelling at teachers and school staff. If you see him a few hours later, he acts as if nothing has happened. There is this toxic sense of hostility, isolation, and "walking on eggshells." It makes it almost impossible to feel like you could safely ask him for help when you have a problem in your classroom or realize you made a mistake. Because if you do, you are likely going to get yelled at or berated. That's why it's easier for me to "stay in my lane" and avoid taking risks in my teaching practice.

Clearly, Mary's assistant principal could benefit from more skillful attention to and regulation of his emotions—no doubt some time dedicated to skill development would be beneficial for him and the school community. Certainly, none of *you* ever succumb to such behaviors! But unfortunately, they are more common than we think. This way of using power—exploding at colleagues and then ignoring what happened—disrupts the psychological safety needed for teachers to feel free to share their thoughts, feelings, and trust. The lack of psychological safety alienates teachers and further widens the historical chasm that exists between administrators and teachers. The presence or absence of psychological safety impacts teacher behavior and performance; eventually, it trickles down to the students and can affect their performance. Amy Edmondson of Harvard University first introduced the construct of psychological safety, which means knowing one will not be punished or humiliated for speaking up in a team meeting. Whether sharing ideas, asking questions, speaking about concerns, or making mistakes, risk-taking is encouraged.[3]

As you continue reading this chapter, take the time to reflect on the messages you send through the behaviors you *show* to others and the skills or strategies that you use to regulate your emotions. Notice whether there are any surprises for you as you reflect. Later in the chapter, you will meet Ana, a superintendent of schools in Brooklyn, New York, who fully embraced this work—and became a champion of emotion regulation!

Review the neuroscience of emotion regulation, explore short-term and long-term strategies that assist with managing our emotions, and listen to the stories of school leaders just like you who are working on their self-management. These research-based strategies are helpful and positive, and they can replace years of unproductive behaviors that negatively impact our relationships and our life choices.

Remember, the first step is to be aware that we are experiencing emotions—that is self-awareness. Next, it is helpful to understand and label our emotions. At the Yale Center for Emotional Intelligence, we call recognizing, understanding, and labeling emotions the "experiencing" part of emotional intelligence. The "action" part of emotional intelligence is how we express and then manage our feelings—that is, how emotionally skillful we are with ourselves. Living and working in a world of people, we also want to be skillful with others—to be aware of their emotions and manage them. Our self-awareness and ability to co-regulate with others (namely, to use ourselves and our own feelings to influence others' feelings) have a significant impact on our relationships—whether we approach or retreat; how we build teams, interact with parents, care for our faculty, provide feedback to teachers; whether we create environments where the adults in the school feel psychological safety, and conflict is handled productively and with care. Creating such schools is easy to talk about, but it takes a lot of work on oneself as well as community work to establish these learning environments—and recognition and regulation are the cornerstones.

SELF-REFLECTION TO ACTION

This capacity implies paying attention to our self-talk—the positive or negative words that we say to ourselves in our minds—on a regular basis as we make sense of our beliefs, values, and feelings and then take appropriate actions. We take our thoughts to another level by taking positive action after reflection. Think of a situation when reflecting on your self-talk led you to behave in a certain way or accomplish something.

Perhaps you committed to an exercise routine or entered a difficult conversation, or you simply did something differently or more creatively than usual. We often self-reflect; we don't always act in our own interest as a result. In the following example, Liz, an aspiring administrator, learns from an unfortunate action of a school leader.

> I've learned that a leader showing emotions can be a way of giving immediate feedback and letting the staff understand what's at stake in the work being done. For example, if a leader is upset with something negative they see going on in the hallway, it can be useful for a leader to be emotional when describing the impact the incident might have on the lives of the children. Without name-calling or casting blame, showing anger might light a spark in the staff. On the other hand, showing negative emotions in the wrong ways might have the opposite effect.
>
> I can clearly remember the turning point at my old school when the principal totally alienated the entire staff. She had been a teacher at the school, then an AP, and finally the principal. She prided herself on being a friend to the teachers and openly discussed how she hated the Danielson framework for teaching, and how she would never ever assess any teacher or give low ratings on observations.
>
> Then, one day, she got a negative visit from the superintendent and addressed the staff crying and upset, blaming us because we hadn't done all the things she had told us to do just the day before to make the school and her look good. At this moment, she lost the staff and became very adversarial and aloof. She was clearly out of control. I have learned from this example to always be authentic. I learned that we can't just think about regulating our behavior, but we have to model positive self-emotion regulation. My self-talk has to guide me in difficult moments, and I need to remember how contagious emotions can be—especially negative ones!

Unfortunately, emotion dysregulation is way more common than we wish in schools.

A dysregulated use of power—exploding at colleagues and then ignoring the emotional consequences for the target or the group—destroys the psychological safety needed for teachers to feel free to share their thoughts and feelings and to work to their fullest potential. The lack of psychological safety alienates teachers and further widens the historical chasm that exists between administrators and teachers in many schools. The presence or absence of psychological safety in the school community impacts teacher motivation, creativity, and performance; eventually, it trickles down to the students.

- **Self-management** is the ability to regulate one's emotions, thoughts, and behaviors effectively in different situations. Self-management is key to shifting and juggling our behaviors, being flexible and adaptable, and maintaining positivity when all may look bleak. Self-management also enables us to set our goals and achieve them: "I wish this teacher could self-manage. She would not experience so much resistance from her students." As leaders, we need to not only manage our own words and actions but also help our staff to do the same in their interactions with parents and young people.
- **Regulating:** The Yale Center for Emotional Intelligence has a definition we use. Regulating involves the *thoughts* and *actions* we use to prevent, reduce, initiate, maintain, or enhance emotions to promote well-being, build positive relationships, and attain goals.[4] It's about remaining calm in the face of stress, and it's also about using a strategy to pick yourself up—for example, when you are emotionally worn out but need to lead a faculty meeting. It's also about recognizing how gratified you feel after a successful event and using an emotion regulation strategy to maintain the good feelings.
- **Emotional self-control** is typically talked about as the act of inhibiting strong impulses: "It took every ounce of my

self-control for me to not eat that last cookie." It refers to the ability to keep our disruptive emotions and impulses in check and to maintain our effectiveness under stressful or even hostile conditions.[5] To use a school example, Superintendent Jane used every ounce of emotional self-control to not scream when she heard that Principal Collins had made the same mistake for the third time. The new cafeteria staff talked about needing a heavy dose of self-control when the kids threw food around or ignored the food that fell on the floor.

- **Co-regulation** is the back-and-forth between people in which individuals mutually influence each other's emotional or behavioral states through their actions and interactions. It involves using our emotions, body language, facial expression, voice, cadence, and words to calm another person's nervous system or to lift their spirits.

EMOTION REGULATION AND OUR BRAINS

In recent years, we have learned from neuroscience about how human brain function impacts our behavior, especially the choices and decisions we make. Let's follow Barry, a principal, as he walks through his typical day. When we asked him how many decisions he makes in a day, he said, "Sixty—about seven every hour in an eight-hour day." With this many decisions to make, it behooves us to explore the impact of our state of mind when we are making these decisions. What is happening in our brains when we are stressed out or triggered by one more mandate from the top, a resistant or needy staff member, an angry parent, or a demanding supervisor—or maybe a family crisis such as a sick child, the loss of a close family member, or a marital dispute? We now know that we can use strategies to shift or change unproductive behaviors and rewire our brains through effective strategies. We know that our brains are more malleable than was once thought. These strategies that help change our behaviors also can change our impact on others.

All of us have, during our lives, acquired strategies to manage our feelings in the moment (many of us inhaled those cookies) or to avoid overreacting—saying something we later regret or ruminating endlessly over a recent interaction with a staff member. (Some strategies are very helpful, others not so much; we will get to that topic later.) The combination of nature and nurture influence the choices we make. The prefrontal cortex, or neocortex—the thinking brain—controls the "executive functions" of the brain: cognition, impulse control, judgment, emotional regulation, planning, reasoning, and relating well to others. This part of the brain is key to self-regulation.

Next are subcortical areas where more simplistic parts of the brain do their work. These subcortical areas work with our memory, emotion, pleasure, and hormone production. Below the cortex, in the midbrain, is the limbic system, the center of emotion, which is found in animals too. This more primitive part of the brain detects danger and exhibits fear. The amygdala connects to the prefrontal cortex via a pathway called the uncinate fasciculus. It provides the opportunity for us to use thought or action strategies to neutralize the triggered amygdala, a critical process in self-regulation.

Finally, there is the brain stem, which connects to the spinal cord and is responsible for basic functions. Known as the reptilian brain, this area controls movement; autonomic functions such as breathing; and the regulation of cardiovascular function, sleep, and consciousness.

EMOTION REGULATION AND THE AMYGDALA HIJACK

The amygdala is activated first in an emotional situation; a conflict; or, at the extreme, a time of threat. What happens between the amygdala and the neocortex in times of extreme stress or threat? The *amygdala hijack*, a term postulated by Goleman in his 1995 book *Emotional Intelligence*, brought attention to the fact that an overabundance of stress can lead to a loss of self-regulation and ability to effectively make decisions.[6] A little cortisol is needed to get up and go and to engage in desired endeavors, but too much can trigger a fear response in our emotion center, the amygdala, and cause us to act in an extreme manner to protect ourselves or another. Such actions can be as simple as sending that nasty email without thinking, totally belittling an employee unintentionally, or committing a serious crime. Neuroscientists have been studying the functions of the amygdala, particularly how it can be affected by chronic stress or produce defensive behaviors to fight off stress.[7] They have identified circuits of our brains that control how we react to a situation or, instead, think it through and choose the direction that best fits the moment. There are automatic responses to emotional situations, and there are voluntary responses to emotions.[8] Automatic responses are not within our awareness; they seemingly respond on their own and can regulate or increase the present emotion.

Voluntary emotion regulation reflects the work that you do for yourself. This involves goal setting that is value driven and often supported by a loved one or a trusted coach or trainer. This is when we make coconscious choices to set on a course of changing behaviors using the emotion regulation strategies we have acquired.

As school leaders, we can feel at times that we have been on the battlefield all day, defending our positions, empathizing with those in need, never quite feeling efficacious because our students don't quite meet academic expectations or their own personal family struggles make it too difficult for them to achieve success. Our emotional selves can weaken, and the stress can take over and lead to burnout. But it doesn't have to be this way—not if we acquire strength from our emotions and use them constructively instead of letting them rule us. Our skills of self-management are critical to this transformation.

STRESS AND SELF-MANAGEMENT

There are compelling reasons that we feel that thinking and talking about self-management is increasingly important at work and in everyday life.

Under pressure from political agendas, racial tensions, and environmental conditions, the school leader's job carries limitless responsibilities. A leader's actions are often shaped by these pressure-filled agendas rather than the leader's own values and mindsets. And, as we put pen to paper, school leaders are working against the backdrop of exhaustion and distress caused by many of these agendas.

According to the National Institute of Mental Health, at the time of this writing, depression and anxiety are present in both adults and young teens at very high rates. One in three adults experiences major depression. Some of these adults may work in your schools and parent your students. Some of these adults are reading this book right now. "Mental illnesses are common in the United States. It is estimated that more than one in five U.S. adults live with a mental illness (57.8 million in 2021)."[9] A *serious mental illness* (SMI) is defined as a mental, behavioral, or emotional disorder resulting in serious functional impairment, which substantially interferes with or limits one or more major life activities. In 2021, the NIMH reported approximately 14.1 million adults aged 18 or older in the US with a serious mental disorder. Less severe mental illnesses, referred to as *any mental illness* (AMI), include many different conditions that vary in degree of severity, ranging from mild to moderate to severe.[10]

None of us is exempt from life stresses. Many of us secretly battle our own anxiety and depression. Others of us don't even recognize that we may be demonstrating a lack of centeredness and calmness or that our eating habits have changed and maybe we can't stay awake while at work. But we train ourselves to outwardly manage our stress, even while inside we are about to burst—not a healthy solution. Look at Assistant Principal Tom's behavior in this scenario, and listen to teacher Lanitra's description of this encounter:

I am known for remaining calm in most stressful situations. On this day, my AP joked with me when he saw me at my desk shaking my head. This particular AP is in charge of school discipline. He is a nearly thirty-year veteran and has a boisterous style in the hallway. He curses freely and complains loudly about teachers in some very disparaging ways. I've heard him refer to one teacher as a "dumb bitch," and while he sort of said it under his breath, it was loud enough that I heard it. I've also heard him joke that he can get away with saying things that would get other people in trouble. Anyway, he saw me shaking my head and said, "Ha! They're getting to you too! Which teacher?" I explained to him that actually I was shaking my head because the internet was moving slowly, unwilling to confront him, and he said, "Oh man, I thought I caught you getting angry."

Sounds like this AP needs some training in implicit bias as well as emotional intelligence! Furthermore, this AP would be a thorn in the side of any principal. As his negativity spreads to others, some may follow suit, and before you know it, you have a toxic culture. Too often principals let this kind of behavior ride, because addressing it would take a lot of energy and time or ruin an age-old friendship.

Fortunately, heartfelt, caring inclusive school leaders never let this negative behavior happen. Some of them are so responsible and committed that even their sleep is interrupted. They worry about everyone's needs being met.

Read the dialogue below from an interview with former elementary school principal Dawn. What parts do you relate to in this conversation?

Janet and Robin: What's a challenge for you especially in these hard times that we've been dealing with?

Principal Dawn: A challenge for me—I guess I would call it work-life balance.

Janet and Robin: Tell us about it.

Principal Dawn: I guess being able to disconnect is very difficult. It's a challenge for me because it takes me away from my life, sometimes. I'm always checking my emails. I always have to check texts so that I am available to people at any time. And I respond.

Whenever people reach out, I respond. It's a management thing for me too because if I don't, things get lost. Things will get lost because then it piles up and there are too many things to try to respond to, so I respond as things come. I think it's part of my personality, but it makes me feel better, to know that something has been taken care of; that somebody reached out about something, and that that is already taken care of. And now my brain can move on to something else.

Yeah, I think that's what that is. So, it's like, even if that something else is getting back to watching my grandkids, if I have something on my mind that needs to be taken care of, I can't be fully present where I'm at. I don't like people to feel like they need something that is unresolved because I don't like that feeling. I've made sure that my parents at my school don't feel that way, and that my teachers don't feel like they have a question, or they have a need that's not being addressed. It's a challenge because I can't stop doing it.

Janet and Robin: What's the emotional/psychological/physical cost for you being so "there" for everybody?

Principal Dawn: It is emotionally and physically draining. It also causes me to lose time with my family. I do think that I practice self-care, you know. But yeah, I'm always looking at my phone, and my email, or I'm on social media because I don't want to miss something, and during the pandemic, it ramped up to a thousand, even more than I usually do. We weren't getting a lot of information from anyone, so we had to depend on social media to find things out to stay abreast of things. And what happened was you went into a Twitter hole. With all the political things happening and everything that was happening in the world, I'd try to find out what the CDC said and there was a breakdown in communication, so I had to stay on Twitter because that's where I was getting my information.

Janet and Robin: It's not the first time that we've heard you say that you can be overextended. What keeps you from really making a positive change? What, deep down inside, is your barrier?

Principal Dawn: I think that I feel like it's my responsibility to do these things.

And I feel that if I'm not doing those things, I'm not doing my job properly.

And so, it feels like I'm not committed or dedicated. I don't like to feel lost, and I don't like to feel out of the loop. And so, it's personal, it's a personal need, you know.

I mean if you ask me when I think it's going to stop, it'll stop when I retire.

Principal Dawn is a super high achiever who cannot rest unless everything is in order according to her beliefs, values, and expectations. Most school leaders are high achievers, and they are relentless. They come into this line of work to make a difference, and that difference isn't manufacturing the latest widget; it's changing the lives of young people. That drive brings with it lots of good stress, until it overflows and starts piling the bad stress into leaders' lives.

THINK ABOUT IT

What is your story about how you regulate your emotions, especially when you are at your wit's end, overly anxious, or on the brink of depression? What kinds of internal and external life events impact your mental health positively or negatively? How do you manage them?

SOCIAL AND EMOTIONAL LEARNING: AN ANTIDOTE

As we write this book, social and emotional learning has been recognized and embraced as essential for young people's development and for the well-being of the adults in the school community, too. Educators are scrambling to bring social and emotional learning curricula to their schools, to learn pedagogy, and to find space in their days to develop both adults' and students' social and emotional well-being. Social and emotional learning teaches us preventive skills and strategies as well as mindsets about inter- and intrapersonal development; it is more than a program. SEL can change the culture and climate when stakeholders accept responsibility for the human development of every child and adult, starting with oneself.

CASEL, or the Collaborative for Academic, Social, and Emotional Learning, was formed in the early 1990s by a small group of very committed adults—academicians, clinicians, educational practitioners, researchers, politicians, and science journalists—who created a movement for developing the social and emotional skills of young people. I (Janet) was honored to be part of that founding group of superstars from whom I learned so much, including Shelly Berman, Maurice Elias, Dan Goleman, Mark Greenberg, Eileen Rockefeller Growald, Norris Haynes, Linda Lantieri, Beverly Long, Mary Utne O'Brien, Terry Pickeral, Tim Shriver, Dave Sluyter, Herb Wahlberg, Roger Weissberg, and Joe Zins. Others soon joined this effort to develop the field.[11] Several of these courageous souls have since passed on, but their spirits will always remain with the work. CASEL recognized that SEL was needed in schools, and all involved were determined to build the field. Together, scientists and practitioners joined hands to make the case for SEL. We started by publishing research studies and writing articles and books that made the scientific case for SEL. While the research scientists were publishing, practitioners were strengthening their programs, evaluating them, and presenting their findings at education conferences.[12] Superintendents and principals were implementing SEL programs at their sites with much success. From these humble beginnings, more than twenty years of meetings, seminal research, and grassroots efforts have brought us to where we are today. Starting with Chicago, one city's SEL policies and curriculum standards served as another state's starting place to guide SEL teaching and schoolwide implementation. In 2020–2021, during the pandemic, educators found these activities very helpful, whether they were meeting virtually or face-to-face with students, for opening a discussion about their fears and hopes. Activities such as morning circles from the Responsive Classroom, FIG TESPN from Social Decision Making, the Mood Meter from the RULER approach, and the turtle from the PATHS program helped adults and children to understand, express, and regulate their often mixed emotions.[13]

Through SEL programs and approaches, students learn to listen to and speak about emotions and to regulate their own emotions. The results? Higher academic performance, less bullying in the classroom, stronger relationships, and better decisions. Schools across our country and the world embrace SEL and the mission to take responsibility for addressing all children's academic, social, and emotional needs. This change has been a long time coming, and it is here to stay. As educational leaders, you are leading the charge by modeling and advocating for successful SEL. Bringing SEL into your schools can shift the culture and climate, as children and adults become more self-aware, build their emotional vocabulary, develop competencies and emotions skills and use their emotional and cognitive intelligence to make decisions and solve problems.

School leaders welcome the recognition that emotions play a key part in the school day for every child. Educators and students can build a shared language to enhance communication and relationships. Schools incorporate emotion skills into their daily schedules and integrate them with core subjects. Adults spend time in professional development learning the skills of emotional intelligence for themselves. For example, schools implementing the RULER approach ("recognize, understand, label, express, and regulate" emotions) educate and train the adults first. Think about it: adults leading districts, schools, and classrooms need to be skilled in emotional intelligence to be the models for their students. What's more, remember the saying "You can't teach what you don't know"? This is so true for emotion skills. In the past few years, with the pandemic as background, educators not only felt the urgency to get help dealing with their emotions but also had access to funds that were previously not available, as the federal government made an effort to meet educators where they were during the pandemic.

The participation of the superintendent is the starting point for all this work in schools. Just as the school principal models for the school community so does the superintendent model for every principal, assistant principal, parent, and student. Moving such an innovation forward requires articulating and stewarding the superintendent's vision. Support for this initiative must be authentic. As we bring this chapter to a close, we'd love you to listen to superintendent Ana's journey in bringing SEL into her school district.

VOICES OF SCHOOL LEADERS: SUPERINTENDENT ANA

At thirty-eight years of age, Ana became the superintendent of a large urban school district. She had sat in all the previous seats—teacher, assistant principal, principal, and deputy superintendent—and for the past twelve years has held her current position. A new initiative had been presented by senior managers in the school system: emotional intelligence leadership. Ana was intrigued by the notion of emotional intelligence, a new concept that made sense to her, and she signed up to participate. "What would it be like to engage with the world from our emotions?" she thought. "And to think about our perceptions of what's happening emotionally for us and others in the social context?"

The program that Ana participated in provided six ninety-minute sessions of individual coaching and five half days of training. In the large-group sessions with other superintendents and senior managers, she learned about the deeper context of emotionally intelligent leadership behaviors. With her colleagues, she reflected on her leadership, noting the effects on her and her followers in areas such as self-regulation, empathy, managing conflict, using her influence, building trust, and integrating change into the larger system. She learned about the burgeoning field of social and emotional learning—what it is and its impact on school culture and climate. In the individual sessions, she learned about how she used her own emotions personally and on the job. She was able to explore questions that she had about her own behaviors in a safe, confidential place. She examined her self-regulation strategies, observed what worked and didn't, and acquired some new ones. Finally, she set short-term goals to practice these new strategies in her private and professional worlds.

It has been almost four years since Ana took this training. We sat down with her to check in and learn what, if anything, she remembered from that earlier work. Her story is noteworthy.

> When I started this work, I wasn't a reflective person. I always resisted that part of the work and was always in a reactionary mode. I was not a person who could take a deep breath and manage the emotions of those around me if they did not have the skills to manage themselves. While I would normally avoid large group sessions, these involved multiple presenters and were experiential. I prefer small group interactions so the individual sessions that the coaching provided were welcomed.

I knew that I needed to explore my emotional states and how they impacted my day-to-day life. I soon learned that how I was reacting to things in the moment was influencing those around me in both the short and long term. Just that realization alone was huge for me, even before I learned any strategies to manage my emotions. The coaching encouraged us to use the strategies we were learning in between sessions. So, for example, if you had boundary issues with a parent or even someone at work, you would practice regulation strategies— say, breathing—and conflict management by asserting your needs.

I use a lot of strategies to manage my emotions. One of my favorites is the Meta Moment that Marc Brackett taught us. This strategy allows me to stop and think before I react. It helps me in frustrating situations where I usually would have been very reactionary, not my best self. When I am in the red zone, I bring myself down to a more productive way of communicating. I don't verbally attack the person so that they are paralyzed and can't hear a word of my constructive feedback. It's changed my relationships with principals. They are very forthcoming with me now about the issues or mistakes they have made. I've developed a deeper sense of empathy. My patience has grown. Sometimes I disengage because I need more time to calm myself down.

This work has been the defining work of my career. It allowed me to be a better manager of people that report to me—administrators, parents, and students. And this is not work that I compartmentalize; it goes home with me, to my family and friends, as well. I recognize that we are all at different levels of awareness and skills in emotional intelligence. This makes me have more confidence in myself and others. I am open to being more vulnerable.

How many of you have walked in Ana's shoes? How often do you struggle with managing your own emotions? What about managing others who are dysregulated? Perhaps you can regulate your own emotions but have a hard time managing those of others—or vice versa.

As school leaders, you have worked with many administrators and teachers who struggle with conflict and classroom management. Teachers enter the conflict cycle because they have difficulty managing their own emotions. The rubber hits the road when the teacher—the adult in the relationship—can't manage his or her own frustrations, so push comes to shove, and strong discipline or even punishment becomes the chosen strategy. The end result? The student is reprimanded or suspended by the school leader. Adults who have power over young people are quick to use it. As school leaders, you too often must spend more time helping the adults you supervise to regulate their own behavior. Though there is a power difference between employers and employees, we have learned that unless a serious infraction has occurred, strong discipline only alienates the adult in question and disrupts the relationship. Forceful punishment never works. Conversation with compassion goes much further. Think about it: if you let your strong emotions get the best of you, the relationship suffers.

Just a quick note about Ana's leadership. Over the past five years, Ana has trained and provided coaching to all principals, assistant principals, and teacher leaders in her district. She also provided training for her parent leadership, followed by training for her parent community. The work in Ana's district has not only changed her leadership style but also shifted the focus to SEL as well as academic learning for everyone.

In the next chapter, we will explore how the leader's social awareness plays a major role in school leadership. We take social skills for granted, as if all adults come prepackaged with them, but this is not the case. Next we will look at relationship management, which makes or breaks the climate and culture of a school or district organization. Appendix C offers a helpful table of self-management strategies.

CHAPTER FIVE

Social Awareness

We're highly social animals—I'm told by scientists that what makes us different from other animals is an acute social awareness, which is what has made us so successful.

—ALAN ALDA

Ours is a time when we are increasingly aware of and digitally connected to others around the globe, yet numerous reports show us alarming data about youth mental health and increasing loneliness and isolation: we feel less and less connected at the human level.[1] Many feel a profound sense of empathic and moral distress caused by the immense sufferings and challenges across the world, which they feel powerless to alleviate or resist. Others struggle with not feeling seen and with emotional disconnection in their daily lives. Even worse, many are recipients of bias, discrimination, and hate.

Too often, educators and mental health practitioners burn out due to empathetic fatigue as they take on the emotional weight of their students' lives. Many lack training in how to remain in one's own emotional space without shutting down the emotional reality of the other. Today, more than ever, all educators need to know how to bring awareness and intention to empathy, to cultivate a stance of compassion and resilient capacity for care from which they can act.[2]

In New York City, from 2015 to 2017, Dolores Esposito, with the chancellor's support, chose to counter some of these challenges by first providing social and emotional development for the top leaders in the system, superintendents.

READING THE SYSTEM: DOLORES'S STORY

Meet Dolores. Dolores has been in leadership roles at the school, district, and central levels for nearly twenty-five years. She was a superintendent of fifty-one schools in the Bronx, ultimately serving in the role of executive superintendent of leadership, supporting the development of all New York City superintendents and their core teams, after being appointed by Chancellor Carmen Fariña.

The professional development Dolores brought to superintendents focused in large part on the skills and competencies of emotional intelligence. This learning process started with top leadership and filtered down to the principals, then teachers, and finally to the target: school children and young adults. When we started working with the New York City Department of Education, few superintendents knew what SEL was. Programmatic SEL is now much more common in New York City public schools.

Dolores spoke passionately about her purpose and how emotional intelligence served her in each of her roles:

> The most challenging part of the work is managing the different relationships and constituencies. We do not know their background

stories, the politics, and the histories of the relationships that are in front of us. Emotional Intelligence coaching allowed me to learn the skills that helped me navigate these different layers before I even got to the actual work. These were skills that we don't receive in the leadership pipeline—like really listening with empathy, homing in on conflict resolution, reflecting on my feelings, avoiding judgment, and being open to the perspectives of others. It's these skills that we need before we can do the actual work of teaching, learning, and leading.

Dolores shared the heart of the challenges that too often occur in school districts when school members have their own agendas, seek power or political position, or fight for a personal cause, in addition to the intended agenda of improving the lives of children and families. These self-interested or often seemingly politically necessary personal goals put added pressure on others as they maneuver the political waters. They are often influenced by those in charge or those who desire advancement. And every four years, when the new mayor replaces the prior mayor, the tide shifts, bringing more new mandates, curricular changes, and professional development. Dolores is well aware that the skillful use of emotional intelligence tools and strategies helps to navigate these challenges in service of promoting the academic, social, and emotional well-being of all students Socially aware educational leaders adapt; they observe those in power and are cautious about what, how, when, and with whom they share their innermost thoughts and opinions. This caution inherently creates a lack of trust and a culture often driven by politics rather than the true needs of the children and families. Those who bear the brunt of this dynamic are the school principals, who are responsible for implementing the new changes, and ultimately the teachers. In smaller suburbs, where school boards make and administer policy, the repercussions of these political waves can be equally detrimental to the constituents. Once you cross the line from teacher to leader, you are no longer protected by a teacher's union, and you are scrutinized by everyone. How you manage yourself in the eyes of others can make or break you. Success in this role requires a strong sense of self and relentless self-awareness and social awareness.

SOCIAL AWARENESS

Social awareness is "the ability to take the perspective of and empathize with others, including those from diverse backgrounds and cultures. [It is] the ability to understand social and ethical norms for behavior and to recognize family, school, and community resources and supports."[3] Leaders' social awareness determines the trust level that others have in their leadership, the relationships they form, and the culture that flourishes in their school or district organization. Central to leaders' competency in social awareness is how empathic they are and are perceived to be by others. Empathy encompasses our ability to know what others feel and to step inside their shoes, cognitively, affectively, or both. My colleagues and I (Janet) conducted a recent educational review that searched more than one hundred studies on the connection between emotional intelligence and leadership. Thirty-five articles highlighted three top competencies cited by principals as the most needed for their jobs: empathy, self-awareness, and social awareness.[4] Leaders with higher levels of these competencies create safe places to deeply listen and be present for others. Empathy heals relationships and can bridge the gap between differences. It is the basis for compassion and our willingness to help others in need.

In this chapter, we learn the power that highly developed social awareness can wield for school leaders. We share individual stories about how organizational awareness is an essential competency for effective leadership. We talk about how empathy can shift mental models and deepen relationships; how empathy, if not regulated, can lead to burnout or indifference; how overzealous empathy can leave you standing too long in someone else's shoes; how cognitive empathy without affective empathy can be dangerous. Ultimately, the stories we share show that empathy is the ultimate attunement with others and, together with organizational awareness, can facilitate the transformative process for school leaders. That said, we realize that harm from hateful behaviors is not healed by empathy alone. Addressing the discrimination others experience on account of the color of their skin, their sexual identities, their socioeconomic conditions, their disabilities, and all other *isms* requires more than empathy alone.

The following story comes to us in the form of a letter to the editor written by our colleague, Deidre Farmbry, former principal of Simon Gratz High School in Philadelphia, in response to a shooting at another nearby high school. Individual empathic responses between the two principals had already been exchanged.

THE BUILDING ISN'T THE PROBLEM
BY DEIDRE FARMBRY

I am a high school principal in Philadelphia. When I recently heard that a student at another high school had been shot by intruders during a "shakedown" for money, I prepared myself for the phone calls I knew would be forthcoming. They are the calls I can invariably count on from relatives and friends whenever there is an "incident" at another school. I know they will ask, "Aren't you glad you aren't the principal of . . . ?" What they fail to understand is I am the principal of whatever school currently has the media's eye. As the principal of The School That Could Be Next, any school is my school, for any school's problem is my problem, too.

Coincidentally, I had a student who was shaken down for money on the same day at approximately the same time, quite possibly by intruders. Thank goodness my student was not as viciously hurt . . . this time. It is this day-to-day reality that heightens the stress level of all conscientious administrators who realize that location is irrelevant when the circumstances contributing to a crisis are ubiquitous.

Florence Campbell, principal of West Philadelphia High School, was very direct while enduring her turn in the spotlight on the evening news. I applaud her candor for pointing out what is all too true for school administrators—we sit and wait our turn.

On the same newscast, Councilwoman Jannie Blackwell referred to the event as "an isolated incident." How common that phrase becomes, reverberating year after year, after each new occurrence. I often wonder about the ultimate impact of the term. Does it foster apathy by perpetuating the belief that what is isolated will not spread? Does it contribute to the masses of parents who school-shop throughout the year, transferring their children from one location to another, in search of the safest environment? As the underlying conditions for tragic incidents are far from isolated, the temporary measures masked as responses are far from solutions.

So, we wait! Yes, more security is needed in schools. I support any effort to supply each school with more resources for security. However, let us not be naive and think that if every door were guarded by a sentry, then, we would all be safe from harm in public places. The problem is larger than the buildings we try our best to secure. Just ask my staff and students, many still grieving over the two students killed and the one student paralyzed since October, all harmed in public places called city streets.

With callous people with no good intentions seeking victims in public places—every private inner space called peace of mind is shattered, as we wait and prepare for someone else's problem to come home.[5]

THINK ABOUT IT

Call to mind a time that someone you work with was there for you, personally, at a critical juncture in your life—a time when you felt the person deeply understood and "felt with you." How did this person show you empathy? What did the person do or say? How did this moment of empathic attunement impact your relationship?

Now, think of a time when you felt deep empathy for what a member of your staff was going through. What did you do to show that empathy? What did you say? How did this person respond? How has this moment impacted your connection?

FROM INDIVIDUAL TO ORGANIZATIONAL AWARENESS

Not everyone has an easy time mastering the emotional intelligence competency of *organizational awareness,* defined as "having the ability to read a group's emotional currents and power relationships, and identify influencers, networks, and dynamics within the organization."[6] This aspect of social awareness is especially necessary for those in managerial positions that are part of the ladder up to a higher-level position.

Imagine being at a work event, a brunch, a social gathering, or an evening presentation, when out of the blue, an unknown, well-dressed person of apparent stature suddenly appears, introduces herself to you and your friends, and begins to chat with you—more accurately, she is chatting *at you.* Ten minutes later, you have barely gotten your names out, while she has shared a litany of her lifetime accomplishments, not interrupting her monologue to inquire at all about you. Finally, she smiles and says, "I want to hear what you do, too, of course," but then she keeps on talking about herself. You, being socially aware and polite, feel your skin crawling due to the lack of awareness this woman seems to have about her own impact and ability to "read the room." All the while she's talking, your positive reframing is telling you to be aware that this woman is new on the job and has a powerful position. You realize that you will learn a lot that will help you build a relationship with her, by letting her talk and talk. You want to escape, but in a way that will not offend her. Thinking about your escape while pasting a smile on your face that you hope signals interest in her story, you say, "Excuse me, so sorry to interrupt, but my admin just signaled to me that I need to join a conversation between two of my teachers. I look forward to the next time we connect." You hold your smile and make a quiet exit, hopefully leaving her with your expression of interest in a next time rather than an insult in your choosing others over her wave of stories. Awful moment—we agree. You may think to yourself, "So glad I escaped." But what about her? She will be stuck where she is because no one will dare let on to how others perceive her.

Maybe your scenario is not exactly like this one, but the actions and behavior of a person who can't "read the room" are often similar. Think about your relationships at work. Maryellen, your superintendent, talks incessantly without taking a breath. You wonder how she can be so efficient when she talks way more than she listens. You don't want to say anything because she is your supervisor. Literally, your head aches when you leave meetings with her. Do you tell her to slow down, or do you sit there and shake your head in agreement with what she says? Isn't this an instance where feedback would be a gift? Depending on the nature of your relationship, you may choose to share your feelings with her in such a way that she can hear you without being offended. However, unless she invites you to give feedback, you will probably keep your feelings to yourself and continue to dread your meetings, falling back on the negative self-talk you use with yourself about her.

Remember, your mental models are at work in these situations. Too often we pigeonhole people into a "type." Our preconceived notions determine our words and actions. The socially unaware person can be a lot to bear for anyone. That said, we must examine our self-talk to be sure that we aren't reacting to our own internal biases or fears and that we choose a right action for everyone.

In emotionally intelligent leadership work, social awareness pairs with self-awareness. Self-awareness is the foundational skill, as we discussed in chapter 3, of recognizing the intrapersonal dimensions of self and how our thoughts, feelings, and behaviors impact our perception of and responses to others. We need to develop skill in social awareness to identify how others might be thinking and feeling. Of course, we will never really know the feelings and thoughts of others unless we ask. Your facial expression that says "sad" to me may in fact be what you display when you are feeling anger. Self-awareness and social awareness create the foundation for how you interact with others and how you regulate your emotions and manage your relationships. The higher up you are in your professional role, the more relevant social awareness becomes, as you are modeling all day every day for staff and students and always represent the face of the institution. In our field of education, a socially unaware school leader can sink a school or a district, for sure. Such leaders dispel the trust of teachers who may find them unapproachable, unpredictable, and unpleasant; these leaders often put off parents who depend on them for their child's welfare and others who could potentially support the school, monetarily or otherwise.

Social awareness, the ability to read and understand others' emotions and respond appropriately, requires focus, intention, and skill. It involves our mindsets, our mental models, and knowing when to show empathy or compassion, happiness, or joy. It consists of listening to the perspectives of others without judgment or blame, all the while learning about those who are different from us and being open to learning about other races, cultural groups, and lifestyles. It also involves our ability to read the environment carefully, pay attention to the social dynamics, and determine where and when transparency is warranted. In emotionally intelligent leadership, the competencies of empathy and organizational awareness are critical to master. My (Janet's) story, which follows, is a prime example of a lack of organizational awareness.

JANET'S STORY

I (Janet) learned early on the importance of being organizationally aware. I was about thirty-four years old when I left the classroom to be an administrator. I was working at a school district in southern San Diego as a bilingual teacher (Spanish-English) and half-time coordinator when a job opening came up that interested me. It was a district coordinator position, a Title VII–funded position in which I would be responsible for implementing bilingual reading labs in five elementary schools. It included professional development for teachers, parent training, and lab-specific training for teachers. When I got the job, I was stunned and ecstatic. I was ready to impact young people more broadly.

About one week after I was hired, I received a visit from the president of the school board. I was curious and concerned. "Why was he visiting me? Maybe," I thought, "it was to congratulate me on my new position." "Quite the contrary, Janet," he said, "I just want to let you know that we did not want you for this position." My heart began to beat extra beats, and I felt the sweat accumulating on my neck. He went on, "We selected a woman who is well-versed in bilingual reading. You are not. You were voted in by the superintendent against our recommendation." Now, my self-talk was racing. "I can't believe this. What should I do? I've never been not wanted. I have always worked hard and have been recognized for that. But I'm not Latina. My Spanish is good but not great. Why did the superintendent want me?" The board president went on, "I just want to let you know that we will not support you. You'd be better off declining the position."

As a teacher, I never had to confront politics. My only concern was preparing my students for high school and beyond. That's what I had been prepared for, and that was where my heart was. I made an appointment to speak with the superintendent and was met by him and the deputy superintendent. "Janet," he said after I explained the context of my visit, "The board needs to accept the fact that you are my choice for this position. We didn't feel that the person they wanted was the right fit for the job. Truthfully, they are angry at me, too. We want you to take the job and we will support you 100 percent."

After some deliberation, I accepted the job. At first, I was so busy meeting with people and learning my tasks that I didn't get bothered by the cold stares that I got from both certain administrators and parent members of the board. I set up the labs and the professional development and began training the parents using the Paolo Freire method of parent training for the parents who were learning English and built-in leadership training for the committee of leaders to be trained in leadership.

After about six months, trouble started. In this position, I directly reported to the federal Title VII headquarters in Washington, DC. I reported accomplishments and challenges to the board to approve the funding for the next two years of the three-year grant. The Washington officer reached out to inform me that he had received a letter of complaint from the parents protesting my hiring and saying that I was incompetent and failing at my job and should be removed. I was flabbergasted! The letter was signed by the very parents who were empowered by the leadership skills and strategies I had been teaching them! Things got harder. I successfully got through the required professional development for teachers and still taught a couple of sessions of the parent leadership work. The reading labs were up and running, and the budget was intact, but I was feeling the stress of the attack on me and felt as if I could not take too much more negativity. I worked late nights, attended to the early-evening and late-night professional development, and was feeling quite a bit of anxiety. The kicker came when that spring, the Title VII Continuation Plan that I wrote with the help of the director of the project was rejected by the board. Rather than support me for another year of the grant, they voted down the proposal, losing hundreds of thousands of dollars. This was my last straw.

I decided to speak to my deputy superintendent and present my case for resignation. After some discussion, he said, "Janet, as my employee, your work is excellent, and I would like you to stay. But if you were my wife, I would tell you to resign. It's not worth jeopardizing your health."

Soon after, I decided to resign, but not until I could have a private meeting with the school board. I prepared a speech explaining that I had succeeded in my responsibilities, but no matter what I did, I continued to be harassed by different community members. I explained that the stress was impacting my health and I had to leave. There was a new board president at this time. After some silence, he said softly, "Janet, we want you to know that we have no complaints about the work that you have done. The reality is that you have been a scapegoat. It is the superintendent that we want to leave. Because you were his choice, you never had a chance from the beginning." I was shocked and relieved at the same time—shocked because I could not imagine the lengths that people would go to make a statement and get what they wanted, and relieved that the board members saw the excellence of my work and that the harassment was unrelated to my performance.

I returned to the classroom shortly afterward. The principal who accepted me into his school had been a friend. I was a marked person now, so I was grateful that he accepted me. I went from eighth-grade teacher to third-grade teacher and learned a whole new way of teaching.

I grew a lot as a leader from this entire ordeal. I learned that teachers are usually in the dark about district or citywide politics. For example, I had not known until months after my resignation that the school district has been led by White administrators forever and that my position was the first time they would have had a Latinx female administrator. I also learned that the Chicano superintendent was considered "too White" and that he did not represent the board's values and ideas. They wanted true Mexican leadership with a position of power to make a difference. Had I realized that the community had been oppressed and that they were fighting for the representation they deserved, I would never have accepted the job. In summary, this event was a "teachable moment" for me; as a result, I committed to sharpening my organizational awareness going forward. It is a skill I am proud of. I know the questions to ask, and my eyes are wide open to see beyond the peaceful landscapes with rolling hills, chirping birds, and the laughter of beautiful children.

EMPATHY

A few pages back, you read Dr. Farmbry's response to the editor of her local newspaper about a school shooting, which clearly displayed her skill in awareness of the institutional problems of the larger system, where violence exists not only in schools but on all city streets. She also demonstrated her empathy for the targeted high school's principal and all principals due to the uncertainty that is part of leading schools today. Empathy is our ability to stand in someone else's shoes—to know what others feel based on our own experiences. Affective empathy allows us to feel what others are feeling and how one is perceived by others. As leaders, we experience and demonstrate empathy and empathic attunement with others throughout our days. Empathy is the top competency that principals speak of when they discuss what helps them do their job well. The capacity for empathy—especially the elements of deep listening and strong interpersonal connections—has often been highlighted as essential in all fields of leadership.[7]

Empathy allows us to tune in and be present with others and their emotional expression. When people experience empathy from and with another, the connection and understanding that follow can heal relationships and bridge the gap between differences. It is the basis for compassion and our willingness to help others in need. Empathy wields an unspoken power for the school leader. It is a relationship builder, shows that you care, and leads to trust. Empathy can shift mental models and deepen relationships; it can facilitate the transformative process and the willingness to engage with people of other races, ethnicities, gender identities, and social classes. True empathy leads to deep healing—it is not just a Band-Aid on a large cut that has not been stitched up so that it can heal.

When most of us think of empathy, we think of the ability to take the perspective of others, which you can do when you "stand in their shoes." In fact, when teachers are working on teaching empathy skills to young children, they often include an activity in which they physically stand in a cutout or outline of the other's shoes on the floor, then speak from the other's point of view before stepping back into wearing their own shoes. It's an activity that makes the point that even in standing in someone else's shoes, you need to hold on to your own perspective and be able to go back and forth if you need to.

Three types of empathy have been named by psychologists Daniel Goleman and Paul Ekman, that are part of human relationships. The first is *cognitive empathy*, which implies that you understand what another person is going through. You may not have experienced the same feelings or situation, but you can imagine what they are thinking and feeling—and understand the suffering of the other person and what they might need. We express cognitive empathy a lot, throughout each day, by letting others know that we are listening and that we will do our best to understand we care. The second type is *emotional empathy*, in which you the listener or witness actually "walk in" the emotional experience of another. Emotional empathy goes beyond a cognitive understanding of what someone is feeling to actually temporarily feeling the same feeling as the other person. It's when someone says, "I feel your pain," and, indeed, they do! The third type of empathy is *empathic concern*, which we know as *compassion*. Compassion moves us not only to feel what the person is feeling but to do something about it to relieve the other person. Seeing a blind woman crossing a busy, crowded street might compel you to ask this woman if she would like your help crossing the street. But if you take her hand without asking, she might be fearful or angry. We can never assume.

When I (Janet) fell and broke one ankle and sprained another several years ago, I was unable to walk for months. My husband, Barry, was beyond kind to me; he was compassionate. He cooked, cleaned, helped me get washed and dressed, and was there for my every need. His compassion was tangible. I could hear it when he spoke to me; I could see it in his eyes.

When I (Robin) was going through a very stressful time a few years ago because my son was facing surgery, all the moms in my immediate social network could "feel" my anxiety. And I could feel their empathic concern. During the lead up to the hospital stay, during the days of surgery and recovery, and for weeks after, my friends continued to show concern and compassion by calling or texting me daily expressing care and support. My daughter and my husband were by my side the whole time and expressed their empathic concern by dropping their own work during the days before, during, and after surgery to be there for my son and with me. My husband made sure we all had regular meals, slept, and took walks outside. The expression and show of care by all family and friends—not just their feelings for me—was evident in their communications and presence, and was so appreciated. To close this story—as you are likely feeling empathy with me in the telling—his surgery was successful and led to greater well-being for my son and for all of us!

Leaders, we know that your empathy and compassion are always at work. Think about it. Everyone who works in a school system is there to educate young people. That's the mission that guides you. That said, because our clients are children, young people, and families, a large part of the school leaders' job is listening and problem-solving. Real listening is empathic listening; it's being present for the child, teacher, parent, or member of upper management who needs you. There is a certain quality to this kind of listening—a full presence given. It requires that you focus all your attention on the person who is speaking, avoid any interruption, and attune with that person so that you can guide the person to choose the next best steps. When you actively listen, it's not about what you need in the moment; it's the other person's needs that matter. Empathic listening can be very healing. When you truly listen with generous space for the other, without contributing your thoughts or solutions, you can move closer and deeper within to get in touch with the other person's true feelings.

What follows are two responses that third grader Shoshana might receive from her school's leader. Notice the different responses Shoshana gives when she feels listened to. She is responsive and secure and willing to listen and trust.

NOT LISTENING

11:00 a.m.: Shoshana arrives at Principal Wrong's office with a note from her teacher asking to see if anything is going on.

Shoshana	"Mrs. W., my stomach hurts."
Principal Wrong	"I'm sorry to hear that," she said, checking her email at the same time. "Did it hurt you this morning?"
Shoshana	"No."
Principal Wrong	"That's good. Well, you go back to class now, and if it still hurts you, tell the teacher."
Shoshana	Shoshana, wiping her tears and holding her tummy, heads back to class.

EMPATHIC LISTENING

11:00 a.m.: Shoshana arrives at Principal Right's office with a note from her teacher asking to see if anything is going on.

Shoshana	"Mrs. R., my stomach hurts."
Principal Right	"Oh, my dear, where does it hurt?" (bends down to be face-to-face).
Shoshana	"Right here" (points to right side of her belly).
Principal Right	"When did it start?"
Shoshana	"It started after breakfast" (her eyes tearing up).
Principal Right	"I am sorry you are hurting. Come with me, let's talk to the nurse about this—OK?"
	Shoshana takes her hand, wiping her tears with the other, and heads to the nurse's office.
School Principal to Nurse	"Shoshana has a stomachache that started after breakfast."
Nurse Helpful	"Did you eat something different this morning?"
Shoshana	"No, but I didn't like my cereal today."
Nurse Helpful	"Was it a different kind of cereal that you don't eat normally?"
Shoshana	"No, but Mommy didn't eat with us like usual . . ."
Nurse Helpful paraphrases	"Mommy didn't eat with you today?"

EMPATHIC LISTENING

Shoshana	"No, she was at Aunt Florence's house, Daddy said. I miss her" (tearing up again). Nurse Helpful rubs Shoshana's back gently, and Shoshana cries.
Principal Right	"Shoshana, stay with Nurse Helpful for a little while and help her. She could use a good assistant." Shoshana's eyes light up, and a slight smile emerges across her face.
Principal Right	Principal Right gently pats Shoshana on the back and says to Nurse Helpful, "I'll head over to Counselor Supportive's office now. Let me know how Shoshana progresses. When she is ready, please send her back to class."
Counselor Supportive	Principal Right heads over to Counselor Supportive's office to discuss what's going on with Shoshana. Counselor Supportive will call Shoshana's father to get information so that the school can help support her during what seems like a difficult family moment.

THE EMPATHY TRAP

As I (Robin) wrote with my colleague, Diana Divecha, years ago, babies come into the world prepared to be empathic. Very young infants cry in response to the distress of others, and as soon as they can control their bodies, they respond to those in need, to comfort or offer a Band-Aid. Children vary in the degree to which they are empathic; there seems to be a genetic component and a hormonal basis to empathy. While progesterone boosts empathy, testosterone does not. But there are no clear gender differences in empathic ability early in life.[8]

Much as the capacity for empathy is built into the nervous system, it is also learned, notably from warm and loving parents reflecting feelings back to their children. Almost all parents treasure the moment when a child spontaneously offers a favorite toy to relieve sadness. Ironically, though, many parents stop "seeing" their children's kindness around age two and a half, and empathic behaviors plateau as parents start to reward more cognitive, achievement-oriented behaviors.

Later, parents may find themselves encouraging empathy again, to shape behavior or nurture a child's own empathy. Think of the adult telling a teenage son, "I understand how important that event is to you; you desperately want to go. And I know that you feel really stifled by our decision." But sometimes children are urged to see things through a parent's or sibling's eyes—for example, setting aside their own interests to visit a sick relative. Many children are regularly called on to disregard their own feelings.

Empathy means connecting with someone else's feelings and paying attention to their needs without sacrificing your own. That is not easy. It is not easy to switch from tuning into your own feelings to tuning into someone else's and then tuning back into your own again. It requires self-awareness of where your feelings stop and the other's start—and, with fuzzy boundaries, it is sometimes hard to distinguish between your own feelings and someone else's. Of course, what makes it even more difficult to switch is that the person receiving the empathy finds the attunement deeply rewarding. Sometimes it can be hard to pull yourself out of someone else's shoes and back to standing in your own shoes, addressing your own wants, needs, or feelings.

ROBIN'S STORY

In my (Robin's) therapy practice, I regularly work with women who ignore their own feelings because they are standing in someone else's shoes just a little too long—or, in fact, getting stuck in those shoes, just as in this story:

Natalie was crazy about her new love, Jessica. They met each other in the mindfulness class (perfect!) and shared many other interests, too. They were drawn to each other not only physically but also, as Natalie said, spiritually and psychologically. But after a few weeks, she began to have some questions about whether or not Jess was really interested in her. Although they made an exclusive commitment and spent every weekend together, she rarely heard from Jess in between dates. Natalie told Jess that the long days without contact were really hard for her. Natalie felt hurt and insecure. Then she started thinking about the conversation they had on their first date. Jess told her a lot about her childhood—that her mom was incredibly intrusive and controlling, always wanting to know everything about her life and whereabouts. Natalie remembered feeling so much empathy for her: how awful it must have been to feel confined and intruded upon! Natalie tried hard to put herself in Jess's shoes. Natalie could imagine how it felt to be accountable all the time. No wonder she didn't hear from Jess in between dates! Her empathic position brought peace to their relationship, and she stopped asking for more; she completely understood. She even understood when Jess went missing on some weekends, not to be heard from and hard to contact. But Jess said she really was "into" Natalie, and Natalie was satisfied that Jess wasn't calling her because she didn't want to be controlled. Natalie's own needs became less and less important over time. She came to therapy because she was feeling depressed.

She told me that she wanted first and foremost to be a good partner. She said it was so important to her to be someone who could really "see" her partner and empathize. She told me that there was a strong empathic connection between them and seemed surprised when I commented that it went only one way. And there was something else she began to notice. Jess's work was flourishing, and she was taking really good care of herself. Natalie, on the other hand, was struggling to meet deadlines (unlike her) and constantly letting down friends outside the relationship (uncomfortable for her). When she began to ask for a bit more in the relationship, Jess accused her of being selfish. Natalie wondered about that for a while and then, through therapy over time, was less risk-averse and ready to accept the consequences of discomfort and tension between them. Standing in Jess's shoes kept the relationship going for almost a year but eventually led Natalie to feel as if she had disappeared and was not important—not even to herself. The relationship ended in a storm of accusations after about two years. Letting go of Jess was one of the hardest things Natalie had ever done. But she never looked back. She had her integrity and went on to look for a partner who believes empathy is a two-way street.

EMPATHY IN SCHOOL

Back in the 1980s, the Resolving Conflict Creatively Program (RCCP), one of the earliest SEL programs created by Tom Roderick of Morningside Center and Linda Lantieri, then a special consultant to the New York City Board of Education, was breaking ground in New York City. Violence was often a daily occurrence in schools. RCCP focused on promoting conflict resolution and diversity work. Empathy was at the heart of the work. At that time, I (Janet) was assistant principal of a large comprehensive middle school of 1,700 students, the Roosevelt Middle School in Vista, California. We were experiencing racial conflict, gang behavior, and the typical adolescent defiance from preteens and teens. I spent entire days suspending kids for minor and more serious infractions. I felt more like a police officer than an educator. When I heard of the work being done in New York, we raised funds to bring Linda out to consult with us. Some of the first strategies that we learned were communication skills such as active listening and assertive language using tools such as "I" messages.[9] We brought students of all races and ethnicities together in a leadership group to learn from them what might help us shift this wave of aggression and apparent disdain. We trained them in the skills of communication, empathy and the ability to resolve conflict and took them on a retreat where we were able to have deep conversations about race.

I'll never forget when eighth grader Stan told his story of being discriminated against repeatedly because he was Black. At one point, one of the White boys, Peter, went up to him, hugged him, and said, "I didn't cause all that pain that you have felt, but I feel so bad that White people have done this to you." He began to cry, feeling the guilt of the many years of hate woven by White Americans throughout history. Stan came over to him and hugged him saying, "Thank you." There was not a dry eye in the room. We were teaching SEL skills such as active listening and assertiveness, but we realized that these essential skills can't be helpful unless the underlying issues are addressed.

Talk about turning around a school! Within three years we were almost where we wanted to be. Teachers were teaching the curriculum in the classroom. Our adults and students had acquired caring communication skills. We had a full-on peer mediation program in place run by our amazing parent coordinator, and all students felt safer with no impending fights breaking out because of nighttime arguments or drug deals gone bad. We had monthly presentations done by diverse students who wanted others to learn about their cultures. By the fifth year, the culture of the school had changed. Kids of color were not subject to lower teacher expectations and stereotypical mental models. Students knew they had a voice to express their concerns and were part of keeping us all safe and cared for. Empathy had increased both in teachers and students, and positive relationships flourished.

CONVERSATIONS THAT MATTER

Key to demonstrating our empathy is knowing how best to communicate with others, both listening and speaking.

Communication skills involve words, tone of voice, and nonverbal behavior.[10] An interesting fact is that "people allocate 7 percent to words, 38 percent to the tone of voice, and 55 percent to nonverbal behaviors."[11] All three are needed for effective communication. We attribute more meaning to nonverbal behavior than other forms of communication. Yet, how often do we think about the expression on our face, or whether or not we are "leaning in" or distancing ourselves from another?

When we trust someone, we don't worry much about how that person perceives us. In fact, we rarely think about the way in which we are saying something or the body language that we are expressing. But the reality is that we should always concern ourselves with our manner of speaking and listening and keeping our conversations positive rather than negative.

Positive conversations release neurochemicals in the brain that give us a positive sense of well-being: dopamine, oxytocin, and endorphins. Negative conversations not only drain us emotionally but can also increase cortisol as stress rises. The late Judith Glaser called positive communication conversational intelligence.[12] For Glaser, one should be taught how and when to use appropriate forms of communication. She believed that there are three types of conversations that people participate in. She referred to them as levels 1 to 3. Glaser would measure the levels of conversation in an organization, including such qualities as trust in the room and expected outcomes at each level, and then work with her clients to set a path for improvement. We think you will find it interesting to reflect on the levels of conversation that exist in your organization, especially the levels that you find yourself and your team conversing at most of the time.

> Level 1, the transactional level, is a space where people are just getting to know one another or attending to a task or organization of a task. The focus is on getting things ready and checking in on who's in the room and what they bring to this space. At this level, we determine levels of comfortableness—achievement, sense of control, and the power held by whoever is present in the room. As we scan the room, we ask ourselves, "Where do I most belong? Where do I fit in the most?" At this first level of conversation, trust is low and we are careful to protect ourselves, keep our feelings and thoughts to ourselves. We ask questions and tell what we want others to know.[13]

THINK ABOUT IT

Think about in what setting you would be comfortable using this level of communication as well as a setting where this would not be appropriate. What feelings come up in this setting?

Level 2 conversations are positional. They are meant for everyone to advocate for their point of view. My goal is to influence you to agree with me. "Can I trust you?" echoes in the silently reverberating self-talk of all present. I am in a learning mode here, inquiring about you and your position on things while advocating for my own. There is conditional trust inherent at this level of conversation, but I am still holding onto my own. People are interacting, and there is an opening to trust slowly lifting the people in the room.[14]

THINK ABOUT IT

Think about in what setting you would be comfortable using this level of communication, as well as a setting where this would not be appropriate. What feelings come up in each of these settings?

Level 3 conversations are what we strive for; they are where the healing happens. These transformational conversations exist so that we can learn together. These conversations can happen only when I let you into my thoughts and feelings. I show an openness to dialogue, learn from you, and share what I must to help you. In this way, we can cocreate with others in a trusting space. We are able to share our empathy for others and join to achieve a common goal.[15]

Having meaningful conversations with others involves transparency, honesty, and trust. It is about caring about your feelings and mine, your success and mine. When school administrators communicate effectively with teachers and teachers do the same with students, everyone feels comfortable, included, and able to express their opinions freely. When freedom of expression is denied, organizational silence grows, and negative thinking permeates the school or district culture. Inadequate communication skills negatively impact relationships with everyone. Teachers and school leaders are no exception.[16]

THINK ABOUT IT

Are there times when you have level 3 conversations with your leadership cabinet or your staff? What are the feelings you have during these conversations? What is the usual outcome of these conversations? What makes it possible to have these conversations with some people and not others? What would it be like if every member of your school or district had the skills to have these conversations?

"Perhaps," Dr. Helen Riess of Harvard Medical School says, "empathy is undergoing an evolution. In a global and interconnected culture, we can no longer afford to identify only with people who seem to be a part of our 'tribe.'" As Riess has learned, our capacity for empathy is not just an innate trait—it is also a skill that we can learn and expand.[17]

In this chapter, we talked about the domain of social awareness. We focused on the two competencies that emotionally intelligent school leaders need to be successful: awareness of the organization and empathy. In the next chapter, we begin to look at the domain of relationship management. The competencies of this domain provide tools for positive change to happen in people and their job performance.

CHAPTER SIX

Leaders Build Relationships

Relationships are essential for effective school leadership—in the past decades we have learned so much about what makes the *best* leaders and what magic they use to build relationships. Let's begin by analogizing relationship building to the story "Snow White and the Seven Dwarfs."

LOOKING IN THE MIRROR

In the story "Snow White and the Seven Dwarfs," each dwarf—Grumpy, Happy, Sleepy, and the rest—had his own special characteristics, which Snow White grew fond of as she lived with them seeking refuge from the wicked queen. While Snow White stayed with the dwarfs, they shared tasks and developed trusting and caring relationships. Snow White's benevolence in cleaning up after the dwarfs and her empathic way of being was deeply appreciated. "It was the least she could do," she thought, in return for them keeping her safe. Meanwhile, the queen's overreaching narcissism led her to admire herself in the mirror as the most beautiful and wisest in the land—until one day when, in response to her question, "Who is the most beautiful and fairest in the land?" the mirror answered, "Snow White." The queen's jealousy, envy, and inflated ego ultimately led her to dominate and try to destroy Snow White. The queen's misery and toxic narcissism kept her alone on her destructive mission.

The claim to be "better, holier, and more knowing than thou" has led many Disney characters to their demise. The moral of the story? Envy, jealousy, and maniacal narcissism in leadership keep us alone. No one is indestructible, not even a school leader! An unhealthy vision—one that is designed to build our own ego to the detriment of others—is doomed to fail. If leadership is not about enhancing the well-being of everyone in the school community, then such a leader will never be respected and followed by others.

Trust will prevail, with psychological safety and caring relationships. We all need to take a good look at ourselves in the mirror and to be truthful with ourselves about the areas we excel in and those that would benefit from some attention. The goal is to secure positive relationships with others—even those who might wish that you would just magically go away!

An example immediately relevant to school leadership would be a leader who demonstrates a strong, negative leadership style that promotes distrust, a lack of care, and a "business as usual" attitude. And the most frustrating aspect of working with this type of leader is that nobody but the person's boss can tell this leader anything about the negative effect he or she is having on others. Fear of job loss or harassment keeps employees from sharing their observations with their leaders. And sometimes, it's not even horrific leaders who alienate others so much as micromanaging leaders, who may love their staff but trust only themselves to make decisions—"No, I'm sorry, but I have to make this decision"—a clear sign of lack of confidence and distrust. Try giving feedback to such leaders? Not happening. If you haven't sat in the seat, you have no grounds for giving any advice. And who wants to risk getting on the leader's bad side? Your opinion is not solicited.

In our Disney story, the relationships between Snow White and the dwarfs were healthy, caring, and trusting. When the seven dwarfs offered to protect her from the queen turned witch, Snow White gladly accepted. She embraced the dwarfs and vice versa; they became family.

On the other hand, the wicked witch hadn't taken the time to care about any other creature in the land, so no one wanted her as a friend or as their leader. Without positive relationships to depend on, she had nothing.

Without positive relationships, we are alone in the world. A lonely, unconnected life can lead to poor well-being and even a shorter life span. Personally or professionally, it's the "kiss of death."

TRUST AND AUTHENTICITY

Earlier in this book we talked about the importance of trust. How leader-follower relationships unfold over time has everything to do with trust and authenticity. Essential to trust are such qualities as care, concern, honesty, and friendship.[1] For school leaders, essential skills and competencies include empathy, self-awareness, self-management, positive communication, the ability to deal with stress, and managing the emotions of others.[2] Having a clear shared vision and ethical core values anchors everything else so that your supervisees believe in you and willingly follow suit.

With so much to think about and everyone to worry about, where do school leaders find the space and wherewithal to concentrate on their well-being and growth mindsets? One place to start might be looking at the competencies in appendix B. Ask yourself, "What are the EI competencies that I use most on the job? Which must I work hard to show, and which come easily for me?"[3]

Consider putting empathy at the top of your list. "It is the foundation that grounds the building of relationships, it allows inner and outer growth transformation to happen, invites us to tend to others' needs and create a culture of caring teaching and learning."[4] If you are already an empathic leader, reflect on the ways you are empathic, to whom, and how.

One very empathic principal we worked with, after taking her 360 ESCI assessment, noticed that people responded that she didn't really listen to them. She was shocked because she believed that she *did* listen to them. But when she reflected on this, she realized that she was always moving from one thing to another and never took the time to ask her teachers questions—such as "How is your daughter doing?"—simple personal questions that would show that she cared about the teachers.

And of course, there is the issue of trust that we have been talking about throughout this book. Followers, be they teachers or principals, must trust their leader, but leaders must be able and willing to trust others too. Julie Wilson and Ann Cunliffe shed light on the relationship between leaders and followers and the development of trust. They conducted a longitudinal study that looked at how trust develops by studying twelve pairs of leaders in a high-tech firm over eighteen months.[5] The researchers looked at the factors that contributed to developing or disrupting trust between leaders and followers over time. They found "that trust included factors such as first impressions and was based on a variety of social and emotional factors such as feelings of liking, integrity, and communication skills." At the beginning of the study, these were all present, but by the end of the study, "disruptions occurred caused by factors such as a person's unpredictability, ability, or a lack of challenge in work." The researchers concluded "that relationship quality is more complex, can shift over time, and is situated in that it depends on a particular relationship—developing in either a positive way or a disrupted way—based on the subjective interpretations of both leaders and staff.

Both were continually assessed looking at the nature and quality of their relationship." In short, relationships need to be nurtured, and certain behaviors or events can either keep them strong or break them apart.

Vulnerability is yet another aspect that can build trust. When leaders show vulnerability, it reveals their humanity. Followers may see them more as human beings than as their bosses. But a leader's vulnerability often produces fear. Many leaders see revealing parts of themselves, such as personal challenges or mistakes they have made, as a risk. They fear losing respect. Brené Brown, author and inspirational speaker, says, "If you don't understand vulnerability, you cannot manage and lead people. If you're not showing up vulnerably as a leader, you can't expect anyone to follow you—period."[6]

According to Tschannen-Moran and Hoy, "one's willingness to be vulnerable to another is based on the confidence that the other is benevolent, honest, open, relatable, and competent."[7] In summary, trust is a two-way street that takes time to build and has to be earned. It can easily be lost by a betrayal or a perceived injustice. Earning trust requires authenticity—there's no way around it.

THINK ABOUT IT

In your role as leader, how hard or easy is it for you to be vulnerable? How has your vulnerability enhanced trust in your leadership? Are you comfortable with vulnerability or not?

I (Janet) share a story of a time in the 1990s when I decided to switch from teaching and return to the world of school administration. A childhood friend who was a teacher at the school informed me about the opening of an assistant principal position. Vince Jewell, at that time the principal of the Roosevelt Middle School in Vista, California, invited me to an interview to determine whether I was right for the assistant principal opening that he was hoping to fill. We met in a coffee shop and had lunch together—something I had never experienced in any New York City hiring process. We both interviewed each other to find out whether I was the right fit for the job. I remember being so impressed by his warmth and vision for his school. He broke down the barriers immediately and opened a relationship of trust. This trust anchored our relationship throughout the years we worked together and continues to this day. His honesty and integrity were valued by everyone on the staff and permeated the school's culture. He had earned the entire staff's trust. He was and, although now retired, continues to be an authentic leader.

As I think back to the years that I worked with Vince, I am grateful for the lessons he taught me. He was the most honest and approachable leader I had ever known—no pretenses, no BS. He loved his kids and cared about his staff. Everyone wanted a piece of Vince, and everyone got one. I never saw him burn out. Although he worked very hard, what I saw was a leader who made time for his personal and professional life. He was a runner and ran daily with others, a sportsman who spent time with his two sons, relaxed with his family, and enjoyed a glass or two of sparkling wine on intermittent evenings. He loved his job. He put me in charge of the rollout of SEL, which allowed me to put theory into action, and piece by piece we succeeded. Never once did I feel that I did not have his full support with the initiative. What a role model! Thanks, Vince.

A BRIEF STROLL DOWN LEADERSHIP THEORY MEMORY LANE

Everyone has a theory about what makes the best leaders. Educational leadership theory has been built on knowledge gained from many leadership fields—corporate, military, legal, medical, and more. All fields stress the importance of building trusting relationships. Before we unpack what we have learned about leadership in our field, let's take a slight detour and review a bit about how business leadership theory has informed us.

THINK ABOUT IT

Call to mind someone you consider a great leader—someone you would like to emulate. What is admirable or even compelling for you about this person's leadership?

From the nineteenth century, we have one of the oldest theories, the Great Man theory of leadership proposed by Thomas Carlyle, a Scottish essayist, historian, and philosopher who stated that certain men are born to be leaders and step up to demonstrate their inborn leadership. This thinking represented the belief that great men, or heroes, are highly influential people due to their natural attributes, such as above-average intellect, heroic courage, and extraordinary leadership ability. This view of leadership was countered by Herbert Spencer and his team, who believed leaders were products of their environment. He advocated that before a "great man" can remake his society, society has to make him.[8] Today, scores of women would jump down the throat of anyone who would espouse the Great Man theory—as would almost anyone who studies great leadership today, especially when we know the leadership success women have had in the workforce![9]

A walk through the early years of school leadership, the days of the one-room schoolhouse, takes us from the late 1800s to the early 1900s. During the Industrial Revolution, leaders were responsible for preparing workers for the assembly lines as mass production was prominent. Relationships were not the major focus. In each economic and political era, a variety of useful leadership styles surfaced. The top-down scientific managers of the early assembly lines soon morphed into the burgeoning bureaucracies of the war years; then came the human relations movements of the postwar years, followed by the mind-expanding explorations of the 1960s and 1970s. We have learned that no one leadership style works in all situations, but the strength of the leaders' relationships consistently matters.[10]

One of the more relationship-oriented leadership styles is transformational leadership. Sociologist James V. Downton created the concept of transformational leadership in 1973, and James Burns expanded on the idea in 1978, talking about how transformational leadership could help leaders and followers both push themselves to higher standards and better outcomes. Bernard M. Bass also continued to expand on this leadership concept in 1985, adding success measures to the process.

Transactional leadership is more directly focused on a structured, directed environment, and relationships take a back seat. This leadership is focused on leading by telling people what to do, giving expectations, and requiring rules or regulations. Transactional leadership often involves using rewards and punishments to get employees to do what they are told. Routines, schedules, rules, and formal authority are key components of transactional leaders' productivity. Transformational leaders are motivated by the need for achievement and usually have a strong desire to set up difficult goals and accomplish them. Many describe leaders such as Steve Jobs, Jeff Bezos, and Bill Gates as demonstrating this style of leadership. Transactional leaders are excellent at the day-to-day management of the organization. Both transformational and transactional leadership styles are helpful in different contexts. So much depends on the knowledge and readiness level of the employee. Much current thinking on leadership is sourced from Warren Bennis, scholar and author, who shared these pearls: "The manager has his eye on the bottom line; the leader has his eye on the horizon. The manager asks how and when; the leader asks what and why. The manager has a short-range view; the leader has a long-range perspective."[11]

Ralph Nader, author and political activist, said, "A basic function of leadership is to generate more leaders, not more followers."[12] This perspective suggests that, at the end of the day, leadership should be elevating and inspiring. Leaders should push the people they lead to new heights, helping them to grow into what they know they can become. Transformational leadership is an important psychological perspective for leaders to study and understand if they want to really influence and impact others. That said, in the reality of leading today's schools, think about this as the target, but know that lots of other leadership steps need to happen along the way.

TRANSFORMING OURSELVES AND OTHERS

Many of the larger problems we face in the world today, from climate change to poverty to racial injustice, ask us to get on the train and become change agents. Old ways are dying, and all of us are tasked, in some way or another, with being a part of the transition to a more sustainable and equitable way of being and operating in the world.

We learned a lot from early studies of group dynamics. Do you remember the experiment that Professor George Elton Mayo conducted in the 1920s at the Western Electric Company's Hawthorne Works? Researchers found that when conditions worsened—lights went dim, breaks were taken away, and the workday was lengthened—workers continued to persevere and work even harder because of the attention that they received from the bosses and the connection that they had with one another. They felt more important because they were being watched; no one had ever seemed to care about their work before. People mattered more than anything else, and the sense of belonging to something larger than oneself mattered more than financial gain or personal comforts.

This finding still carries great weight today. Think about the Great Resignation that happened not too long ago, spurred on by the pandemic. Workers began leaving their jobs in search of other ones more suited to their lifestyles. Others retired. It seemed that workers began searching for another way because they now viewed personal life—family, well-being—as more important than getting a paycheck.[13] People matter. Relationships matter. That is why the development of "soft" skills—such as empathy, positive communication, compassion, and other people-oriented skills—is encouraged. Most corporate leaders have an executive coach to help with these skills as part of the job and hold regular meetings to develop their teams' communication and interactions.

Bennis said in a 2009 interview, "The process of becoming a leader is similar, if not identical, to becoming a fully integrated human being." Both, he said, were grounded in self-discovery.[14] Bennis's vision was about developing human potential through an integrated approach to leader development. What we are recommending in this book is exactly that—a new way of preparing our school leaders grounded in emotional intelligence.

Among all competencies measured under the construct of emotional intelligence, we have mentioned earlier that empathy is the strongest connection between emotional intelligence and transformational leadership.[15] Transformational leadership proposes that leaders should engage with others and create a connection to raise the level of motivation and morality in both the leader and the followers. Bernard Bass indicated that transformational leadership was centered on the followers and emphasized motivating followers to reach beyond leaders' expectations.[16]

Front and center in the school leader's mind is how to best develop teachers who have a direct line to student success. Doing so requires establishing a culture in which growth and transformation are the goals, our best selves lead, and feedback is not just promoted regularly but expected by all and openly shared. In lifting student achievement, you are second in your influence on students only to teachers. You are the model! To build a culture where transformation can happen, one must start with oneself. Former chancellor of the New York City Department of Education Carmen Fariña shared, "Every year I sat with the principal for one-and-a-half hours. Nobody said I need to work on this or that. So, I modeled, 'Each of you needs to take responsibility,' help them find their area of growth. I listened as they shaped their individual work."

THINK ABOUT IT

What do transformational leaders do? There are many characteristics of transformational leadership that matter to us in schools. Where do you see yourself?

Transformational leaders have the following qualities:

- They don't micromanage. They foster a culture of employee independence and ownership.
- They demonstrate their own creativity and innovation, becoming role models for employees, and then inspiring employees to follow in their steps.
- Transformational leaders use intellectual stimulation and inspirational motivation to help add to employee empowerment and job satisfaction to find success.
- They continuously seek new routines in pursuit of improvement or something new and different.

Chancellor Fariña's approach to developing leaders is a perfect example of the qualities of transformational leadership. And while individual development is key, the development of the collective optimizes student success. In the 1990s, we began thinking of leadership in organizations more systematically. Schools were no exception. Brilliant minds such as Peter Senge and Otto Scharmer introduced the idea of turning into our inner consciousness to "sense and see" systems and lead them forward toward positive change. At the same time, Dan Goleman, Peter Salovey, John Mayer, David Caruso, and Richard Boyatzis were approaching leadership from the lens of emotional intelligence anchored by the neuroscience of the brain. The field of mindfulness burgeoned. *Self-care* has become the term used to describe taking action steps to avoid burnout and positive well-being. Let's just agree that educational leaders are often remiss in taking care of themselves in wholesome ways—with good nutrition, exercise, sleep, and connections—as we discussed in chapter 1. And if we have learned anything by now, we have learned how essential it is to take care of ourselves and our loved ones, as well as our schools' children and families.

AND THEN, THE PANDEMIC

One superintendent said, "During the pandemic when I was working from home, I realized how much time I give to the job and how little to my family." She was so happy to "get to know" her son again, cook dinner, and even watch television with the family occasionally. Although at the time of this writing, vaccines have been found to reduce the severe effects of the virus for some, many are still becoming sick from these viruses. Most educators are still fearful of the potential impact that COVID and its variants can have. And the winter flu last year was also severe.

Anxiety-provoking uncertainty about well-being can lead to physical and mental exhaustion, resulting in rethinking our commitments to the jobs we love. Our emotional intelligence skills and competencies help us to maneuver the waters, feel our feelings, think clearly, and make the best choices possible during difficult times. We have witnessed the power of school leaders' personal interactions with staff members who bring their worries to the leader. Effective leaders are steadfast in their use of active listening and empathy. Necessary difficult conversations still occur, but with caring words coming from the heart as well as the mind.

Before the theory of emotional intelligence was established, most people distinguished a good leader from an average leader on the basis of the characteristics, traits, and qualities the leaders possessed. Trait theory proposed that every human being has a personality that consists of a variety of traits. Different theorists considered effective leaders to have certain traits over others. Ralph Stogdill identified ten traits and skills of born leaders. Three of them are directly related to interpersonal communication: "ability to influence other people's behavior," "capacity to structure social interaction systems to the purpose at hand," and "readiness to absorb interpersonal stress."[17] Psychologist Raymond Cattell's sixteen trait factors are still used in career and other types of counseling today.[18] Both Rensis Likert and Gary Yukl proposed that participative leaders should show great concern for employees, listen carefully to their ideas, and include them in the decision-making process.[19] Mehmet Bellibas et al. suggested that school leaders who include teachers in decision-making processes improve overall job satisfaction, motivate teachers to work more collaboratively, and therefore indirectly improve instructional practices.[20] Interestingly, none of these traits of leaders has been studied over time to observe how the traits show up. But many of them can be seen reflected in some of the strategies stemming from emotional intelligence.

We talk about leadership today as a combination of leading with the head and leading with the heart. Getting at the heart of changes over time and hearing the stories of leaders give context to our learning about effective leadership. When Boyatzis and Goleman developed their Emotional and Social Competency Inventory (ESCI), they interviewed hundreds of leaders using a behavioral event interview approach that allowed them to hear leaders' stories. This lengthy process was fruitful, however, because it extracted the actual words of the leaders, which were later categorized and coded as individual competencies. The original twenty-four competencies were eventually collapsed into the twelve behavioral competencies that we use with our leaders today. They have consistently held up as very effective in defining leaders' emotionally intelligent leadership behaviors.[21]

Every school district and each individual school within that district is a unique entity, different from the next, based on families' and student needs, available resources, access to professional development, and mental models of the leaders. A leader who understands this knows that one leader would be great for a particular cultural environment, while another would not. The more we know about a leader's intrapersonal and interpersonal strengths and challenges, the competencies that are strengths, and those that could use some work, the better the match should be. Furthermore, stories about our experiences lift commonalities up and provide comfort to others. In our next story, colleague Deidre Farmbry eloquently writes about her "stop" as a principal and how she maneuvered being the right "fit" to change the culture of the school.

Destination: The Principalship

My first principalship was in a place I knew well. I had taught for eighteen years at the high school where I was ultimately appointed as principal after a five-year hiatus during which time I worked in a supportive capacity to a superintendent. I felt extremely confident returning to the school to serve in the top leadership position, believing that my knowledge of both people and place would enable me to rise to the expectation that had been outlined for me by those who had decided to send me "home" as principal. I felt no need for a road map, for I knew where I was going . . . or so I thought!

Instead of stepping into the context I expected, I stepped into a situation where in five years, teacher morale had declined, serious behavioral infractions had escalated, and academic expectations for students had plummeted as a result. The first indication of the extent to which the landscape had shifted came in the form of a teacher's comment during the summer when I held informal focus groups to gain information to shape my entry platform. All she said during the ninety minutes I met with her and four other teachers was, "Make me feel safe, and I'll do whatever you want." While other teachers brought me up-to-date on what had occurred in the development of small learning communities during the five-year period I was gone from the school, the desperation reflected in that one teacher's statement shifted my thinking from what I wanted to do my first year to what I might need to do instead.

Given her statement, not only did I, as a leader, need to revisit and redefine what I had the will to do, but I also had to grapple with what I had the skills to do. Did I have the capacity to make this teacher, or any other staff member, feel safe? What was needed beyond currently existing resources to make people feel safe? How would I balance the expectation that it is the principal who provides a safe climate with my personal belief that safe environments hinge on collective responsibility and ownership? And in terms of professional accountability, to what degree, did I, as the official school leader, want to allow others to judge my effectiveness as a principal on an indicator I had not anticipated and did not especially want as a measure of my success as a leader?

All these questions swirled around in my head, placing a major roadblock to my previously intact sense of self-confidence regarding my capacity to lead, especially at a school I considered "home." Faced with that one request—"Make me feel safe . . ."—I went from traveling down a familiar road to the state of being lost! I needed help in overcoming this roadblock, especially when I realized how pervasive the climate of fear was in the school, rendering impossible my desire to focus initially on anything but safety and security. So, I did what lost travelers do . . . I asked for guidance; and, in the process, I developed my skill in garnering resources and developing partnerships to help me survive my journey on this particular road. The two most helpful traveling partners were a prominent sociologist and a probation officer, both of whom provided different road maps for helping me through this detour off the path of what I had assumed would be my leadership priorities during my first year. Drawing comparisons between the streets and school hallways, the sociologist helped staff improve their ability to navigate shared space respectfully with students perceived to be threatening. Meanwhile, the probation officer—placed at the school due to my persistence in appealing to the powers-that-be in the juvenile justice system—provided some assurance for wary staff that the most troubled youth were under his observation while at school.

In the course of making it through this detour, I had to address issues of race, perceptions, and stereotypes—topics not discussed in my leadership preparation classes. I had to seek balance and perspective before making critical decisions about how to allocate resources, including my own energy, to address this issue of fear, lest it become all-consuming. While I was committed to being a leader at this particular school, my "home" school, I was not committed to remaining lost on an issue that too often becomes a derailing factor in urban settings, so I was quite proud of the stance I took, enabling me to eventually get back on the road where I wanted to be.

Deidre's story resonates strongly with us, for the road is never straight and narrow in the business of schools. There is no road map to follow. Adaptability—the ability to roll with the punches, as Deidre did, while considering the sudden detours as lessons learned—is a prerequisite for effective school leadership.

CONFLICT IS INEVITABLE

Conflict is not always negative, although many think it is. Most of us find it uncomfortable and challenging unless we have learned strategies to resolve conflict in productive ways. Schools are places where children work out their social relationships as well as form their identity and develop self-awareness—and emotion regulation. Adults in schools are prone to avoiding conflict and gossiping about situations with others rather than confronting them. Conflict is often the subtle elephant in the room. Whether this is the case in a particular school or district depends on organizational norms regarding one's responsibility in conflict, individual behavioral expectations, and skills acquired. If we are skilled in conflict resolution strategies and skills, we have the potential to promote a peaceful climate. But it does take a village. . . .

School and district leaders set the tone for both the culture and climate of the district and school. The way that they model how to manage emotions positively impacts how they respond to conflict and how they expect everyone to follow. Without established norms of how conflict is addressed, anything goes. This lack of agreement allows conflict to be either handled well or left to escalate.

Demonstrating empathic behaviors in solving conflicts, when needed in the workplace, can help bring both parties a win-win solution. Keep in mind that intellectual understanding of others does not guarantee empathic concern. Conflict can result in positive outcomes if leaders pause, reflect, and seek to understand others' perspectives.

Notably, high-powered leaders have been found to be more likely to rely on their own vantage point and to be less inclined to adjust to others' perspectives. Such leaders have even been found to be less accurate than others are at reading other people's emotions. For leaders, it is important to be aware of specific situational triggers to be more effective communicators and detect potential conflicts. Furthermore, when leaders don't feel empathic toward someone, it's difficult to hear that person's perspective. The more you sincerely express empathy, the stronger the relationship bond will become, and the easier it will be to work with others in addressing conflict with them or between them and others.

As a leader, it is wise to use different conflict styles to handle unique situations and assist followers. For example, you don't want to collaborate in a crisis. You need to use an immediate direct approach to stop someone from getting hurt or ward off a conflict from escalating. Nor would you accommodate someone who could be a potential danger. But given a situation in which a student is angry with another student, bringing them together to talk about the issue and helping them to negotiate their conflict will resolve what could have resulted in a physical altercation. Helping two teachers collaborate and talk out the conflict resolves the problem and sets an example for how conflict is resolved in this school or district.

Challenging staff to be problem solvers and coaching them to handle conflict productively communicates to teachers your expectations about monitoring, regulating, and managing our own emotional experiences and expressions.[22] Our personalities also influence our interactions with others and can create a harmonious work environment or a toxic one. Our influence triggers others' reactions and affects subsequent actions. Emotional dynamics could either interrupt or facilitate the communication process between the leader and others.[23]

How we embrace our own development can make or break our leadership success. The professional development opportunities we give our staff can help transform the culture and climate into a peaceful, caring place to work.

As an assistant principal, I (Janet) influenced the climate of my middle school by upskilling all faculty with conflict resolution skills. What a lifesaver! The ability to say strongly but kindly what one wants or needs empowers a person. In conflict, the skill of active listening is a powerhouse. Why? It provides a space where all parties feel heard and are heard by the other parties. Having the skill of active listening makes it possible to create this space. Similarly, "I" messages empower the person who is feeling hurt, angry, or sad, and who may be prone to avoidant behavior and depressed, to voice those feelings and be heard by the listener. I have seen discipline problems melt away when teachers used these strategies with their students. Rather than scream, shout, and throw a student out of their classroom, they learned how to calmly express their displeasure; in most cases, the students backed down when they were no longer the center of attention. Teachers became better equipped with these two strategies, which opened the conversation and prevented conflict escalation. With these strategies under our belts, we can control our triggers and work through trying moments. I have told prospective school leaders that if I were to lead a school tomorrow, the first thing that I would do is ensure that all adults have the skills of listening and positive assertiveness. Empowering adults with these skills reduces conflict between adults, between students and adults, and between students. Teachers who had been at one another's throats, asking you to resolve their differences, became willing to work out their problems with one another together.

When I (Janet) was working as an assistant principal, handling discipline was a big part of my role. Once we fully implemented our SEL program, referrals, which had made for all-day traffic in the past, were reduced to about 9 percent of what they had been. Adults practiced negotiation skills, and we set up a peer mediation program for students who needed adult supervision because of fear of ongoing bullying. This program also served to diffuse all the minor issues that middle school–age youngsters saw as grave. The campus became so peaceful, and I was finally able to focus on instruction.

Adults also benefited from reflecting on how they learned their conflict style during their youth from their own families. Many of us did not have parents who were equipped at handling conflict. My (Janet's) mom was a screamer when really upset, and my dad would sit quietly steaming. Of course, most of these arguments happened at the dinner table, so my sister and I were privy to them—not a healthy model for us. My approach to handling conflict arose out of those heated dinner-table conversations: avoid conflict at all costs. My sister became the mediator, a thirteen-year-old analyst in the making. I, on the other hand, saw no resolution resulting from her techniques, so escaping into my room or going outside to meet my friends served me well. As an adult, these early events molded my conflict style preference—avoidance was my number one preferred style for many years, much to the regret of friends who wanted to talk things out. When I started learning about how I faced conflict, I was mortified by my avoidant approach. I learned that we could shift our dominant styles and get results that both parties feel good about. I voiced my opinion more and made myself more vulnerable without fear or embarrassment. As a professional, I spoke up for the inclusion of SEL into school curriculums. I became an expert in the very area that had once challenged me. We are often drawn toward areas that we felt helpless about as children, when we realize that we are adults and can discard unwanted behaviors from our pasts.

What is your conflict style? Thomas Kilmann's framework for determining our conflict styles has been a powerful tool for us in our coaching work and trainings. The Thomas-Kilmann Conflict Mode Instrument (TKI®) was developed to help people deal more effectively with conflict situations and is based on forty years of research and implementation by the authors, Kenneth Thomas, PhD, and Ralph Kilmann, PhD, both professors of management at the University of Pittsburgh. Inspired by the managerial grid model of Robert Blake and Jane Mouton, Thomas and Kilmann developed a neat, accessible model that people at any level in an organization could use to deal with conflict quickly and effectively. Since the researchers' early work, their model has become the leading measure of conflict-handling modes, backed up by hundreds of research studies.[24]

We bring to conflict two behaviors: being assertive and being cooperative. Our approach to conflict depends on the balance of these two behaviors. Kilmann suggests that we have a primary and secondary conflict style that we often call upon. If we are feeling not so cooperative or assertive, basically, we are saying, "Leave me out of this." If our cooperativeness is low and our assertiveness high, we find ourselves in a *competing* mode. This style can be excellent in making quick decisions, but if used for the wrong reasons, this style can result in the person being seen as someone who is not in touch and who loves controlling everything. Competing is often very useful in getting the job done, but it is not so good for resolving conflict. In fact, competitors see conflict as a game—someone wins, and someone loses—which is not very helpful when one is trying to forgive or heal a situation.

Accommodating is what we do when we want to preserve the relationship. In accommodating, we are overly cooperative and assertive. Our end goal here is to give the other person the benefit of the doubt and hope that they will rise to the occasion. I always use the pencil metaphor to explain. Many teachers have a long-term battle with giving out pencils when a student consistently comes to school without one. Rather than accommodate them with one that belongs to the class, teachers make the pencil the center of the conflict. They refuse to lend the student a pencil because that student will never learn responsibility. Subsequently, the student with nothing to do gets bored and further interrupts the class. Nothing is gained, because that student has neither learned a lesson nor participated in the current class assignment. In my opinion, here is where we should accommodate. This child may never bring a pencil to school but will participate and learn when lent a pencil.

Collaborating is the way we hope to behave in most conflicts. In collaborating, cooperativeness and assertiveness come together: we use our words to describe our feelings and politely seek to meet those needs; we can sit next to one another and together find options for mutual gain, and a common purpose; we can work out a solution to the problem and hold one another accountable.

Finally, there is *compromising*. Many think that this is the best solution. It sometimes is, but not as often as you would think. When we compromise, we must give up something to gain something else. Compromising involves give-and-take, which can be helpful but most often not sufficient. This approach to conflict can work depending on the problem at hand. The next time you go for a compromise, try to push yourself further and ask yourself, "What would it take to get the two parties to a place where we both can get our needs met by negotiating and not have to give something up?"

I'll never forget the time when two of our eighth graders came to me to tell me that there was going to be a gang fight that night that stemmed from the two middle schoolers, the brothers of local gang members. This student asked me to bring them together in my office to talk and see if the fight could be avoided. I remember being a bit uncertain about trusting the boys, so I put them in my office; after setting the ground rules, I sat outside the door where I could hear if anything went awry. Those two boys came out smiling after making a pact to not let their brothers take this into their own hands and to let them know that the two boys had worked the conflict through. I sighed a deep sigh of relief and was thankful for the respect everyone had for one another. For me, this was the pièce de résistance.

Shifting our conflict style isn't easy, but it can and must be done if your current style isn't working for you. Three techniques that can help us shift obstructing paradigms are reframing, shifting shoes, and affirmations.

Reframing is the mental act of looking at the issue in another way, a more positive light. For example, you might think to yourself: "If I address this issue, it'll slow down the meeting." Consider this thought: "If we negotiate this difference now, trust and creativity will increase."

Shifting shoes is another technique used to practice empathy by mentally "walking in the shoes" of another person. You answer questions such as "How would I feel if I were that person being criticized in front of the group?" and "What would motivate me to say what that person just said?" Affirmations are positive statements about something someone has accomplished or a positive quality of a person. These positive statements often represent something you hope to be true, and positive thinking might make it so. For example, instead of saying to yourself right before a negotiating session, "I may be calm now, but I know I'm going to blow up," force yourself to say, "I am calm and I am prepared, and if I am rattled, I have strategies to bring myself to calm." If we can learn to shift any negative mental tapes to more positive ones, we will be able to shift obstructing paradigms and manage conflict more effectively. As leaders, knowing these differences will help us model positive conflict management for all teachers and students and provide training for them to acquire the skills themselves.

In the magical world of Snow White, the dwarfs' team effort resolved her conflict with the wicked witch and healed her from the negative effects of the witch's apple. In our world, our conflicts are left for us to manage, but if we empower our staffs and our teams with the skills they need to handle conflict, we can shift from the dynamics of disempowerment to a culture where every member of the school community can resolve their disputes.

CHAPTER SEVEN

Managing Our Relationships

Great team players lack excessive ego or concerns about status.
They are quick to point out the contributions of others and slow to
seek attention for their own. They share credit, emphasize team over
self, and define success collectively rather than individually. It is no
great surprise, then, that humility is the single greatest and most indis-
pensable attribute of being a team player.

—PATRICK LENCIONI, *The Ideal Team Player:*
How to Recognize and Cultivate the Three Essential Virtues

It is not a luxury to have work teams that can perform effectively in a thriving or turbulent environment; it is a necessity. And, whatever the initiative, if we are willing to distribute leadership with other leaders, teachers, teams, parents, and students, the tasks will get done and everyone will be more invested. To manage change effectively, school leaders need knowledge and skills in emotional and social intelligence, and they need to create opportunities for education and training in emotional and social skills for their leadership teams and school communities—first creating a culture of psychological safety among educators and staff wherein these safe spaces and expected norms allow people and teams to take risks and to be creative and innovative. When leaders have a clear vision and a positive outlook, and when they engage in caring communication and engender trust, they can develop communities where collaboration is affirmed and practiced and where resistance is aired and discussed.

In this chapter, we continue to look at the leadership competencies that are part of the domain of relationship management: influence, teamwork, and inspiration. The more leaders demonstrate these competencies, the higher performance they will achieve. Let's explore what these competencies look like for school and district leaders.

POWER TO INFLUENCE

We create collective efficacy by "clarifying school goals, providing meaningful capacity-building, and collaborative opportunities for staff, such as participating in professional learning communities and engaging staff authentically in school decisions."[1]

"Sometimes it feels like we are constantly selling to them. Because we are a democratic system that includes a protective teachers' union, we are constantly trying to get our teachers to 'buy in,'" shared principal Elaine. "There are times when the union supports a teacher to the detriment of student learning."

Depending on your leadership style, these setbacks may be overcome easily or may be difficult for you. And then there are those staff members who just won't give you a break. They resist every kind of change. They are the one-third that want control and will take it however they can; there's no convincing them. They just don't give up. This puts extra stress on you, the school leader. Having a good handle on your emotions doesn't make the stress go away, but it does give you a better way to cope with it. So much of the way you deal with these naysayers has to do with your emotional intelligence.

Influence can be your friend in these moments. As school leaders, you are always networking, not only with faculty but with all school stakeholders—parents, politicians, and community members. Knowing how to influence others is a much-needed competency. A 2004 report by the Wallace Foundation of New York City presented evidence about how school leaders lead school change by inspiring and influencing teachers to ensure that students achieve. A 2021 update to this report confirmed the earlier findings. It found that "the cultivation of high-quality school leaders could yield one of the highest returns on investment in K–12 education."[2] By upskilling our leaders, we have the potential to assume the kind of leadership that is needed.

THINK ABOUT IT

Let's spend a few moments thinking about your influence on others. Do you consider yourself to be influential? Would others say the same if asked? What is the language and what are the behaviors that you use to successfully influence others? What behaviors would you like to develop to grow your influence or enhance your skills?

Superintendent Ana is a great example of someone who is influential. Of course, she has a position of power, which automatically gives her influence. But Ana has qualities as a person and a professional that allow her to be able to influence others without much difficulty. For one thing, she is empathic. You can feel her empathy when she speaks to you. She is kind and caring to others, and she is sincere. When she asks those around her to do something, they do it because they want to please her and because they know she "gets" them—and understands what will benefit the school district or individual community. Finally, she is straightforward and transparent at the same time. When she told her school leaders that participating in our training and coaching had changed her in so many ways, they immediately signed on the dotted line to enroll. That's referent power—the power that Superintendent Ana is given by others because her authenticity, values lived in action, and high-level interpersonal skills allow them to trust her. Now, if she were here right now, she would say, "Listen, I wasn't always like this. It's the work that I did with you both and Marc Brackett and with my coach. I wasn't as nice before. But now I strive to be my *best* self at all times. And it's made a difference in my leadership and the relationships I now have with my principals."

If you know Marc Brackett, by the way, you would see his influence on others—not just in what he says, but in how he says it, with a combination of high-level science and fun-loving humor.[3] When we look at French and Raven's power structures, Marc has them all. He has formal power—both coercive and legitimate power—because he is the director of the Yale Center for Emotional Intelligence and a Yale professor. His vision becomes a shared vision and guides the work of others. He has the ultimate say in all decisions. He compliments and gives public shout-outs to employees. But more than this, he has personal power, both expert and referent, by the nature of his interpersonal relations with others.

Now we aren't all Marc Brackett, Dan Goleman, or Richard Boyatzis, but we have the same potential to influence those whom we lead. Terry Bacon, author and former CEO of a global consulting firm that specializes in executive and professional development, is known for his writing on power and influence. He describes power as consisting of eleven factors:

1. *Knowledge power:* what you know and what you can do; your knowledge as well as your skills, talents, and abilities.
2. *Expressiveness power:* your ability to communicate powerfully and effectively in speech and writing.

3. *History power:* shared experiences, familiarity, and trust with people close to you.

4. *Attraction power:* your ability to cause others to like you and want to be with you.

5. *Character power:* your character, including your integrity, honesty, fairness, courage, kindness, modesty, and prudence.

6. *Role power:* power derived from your role in an organization; the legitimate power and authority vested in your role.

7. *Resource power:* your ownership or control of important resources (such as wealth or natural resources).

8. *Information power:* your access to and control of information.

9. *Network power:* power derived from the breadth and quality of your connections with other people.

10. *Reputation power:* how you are thought of by others in your community (team, organization, or society).

11. *Willpower:* your desire to be more powerful coupled with the courage to act.[4]

In this long list, you are bound to find several powers that you recognize in yourself. It can be very helpful to spend time reflecting on the kinds of power and influence you rely on as a leader. We find of particular interest *willpower*, which Terry defines as

> power based on your desire to be more powerful coupled with the courage to act. This power comes from within and can magnify every other source of power. It depends entirely on your decision to act on your passion and commitment, but also on your energy and action. Willpower is different from desire and longing. It comes not from the impulse to act but from acting on the impulse. The most important power source of all. Compared to low willpower, high willpower can increase your leadership and influence effectiveness by a factor of ten.[5]

After reading through this discussion of power, are you left feeling you would like to have more influence or would you like to be more powerful? Strengthening your emotional skills and behavioral competencies will help you. Even if the system you are working in tries to hold you back, we invite you to include *influence* in your mental model of your best self in your personal and professional life.

THINK ABOUT IT

Reflect on the powers that you believe you have and those you would like to own. What do you gain from leaning into the powers you currently have? What would additional powers bring you?

SHARING LEADERSHIP THROUGH TEAMWORK

In the corporate world, teams are the life force of an organization. Investment in development of employees is primary to organizational success. Emotionally intelligent CEOs promote employee development. Coaches are commonplace for top and middle management. Increasingly, leaders at all levels are coaching employees rather than weighing someone's worth based on a performance assessment alone.

Schools, being public entities, don't readily have the financial ability to provide ongoing executive coaching to their leaders. Even professional development, now more than ever before, is limited due to time and finance constraints. Instructional coaches are available and relied on to raise the level of teacher interaction and the instructional level of their students. The instructional coach works with the development of skill sets in teachers. These coaches organize curricular meetings and events; they teach by modeling and observing. They are a huge help to administrators who get bogged down with so many other needs to address. Distributing leadership to teams accomplishes three very important objectives: sharing the responsibilities to coach and mentor teachers in need, creating a feeling of belonging, and enhancing trust.

In this section, we explore how emotionally intelligent teams are assets for the school leader.

THINK ABOUT IT

When was the last time you worked in a team, and you respected all team members and found the time spent very productive? How did you feel in this team? What was present in the team that made it work well?

On the other hand: Ever work in a not-so-good team? We know—horrible. You might even end up thinking, "I'm never working with a team again!"

One of the best classes that I (Janet) ever took was a group dynamics class. To this day, I continue to use the theory and practices I learned in that class. It is through the study of groups that Robin and I have been successful in leading teams to look at the hard stuff and make personal and professional changes.

The power of teams has been recognized for decades, but teamwork has taken on greater meaning since the pandemic made it a more viable way of working. A recent Forbes article tells us that remote working is here to stay: "25% of all professional jobs in North America will have become remote by the end of 2022, and more opportunities will continue to increase through 2023."[6]

So, what does teaming look like in schools? How do teams benefit staff members and the school leader? Research shows that collaborative problem-solving leads to better outcomes. The reason may be that team members take more calculated risks. Maybe the team's energy motivates them. Working in a productive team can also lead to happier team members. Happier team members experience less burnout, boosted productivity, fewer mistakes, and expanded creativity.

Some of us love working in teams, and others shun it. Working in a team makes us more accountable to one another. I (Janet) once taught a class in which one of the teams was experiencing conflicting points of view. A team member was called out by another team member for her lack of participation in the group. Rather than work it out with her team or have me mediate the team, the student dropped out of the class. That's how unprepared she was to confront her own shadow side or voice her feelings about the other member. The more a staff member is reluctant to put feedback into practice, the more our frustration increases. Unmanaged, this can cause us to grow weary and even angry at the bite-size changes we observe. What we say or do in our positions of power can get in the way of the relationship and lead to more resistance in the staff member. When a team is generative and works well together, ideas flow, creativity sparks, and personal and professional growth happens.

The times are changing. We believe that school leaders and teachers need to be facilitative leaders and to guide and coach their employees and students to learn by doing, solving problems, inquiring, and exploring their creativity. That way, they acquire skills and ways of being designed for the times, rather than the way we learned. *Fun with Dick and Jane* taught us how to read but not how to think. We need a paradigm shift—how and what we teach has to change. We have to teach skills, not content, to adults and young people. There is plenty of content available on the internet for everything we want to know. Today's world asks that graduates can figure out how to use their knowledge.

Here is an example of a new way of thinking about school: While we were writing this book, former police captain Eric Adams became mayor of New York City. For the first time, the city is starting a virtual/hybrid school without walls for incoming ninth graders. This "out of the box" school offers both a hybrid and virtual program to approximately six hundred students. Ninth-grade student Pete talks about the program, "At a School Without Walls": "I learned that creating a positive and supportive environment isn't just dumb luck. I used to think having a good community just came from certain personalities meshing together, but this showed me that building a strong community is something that can be worked toward. Creating connections and trust within a community can be achieved by creating opportunities for team building and getting to know one another." Pete and other ninth graders will be codesigning their learning beyond problem-based academic subjects to a selection of courses of high interest, including coding, anime, visual arts, theatre arts, web development, digital animation, music production, podcasting, and video game production, and so on.[7] This ninth grader's experiences of working as a team with the freedom to problem-solve, invent, create, and appreciate the accomplishment of the collective will be carried forward with him for a lifetime. He has learned the strength that lies in connection, which one can have through working with proactive teams.

THINK ABOUT IT

Have you had a similar experience of working with a team on a new-for-you digital platform? Or the creation of a podcast? Is this an area in which you must upskill?

Fortunately, as educators we find ourselves continuously challenged, because new ideas bring with them the mandates that educators must learn, adapt, and teach their students. Change is never easy, but it is necessary. As a school leader, you confront this challenge daily, not just in yourself, but in the voices and facial expressions of your staff. The responsibility of providing them with support and encouragement rests on your shoulders. *How you check in with team members and monitor the team's productivity makes a world of difference in the outcomes of their work.* Setting them up as a group and letting them go without supervision and a network of support is fruitless. Distributing leadership can reduce your stress level and empower staff, but without accountability, your leadership will lose its effect on the school culture.

SELECTING YOUR EMOTIONALLY INTELLIGENT TEAM

Let's take a step back to explore the knowledge one needs to select the right people for the right teams. First, consider the type of team the member in question will participate in individually, how ready or prepared they are for participation on this team, the balance of racial and other diversity on the team, the background in the subject that each member brings to the group, and personality traits and leadership skill strengths.

The power of an effective team depends on the commitment that members are willing to make to the team. Work teams need people with high interpersonal skills who can both work alone and "play nice in the sandbox" with others. The teams should be diverse in multiple ways—someone has to be the visionary, and someone has to ensure that the work gets done well. If the same members always take on most of the work, the doers will become angry and could pull out. The team runs the risk of member burnout or worse: member turn-off.

These are a few other things to think about when selecting team members: Look for excellent communication skills, self-discipline, individual talents, diversity, commitment to your vision, belief in equity, and excellence in connecting with others—adults and students.

I (Janet) remember when I was interviewing for the faculty of the Administration and Supervision program at Hunter College. Tony, the faculty member who was running the search, made a point of selecting me because my experience and personality balanced the current team. Tony told me, "I selected you because you were not like me or other members of the faculty. You have the skill sets that we are lacking as a team." I was impressed to learn this; I believed that statement, and I was curious to find out how the faculty members were different from me. In fact, we couldn't have been more different, and with our individual talents we filled in gaps for one another.

EMOTIONALLY INTELLIGENT TEAM PROCESS

One missing piece that we have not discussed yet is the process of developing an emotionally intelligent team. "Yes, an emotionally intelligent team. Oh, you mean a group of people who are each emotionally intelligent?" you ask. Well, not exactly. Yes, you do want to include people on your teams who have EI, but more than that, you want to work with the team as a whole to ensure that they work as an emotionally intelligent team.

Groups have their own personalities and identities. The group identity encompasses the personality of the entire group. It reflects the group's values, norms, purpose, and vision. Its identity is formed by the team's behaviors (including words and conversation). Of course, the individual members' actions represent the group, but these actions are also seen as one person's behaviors. When you join a group and, over time, feel a sense of belonging, you take on the essence of that group. The dispositions of the group are assigned to you. "Emotionally competent teams don't wear blinders; they have the emotional capacity to face potentially difficult information and actively seek opinions on their task processes, progress, and performance from the outside. For some teams, feedback may come directly from customers."[8]

What does an emotionally intelligent team look like? Well, first of all, it's a team in which all members want the same thing—there is a shared vision—to jointly reach the goals that they establish with care for one another, honesty, and commitment to using their emotional skills. Drs. Vanessa Druskat and Steven Wolff developed the TEAM EI Survey.[9] It helps team members diagnose problems the team is facing, including issues such as someone not pulling his or her weight, or hurtful gossiping behind someone's back and fear of speaking up in a meeting due to possible verbal assaults. Druskat shares, "Our research tells us that three conditions are essential to a group's effectiveness: trust among members, a sense of group identity, and a sense of group efficacy."[10] As we discussed earlier in the book, most people avoid confrontation and never speak their mind, especially not to the boss. The key to being able to get to a productive place, according to the two designers of the survey, is by building what is expected not only of individual members of the team but also of the team as a whole. The authors use three types of norms that work nicely together: individual norms, team norms, and external norms.

Let's look at the first bucket, *team fundamentals*: these include the roles and responsibilities of the team members, the procedures they set up for their meetings, and the goals and objectives they desire. These are the basics that any competent leader takes charge of in meetings. When the team neglects these fundamentals, the team lacks the skeleton that supports the rest of the meeting. The result can be confusion and a feeling that anything goes. Team fundamentals provide a structure that is repeated time and time again, is expected by all team members, and can be led by any team member should the team leader be absent.

The next bucket is about *building social capital.* "Social capital allows a group of people to work together effectively to achieve a common purpose or goal. It allows a society or organization, such as a corporation or a nonprofit, to function together as a whole through trust and shared identity, norms, values, and mutual relationships."[11]

Social capital involves how the group interacts with others. It's how the group presents itself—its identity and safety protocols. It's about the reputation of the group, how it is perceived by others, and where it stands among other groups. The more social capital a team has, the more likely it will be able to accomplish its goals.

The third bucket consists of *nine norms*, divided into those that are for individuals, those for teams, and those in the community environment. We have found these norms to be helpful in our work with school leaders and their teams. They create a structure for the effectiveness that you may be seeking. They create safety for team members to know what is permissible and what is not. When norms are agreed on and followed by all team members, people know what will move the team forward and what will take it several steps backward. The nine norms include interpersonal understanding, addressing counterproductive behavior, caring behavior, team self-evaluation, creating emotion resources and an affirmative environment, proactive problem-solving, organizational understanding, and building external relationships.

The assessment that Druskat and Wolff created and promote through EI World, a global consulting company, is very helpful in fostering transparency of thought among team members and between the team and the school or district. Depending on the culture, the leader will receive pushback and potentially hurtful comments. Through individual coaching sessions, the leader is briefed beforehand by the coach or facilitator about how to handle the pushback. Effective leaders welcome the comments, as hard as it may be to hear them, because this transparency will allow the leaders to know the true feelings of team members and the staff members they represent. Only by inviting others' voices can we know how our actions may positively or negatively impact employees. Of course, Drs. Druskat and Wolff encourage team members to contribute not only negative feedback but gratitude for positive aspects of the organizational changes they embrace.

Turn to the world of sports to observe how some great coaches work with their teams. Connor McDavid, of the Edmonton Oilers, a Canadian hockey team, is perhaps the greatest individual player in the history of the sport, but the team has yet to come together to win a Stanley Cup championship. Perhaps the reason is that the individual members of the team may not thrive in an environment where one person is so much greater than the others. Their narrative may rest on wanting to shine individually, but they cannot compare to a superstar of such magnitude. In an interview, McDavid shared his thoughts about why they were not winning: "Everyone has to buy in and work towards a common goal." Sounds like a team problem to us! On the other hand, the former coach of the Chicago Bulls, Phil Jackson, knew that by focusing his understanding on the intrinsic motivator for each team member's desire to serve the greater team, he gave team members the freedom to create their personal athletic identities. Only then did he coach them to be the best players they can be within that team. He was emotionally intelligent. He brought practices such as mindfulness to the team. He made room for the individual egos and talents of the members. When you have a Michael Jordan or a Connor McDavid on your team, you need teammates who complement the greatness of the star performer. Each player's greatness makes the other players' greatness even bigger. Michael was all about winning, and that's what he did.

From the other side of the globe, South Korea, and the world of entertainment, comes the seven-member team of BTS, internationally renowned K-pop performers, loved by millions of fans. The boy group's team experiences provide a different example of the power of a committed team, with all members sacrificing their individual star qualities to form one unit that is greater than the sum of its parts. This group has created an international mega-storm. Their commitment to one another has required them to sacrifice their individual growth for the good of the team. But as we just saw with Coach Jackson, members of the team also need the room to grow their individual talents. Remember the Beatles? George struggled because he wasn't given the same opportunity to put his songs on the Beatles' albums as John and Paul were. Had they been able to work this out as a team, perhaps they would not have had to split up so soon. All voices must be heard in a system of communication that makes it safe to share your innermost thoughts and feelings.

BTS members are committed not only to their team but also to their fans. They realize that the fans brought them to greatness, and the members of BTS constantly express their appreciation. In June 2022, they announced they were going on a hiatus to develop their personal identities. They had been living and working together for ten years and finally got their own apartments. RM, the leader of the K-pop group, told *Rolling Stone* "the relentless pressure to make music all the time doesn't give artists time to mature. . . . There's no time left for growth." He later added, "Right now, we've lost our direction, and I just want to take some time to think."[12] During the time the team has taken off from performing together, several members have performed individual concerts, and members will also fulfill their military obligations.[13] The group is slated to return to the stage as a group again in 2025—Janet's eighteen-year-old daughter sure hopes this is true!

What do these examples bring into this discussion for school leadership? The school leader needs a team that is eager to follow and supports the leader's ability to lead. Simultaneously, the team needs to have implicit trust in the leader and one another. Team members also need to be honest about their feelings and thoughts and to be authentic and quick in communication. Team members, in our case mainly teachers, need to continuously move forward on their own personal and professional journeys to become their best selves. Collaboration among all team members, including the school's principal or, at the district level, the superintendent, is essential, as is the commitment to the team and its goals. A team inspired by the leader's vision will share in that vision and make its achievement possible.

Earlier we mentioned that we have been working with a wonderful group of principals who were selected as part of a fellowship called the Gray Fellows. They are a dynamic group of leaders who are exploring the transformation of themselves and others by incorporating contemplative practices into their own and others' lives. This fellowship, developed by Principals Noah Angeles and Kevin Froner, empowers its members with mindfulness, brain-body exercises, and more within a strong community that encourages healing and well-being. The principals travel annually to Kripalu, one of our favorite retreat centers, where they practice lessons for healing the body, mind, and spirit. They eat wholesome food, honor the gift of silence, and practice meditation and yoga. The project focuses on individual transformation, which then extends to schools in the form of change projects. As part of this project, the fellows received EI-based coaching, which aligned with the inner work they were already doing. Several cohorts have taken part in this one-year program, and some of the fellows have gone on to become coaches to work with new cohorts of principals. One of them, a high school principal, Moses, signed up to become a coach so that he could improve his leadership and learn new strategies to develop this team's interrelationships and commitment to the vision and to one another.

When we make ourselves vulnerable, put down our masks, and show our emotions, we become human. Author and speaker Brené Brown says, "The definition of vulnerability is uncertainty, risk, and emotional exposure. But vulnerability is not weakness; it's our most accurate measure of courage. When the barrier is our belief about vulnerability, the question becomes: 'Are we willing to show up and be seen when we can't control the outcome?' When the barrier to vulnerability is about safety, the

MEET MOSES

Moses is currently a Latinx principal of a large vocational school with 2,200 students—the very same school that he attended for high school. We asked him why he wanted to become a coach.

He told us that he has known for some time that he was lacking the skills of a coach. He shared,

> I felt responsible for how my APs are leading. I gave them too much freedom and trust without modeling the same. It came back to bite me. Teachers circumvented the APs and came to me to complain about what the APs were doing. Ten is a lot. I started mentoring and I realized that I need coaching as well. When my coach talked about it, I realized I knew more than I thought, but still had a lot to learn. I knew I needed to reflect on how I was going to do this. I got into the Gray Fellows because they offered coaching. I recognized that my team of ten assistant principals was not functioning as a team. They were, each of them, involved in their own departments, and these boundaries were rarely crossed.

Moses had been thinking a lot during our discussions. He blamed himself for the present state of the APs. He had not developed them as individual leaders nor as a team. He shared,

> At the beginning (when first promoted), I had a hard time with them. I would close my door and yell or kick it to get my anger out. I'm not that person anymore. I don't lose my cool. I tell them, "I hear you, but I don't agree with you." I want the APs to learn skills, coaching, and modeling for their teachers. Three years from now I hope the finger-pointing is gone and there is more collaboration, and they can regulate their emotions. You can't take back what you say.

He shared that early on he lacked the language for positive communication; he would often raise his voice and shut his employees down from sharing anything with him.

> As a mentor principal, I learned new ways of getting things done without expressing anger. When I first started, it was so hard to receive constructive feedback. I would take it personally. My mentors would tell me it's not personal, it's business. The minute I started to think that I can't do this job alone, I began thinking of others first. I allowed people to give me feedback. I am in a better place now, healthy and happy. If you fix yourself, everything else will get fixed. Know yourself and be honest. Know your areas of improvement. If you work on the areas you need to improve your energy, everyone else's will be affected.

Moses and his team spent this year together with us bringing all the "elephants into the room" and listening to one another. They are working toward positive steps in their own behavior and for the team. Kudos, Moses!

question becomes: 'Are we willing to create courageous spaces so we can be fully seen?'"[14]

We would be remiss if we didn't mention the great work of Patrick Lencioni. His book *The Five Dysfunctions of a Team* has helped many teams to unravel the issues that inhibit them from high performance and provides ideas on how to improve. To refresh your memory, here are the five dysfunctions that Lencioni says usually get in the way of team effectiveness: absence of trust, fear of conflict, lack of commitment, avoidance of accountability, and inattention to results.[15] These dysfunctions can be shifted with a concentrated focus on them by everyone on the team. It all begins with the leaders' willingness to be vulnerable. Others will then follow suit. In the story above, Principal Moses was completely vulnerable with his staff. When we began the work he said to them "I haven't done a lot of things right in leading you and I want to change that." True to his word, Moses and his team are on their way to high performance.

In a more recent book, *The Ideal Team Player*, Lencioni focuses on what he calls virtues that individuals should possess in order to play an active role in a team. He believes that each member of the team should be humble, hungry, and smart. We include his model here to give context to his reasoning for selecting these three virtues:

- **Humble.** "They lack excessive ego or concerns about status. Humble people are quick to point out the contributions of others and slow to seek attention for themselves. They share credit, emphasize team over self, and define success collectively rather than individually."
- **Hungry.** "They are always looking for more. More things to do. More to learn. More responsibility to take on. Hungry people almost never have to be pushed by a manager to work harder because they are self-motivated and diligent. They are constantly thinking about the next step and the next opportunity."
- **Smart.** "They have common sense about people. Smart people tend to know what is happening in a group situation and how to deal with others in the most effective way. They have good judgment and intuition around the subtleties of group dynamics and the impact of their words and actions." [16]

THINK ABOUT IT

Stop to think about the members in your teams. Are they the "right" people for these teams? How did you choose them? What does the entire team do well and not so well?

Now, think of all the people you supervise. Do they live by these virtues? Don't you wish they did? Do you live by these virtues?

INSPIRATION

Close your eyes and think about a time when you felt truly inspired. Was it a person who inspired you—a speaker, a teacher, a student, a child? Did something you read resonate with you? What did you feel in your body? Were there tingles? Did a smile come over your face? Was there a warm feeling inside? Did your heart race with excitement? How long did the feeling last—a few hours, a day, longer? Did you take action as a result of this inspired moment or period of time? How did it impact you over time?

The Latin roots of the word *inspiration* mean, literally, to breathe in or to take a breath. Our colleague Allison Holzer, in the book she coauthored, *Dare to Inspire*, defines the initial moment of inspiration as "the spark, the intersection of possibility and invincibility."[17] Those moments of inspiration feel wonderful. We feel that so much is possible, that we can accomplish anything. Unfortunately, these moments do not always translate into reality. A spark of inspiration can remain just a spark, or we can make it sustainable. Holzer's book deepens our understanding of inspiration. How can we turn those moments of inspiration into something that endures over time, that results in something desired? In what ways are you inspirational and how much inspiration do you bring to the table? How can we use the competency of inspiration as a tool for growth and change in our personal and professional lives?

Through their research with more than 350 leaders, Allison Holzer and her colleagues found five truths about inspiration:

- Inspiration is highly personal, and it evolves over time; everyone is inspired differently.
- We have agency and choice about inspiration in our own lives. (Be sure not to force others to see inspiration as you do.)
- There are reliable engines—pathways that can spark inspiration.
- Inspiration can be sustained over time.
- Inspiration is contagious.[18]

Let's not forget that there are different ways to think about inspiration and that different groups of people are inspired by different people, events, and practices. What inspires us may not inspire you. In a culture where Whiteness is valued over and above other races, different approaches to inspiring may be overlooked. As leaders, knowing these differences will help us in inspiring all teachers and students.

Before we read Holzer's book, we never thought too intensely that you can choose to be inspirational in various ways. The personal, relationship, and circumstance "engines" discussed in this book allow us to think broadly about how to be inspirational and set a goal in place to develop these engines and integrate them into your leadership.

Let's explore further what inspires each of you, how you inspire others, and the ways you can ramp up your ability to inspire.

THINK ABOUT IT

Start by thinking about someone who has inspired you. What was it about this person that inspired you? Was it their presence and what they said or did? Was it the principles and morals they stood for? Was it their accomplishments? What was the quality of their communication skills? Were they great storytellers? What else has inspired you? *Hold onto this reflection as we will return to it shortly.*

I (Janet) have been inspired by a number of people in my lifetime. But the one moment that stands out for me was when I was in Costa Rica with my friend and colleague Linda Lantieri, at the University for Peace. Linda managed to arrange a meeting with Robert Muller, former assistant general secretary to U Thant, secretary general of the United Nations. Robert was known for all he did to make peace in the world. I had become a fan of his after reading several of his books. To me, he was a hero, having fought for peace in many ways, including spending a week in a German prison during World War II. Robert learned about the foolishness of war and the benefits of peace as a young man. He lived in Alsace-Lorraine, a city on the border of France and Germany. These two peoples lived harmoniously for many years, but during the war, they were not only enemies but murderers of one another. He thought, "How could they be brothers one day and enemies the next?" This event greatly influenced him in his quest to build communities of peace. Simply crossing a line changed who your enemies were!

Robert lived in a small, rustic home on top of the lush, leafy campus of the University for Peace. We sat on a bench on top of the mountain talking with him for hours. His mere presence made me tingle. I learned so much from him that day. I asked him to share his thoughts about how to shift education to teach peacemaking skills to students. He said with passion, "First we have to change our thinking about what children should learn. For example, why are we teaching the history of war, when we can teach the history of peace?"

To this day, those words echo for me and bring me back to that special time on top of the mountain. The late Robert Muller was a very extraordinary man to me and many others. Thank you, Robert, for your continued inspiration.[19]

The visit with Robert that day sparked my inspiration big time. This falls under the engine called "admiring our mentors and heroes." The visit also engaged my *belonging* engine in that as Robert spoke, I felt affirmed in my values and beliefs about education and realized that all three of us shared a mission with other peacemakers around the globe.

THINK ABOUT IT

Go back to that person you visualized earlier and locate the inspirational sparks that you felt or feel when you are with that person. Are these your go-to engines? Skim through the other engines that you would like sparked. What would it take for you to be inspired in these ways? How are you inspiring others in your work environment and at home?

In this chapter, we deepened our understanding of three of the emotional intelligence competencies that make leaders effective in building relationships, teamwork, and inspiration. These competencies, when rated highly by others, demonstrate the leader's abilities to move change forward. In chapter 8, we will explore the world of emotionally intelligent coaching, a gift of reflection and care for school leaders.

CHAPTER EIGHT

Our Coaching Journey

Twenty years ago, when we first met, we would never have predicted that we would develop a leadership training and coaching series that would make a positive difference in the personal and professional lives of school leaders. We wouldn't have predicted that we would share our work with almost all superintendents and hundreds of school leaders in New York City. We would not have predicted that former chancellor Carmen Fariña would assign executive superintendent Dolores Esposito to the task of seeking the best training for all her superintendents and that she would choose STAR Factor for coaching and training in emotional intelligence leadership. That decision brought us to New York City to coach all of her superintendents and deputy superintendents. And when these district leaders got their arms around the infusion of emotional intelligence at a systemic level, they brought the Yale SEL program, the RULER approach, to their districts for both pre-K–12 students and some five hundred principals, to embrace adult emotional intelligence.

We also would not have predicted that after her retirement from New York City schools, Dolores, once again, would lead a transformation in the city's educational leadership by training coaches at the Council for Administrators and Supervisors (CSA), the administrator's union. At the heart of this work, Dolores positioned training school leaders to rethink their own leadership from the context of their emotional selves—the piece that had been missing entirely from their leadership. Finally, leaders had the tools and strategies to include their own and others' well-being as part of the process of leading schools.

Our work together began when we enrolled in an accreditation course in the use of the Emotional and Social Competency Inventory (ESCI). We knew that there was great value in the assessment that we gave educational leaders as they took their places in charge of schools and districts. The assessments offered a way for each leader to understand his or her strengths and challenges in the competencies of emotional intelligence. But we were frustrated that it stopped there. Once leaders took the assessment, what were they supposed to do with the information they learned about themselves? Over a period of weeks that stretched into months, and with the help of a young colleague—Courtney Martin, who was beginning what would become an exciting career as a widely published author and social activist—we put pen to paper and together outlined a coaching model for an experienced educator trained in the assessment to coach someone in a safe space to share their leadership challenges.[1] Thank you, Courtney.

Beginning with the client's vision, coaching was designed to be a holding environment in which coaches would help clients create an action plan to leverage their strengths to meet their goals. We knew we would need to train a cohort of educators to be a pilot group, to go through the learning process we would design; then we would make it a turnkey process and train other leaders in the same way. We worked with a dedicated group of recently retired principals to design the modules based on the realities of sitting principals' experiences. We knew they would need to be trained on how to carry out the new coaching model and supervised while they were coaching their first few clients. We thought deeply about the process to move people forward, stepping into their personal or professional vision and making it happen.

We knew the research about the power of emotions to impact all aspects of our lives, and in the specific case of educational leaders, we knew how emotions impact all aspects of their jobs. We each had spent years developing our own emotional awareness and interpersonal skills—although not until the late 1990s did we have a rubric for the competencies and behaviors of emotional intelligence, with the ESCI and the theoretical constructs of Richard Boyatzis and Dan Goleman. We took the best of our knowledge from the fields of psychology and education and scaffolded our coaching around these and other theoretical frameworks from both disciplines. We wanted the coaching process to be user-friendly for educators, so we created a blended model that allows for both mentoring and coaching within the sessions. We also created a scripted manual to accompany each session and built the sessions using the best pedagogy we know for teaching and learning. Robin's years of preparation and clinical work as a psychoanalyst and Janet's years of teaching and leading in schools provided the architecture for the coaching model.

We knew we were on to something important that could impact how educational leaders lead, model critical EI skills for their teachers and colleagues, build trusting relationships, and create psychological safety, by being vulnerable and transparent in the presence of one significant, empathic, caring person—their coach. The coach would guide leaders through a reflective process that allowed them to venture out of their mandated charges and opened the gateway toward aspirational thinking about their own dreams for their schools and their leadership that would encourage and help their teachers to transform themselves and infuse emotion skills into their students' curricula.

We built a process that originally consisted of eight sessions. Six sessions, each ninety minutes long, took place every other week for three months. Two additional sessions were to follow, each session a month apart. This design would allow support up to two more months after the original coaching sessions while participants lived the action plans that had been created. Our thinking was modeled on the work of Cary Cherniss, Robert Emmerling, and other researchers who have been studying similar programming from the corporate world. These guidelines can be found on the website of the Consortium for Research in Emotional Intelligence, a group of scientists and practitioners worldwide who have been studying EI leadership program effects.[2]

We knew that the relationship with the coach would be very important. The coach is an empathic, knowledgeable guide, able to create a safe emotional container for leaders to envision themselves three years into the future aspiring to the dreams they would love to see in place both personally and professionally. This vision is anchored in emotional intelligence, empathy, communication skills, equity, deep-rooted conflict management, and well-being. The anchored vision becomes the motivating factor for the leader to explore his or her strengths and challenges and willingly identify actionable steps to make the vision happen.

Given our unique partnership and complementary backgrounds—with Janet being an educational leader and Robin a psychoanalyst—we created a model that combined the teaching and learning of EI skills and competencies with the training process that I (Robin) went through as an analyst in training; I had to not only go through my own course of psychotherapy but then also attended supervision when I began to work with patients. In our coaching model, critically and perhaps uniquely, the supervision process is required and demanding. Each coach-in-training, in the first months of seeing clients, is required to write an anecdotal description of segments of sessions, so that when presenting the case in supervision, the focus will be on the coach's thoughts, feelings, and actions when interacting with the client, followed by unpacking what happened as a result with the client. Taking a page from self-psychology (and in consultation with colleague and therapist Lester Lenoff), if the environment surrounding the client is responsive, nurturing, and affirming, clients will naturally move forward in a positive direction toward their goals.

We knew that there were many things we wanted coaches to take away from the training, and we built our model and the steps for each individual session around the expectation that coaches would walk away from training with significant benefits for themselves. Their personal growth would serve them in becoming responsive, empathic, and motivated coaches for the next cohorts.

And we had in mind a *very* big goal: we wanted to impact the transformation of education in New York City, starting with how school leaders learn to be leaders.[3] We are happy to say that our dream is slowly becoming a reality. In addition to the superintendents, deputy superintendents, principals, and other school leaders we have trained through the years, we are currently training some fifty sitting and retired principals to become coaches. We have partnered with two organizations that are aligned with our vision and values and are using the model to coach principals throughout the city. At the student level, SEL is alive and well and increasingly being integrated into teaching and learning.

The Council for Supervisors and Administrators (CSA), the union for school leaders, has a stellar reputation for offering outstanding professional development to leaders through its Executive Leadership Institute. By spring 2023, twenty coaches will be available to provide coaching to school principals and assistant principals. Each year, the CSA will add to this number, making coaching available to many school leaders in need of acquiring skills in emotionally intelligent leadership.

The Gray Fellows, the grant-funded transformative education leadership partnership with Hunter College of City University of New York, previously mentioned in chapter 7, provides training on transformative change at the individual, school, and systems levels. To date, the partnership has trained some twenty principals as coaches who will, with guided supervision, coach a new cohort of principals annually—coaching infused with self-care, mindfulness, and systemic change. It took more than ten years to get to this point, and we are determined to reach the leadership of all 1,700 New York City schools, one superintendent and one principal at a time.

OUR MODEL OF DEVELOPING SCHOOL LEADERS

We coined the name of our model, the STAR Factor coaching model, after hearing our friend and mentor Daniel Goleman refer to leaders who are high in emotional intelligence as star performers, the best of the best. The added dimension of EI continues to separate out the successful school leaders who are good from those who are great. The model of executive coaching development builds on the Goleman framework of EI leadership: self-awareness; self-regulation; social awareness and relationship management; and the utilization of specific emotion skills—to recognize, understand, label, express, and regulate emotions—present in Peter Salovey and John D. Mayer's ability model of emotional intelligence and espoused by the RULER approach at the Yale Center for Emotional Intelligence. As we shared earlier, the STAR Factor coaching model is a blended model: it uses mentoring and coaching informed by the evolution of leadership theory, and it is also strongly anchored in intentional change, the work of Richard Boyatzis, adult development, motivation, transformative learning theory, self-psychology, and systems thinking.

The EI-based coaching consists of the following: trust building and exploration of one's personal and professional vision, EI behavioral competency assessment and feedback, identification of gap areas for development, assessment and feedback on conflict style, bias awareness and intervention strategies, goal setting anchored in emotional and social skill development, and planning how to move learning systemwide. We hope and have heard that coaching leads to transformative change in people and in structures such as the school climate, how instruction happens, student placement in classes, team performance, teacher trust in leadership, leaders' growth, and so much more.

We have learned that the interactions between the coach and the client are the most important factor in achieving successful outcomes from a coaching process. Therefore, we put great emphasis on the coach's development both in initial training and in subsequent supervision. Becoming a coach doesn't happen overnight. It's a minimum of a year of training with continued practice and supervision as you grow. Our principals and others who train to become coaches are often meeting a double purpose—they are preparing themselves to coach others, but at the same time they are learning a new style of leading, a coaching style, that guides and supports versus telling and expecting immediate results.

During the initial five-day training, the trainee learns the coaching process from experts including veteran coaches. This initial cognitive and experiential training prepares the coach-in-training to begin the process of coaching with one willing client.

Shortly after the initial training begins, the coach trainee receives six one-on-one coaching sessions from a certified coach. These sessions take place preferably every two weeks. By engaging as a learner, coach trainees learn more about their own emotional skills and leadership competencies; they identify their own strengths, challenges, triggers, unique style of managing their feelings, social skills, and more. This self-knowledge deepens and enriches their work with clients. It helps them to see clearly in the coaching relationship and to be mindful of boundaries. Both coach and client bring something to the relationship; both take responsibility for the relationship's success. These coaching sessions provide the time to experience the process. It isn't often that we are offered the precious gift of someone's heart and mind to support us.

During this STAR Factor internship period, each coach practices with a minimum of one person, ideally two. During this time, as the foundation for conversations with a STAR Factor supervisor, the coach trainees submit written anecdotal reports from their coaching sessions. The coach-in-training selects part of the verbatim transcript—a small portion of the dialogue between the coach and client—much as school leaders conduct a lesson observation. The discussion, however, is on the language and actions of the *coach* more than on those of the client. Together, the supervisor and coach unpack the coach's thoughts and feelings and examine the choices of questions the coach used to guide the client to move the client closer to his or her vision.

The coach brings this anecdotal report to the supervision session with his supervisor. The coach talks about the thoughts and feelings that are guiding the questions he has asked his client to take her toward her vision. In supervision, the coach explains that his client can be impulsive, as seen previously in the emotional self-control competency results of her ESCI, and that he has made a move to slow her down and think about the function of this team as well as the selection process. In this conversation, the coach supervisor helps the coach examine his thinking, feelings, and motivations for the direction he went with his questioning techniques.

Selecting and discussing these anecdotal reports helps coaches take a closer look at their own process, habits, and tendencies in the session and their impact on their client. Their own feelings as a coach constitute information that all coaches, but especially coaches in training, use to understand their coaching process, sharpen their skills, increase their presence, and be confident in their coaching style. Coaching partners benefit from this gift of coaching at the same time as trainees improve their skills.

During the internship, trainees are required to attend supervisory sessions with their coaching supervisor and can conference individually. The purpose of the supervision meetings is to deepen self-awareness and understanding, refine and sharpen trainees' practice, strengthen competency in the model, practice specific coaching strategies, and participate in debriefing sessions. Feedback from a coaching supervisor and other coaches in training is an invaluable part of the learning process and builds the STAR Factor community. All coaches continue meeting for supervision even after they begin to practice. We never stop growing and learning.

TWENTY-FIRST-CENTURY LEADERSHIP

Extensive field-based experiences supported by site-based mentoring or coaching continue to be among the most desirable approaches for aspiring leaders' development, but the costs to sustain such models limit their availability. And even with such a rich experience, there is no guarantee of leader effectiveness. Furthermore, as we have discussed throughout this book, fewer people strive for the position of principal, with its heavy accountability markers tied to student achievement on standardized tests and expectations of school "turnaround," often within a year of stepping into the leadership shoes. Likewise, the superintendency, with its often-quick changeover from one school board to another, is unattractive to many leaders who want security in their jobs and do not seek the transiency that often comes with this role.[4]

As the role of school leaders in improving student learning has become paramount, so too has the importance of these leaders' development. School leaders must master skills from teaching and learning to management and community outreach. Howard Gardner's multiple intelligences continue to speak to the position of school leaders, and the interpersonal and intrapersonal intelligences align well with our work.[5] Leaders who motivate and enhance others' growth are best positioned to create a culture that supports needed change. But a focus on the skills to do so has been missing. We have looked carefully at the types of skills that school leaders need—the skills and competencies that you have been reading about throughout this book.

Moving theory into practice requires the application of skills that are visible in behavior—skills that transform the self, others, and the organization. To be able to meet the extensive expectations placed on them, school leaders need support in fostering actionable self-reflection, building generative relationships, enabling meaningful conversations, and thinking systemically. These skills, often regarded as "soft skills," lie at the core of our being—the way we think, the way we perceive and interact with others, the way we listen, and our ability to maneuver the daily challenges of the job with professionalism and grace—and are foundational to adult performance and success.[6] Furthermore, embedded in each of these four capacities are the emotional and social skills and competencies of emotional intelligence.

What follows is a compilation of the benefits that have consistently been reported to us by leaders who have participated in our work. Each theme is supported by a sample case that is representative of hundreds of school leaders.

COACHES AND CLIENTS OBSERVE THE BENEFITS

On the following pages, we are proud to share with you the takeaways that we have learned over the years that benefit school leaders through participation in STAR Factor coaching. When we asked school leaders, principals, superintendents, assistant principals, and teacher leaders how they benefited from the coaching, we learned that the experience was different for each person, depending on their vision and the goals they each chose to develop in their sessions.

1. *I got the time to reflect that I never had.*

   One of the most common responses that we hear from school leaders is that through the coaching process, for the first time, they can think about *themselves* as leaders and about their practice in a safe place that is confidential. For example, many are overburdened by the continuous mandates placed on them, always with urgency. Some matter, but not at the expense of leaders' ability to think; reflect; and be curious, creative, and open to new ideas about the young people and adults at their schools.

   Case: Coach Carol

   Coach Carol shared a story about her client, a school leader who discovered that she wasn't able to complete her own tasks and meet others' needs because she was pulled in so many directions and had such limited time. She was able to get to a place through her coaching to voice her needs and let her supervisor know that she had too much on her plate. The client's need for assertiveness was also present in her personal life, as she had similar issues with a family member who expected the client to comply with her wishes right away. Coach Carol helped her client to see this similar pattern. The client learned to speak her truth using her newly developed skills. By the end of her sessions, she was able to assert herself at work, heal her relationship with her family member, and better care for her own well-being.

2. *I set expectations for my Best Self and strategized how to get there.*
Seldom do we set out on a course of self-development with such a knowledgeable and empathic cheerleader! STAR Factor coaches guide the process for their clients to develop and enhance their Best Self. Borrowed from the RULER approach, the Best Self is a key component of the Meta Moment tool. The Meta Moment is the space in time between when you are triggered and when you respond. The Best Self is a mental model of the "you that you want to be and the you that you want others to see." It is a values-based and aspirational way of anchoring yourself at a moment when you are suddenly experiencing big feelings. Invoking an image of your Best Self means that you took a Meta Moment: you paused, took a deep breath, and called to mind your personal representation— an icon, an old memory, or a representation of your ideal self in combination with your hoped-for reputational self. Think about the power this holds. It is important to note that we don't have to wait until we are triggered. We can invoke our Best Self before we walk out the door in the morning, before we enter a meeting, or before we sit down to write a chapter in a book we committed to.

Case: Superintendent Donna
"We can't implement SEL without leadership," says Superintendent Donna during an hour-long interview in the summer of 2022. Donna, a native New Yorker, always puts a smile on our faces as she tells stories and cracks jokes—about herself mostly. She admits that sometimes she is overzealous and overreactive with employees who are not "cutting the mustard" in their schools. Very emotional,

Donna rarely holds back her thinking or feelings. Consequently, she could spontaneously compliment you or criticize you in front of others if you didn't meet the mark. Donna recognized that she would benefit from gaining more skill in self-management, especially emotion regulation.

Knowing this about herself, she was committed to improvement. She adored her coach, Miriam, who visited her twice a month. After about nine months of working with Miriam, Donna said, "I drank the Kool-Aid!" Donna had learned and committed to practicing emotion regulation skills, communication strategies, and conflict management. She felt like a new person and shared this revelation with all her principals. Seeing the change in Donna, most of the principals wanted to experience the training and coaching, too. As a result, she offered training and coaching to her principals, followed by her assistant principals, and then counselors and related staff who worked with young people with mental health issues. Teachers received training in the RULER approach and other SEL programs. Within two years, Donna had trained most of her district, and SEL was thriving in the district schools.

3. *I know now that it is OK to show that I am angry—but with the right person, at the right time, in the right place, and in the right way.*
   Aristotle made this clear thousands of years ago. Still, so many of us use either avoidance or aggression to express anger. School leaders in particular, who are in constant emotional labor (forced to show emotions that are very different from the feelings they have in the moment), have nowhere to go with their anger, and anger unaddressed can leak and lead to all kinds of unhealthy, dysregulated actions and reactions. But pausing and using a favorite strategy to bring us to calm—such as the Meta Moment, deep breathing, or a mindfulness mantra—can give us the time to be our Best Self and communicate our feelings in a helpful way or to choose a different time and the "right" person with whom to express ourselves.

Case: Superintendent Donna, continued

Donna told us, "I have to really tap into my social and emotional self. I go into the side room by my office for several minutes and reflect. Sometimes I wait twenty-four hours to think a situation through. I think about the human side of the person.

"When I see myself getting super stressed or angry, I see it in my body. It's weird. And I say to myself, 'I don't want to do that anymore.' I get what I want when I am nasty, but I don't get people to follow me. I can control the things that I can control and that's what I do beautifully. Every day I try to model this way of being to my principals."

4. I am more self-aware.

Self-awareness, we know, is the foundation of the ability to be socially aware and self-managed and to build positive relationships. We felt it was important to be sure that coaching gave a window into knowing our strength and challenge areas, connecting with our values, knowing who and what triggers us, knowing what we need in the morning to settle and at midday to keep us sharp and energized all day, and knowing where we want to go—what is our vision, revisiting that over and over again. We were excited to spend so much time on this key competency of self-awareness, as most of us are not as accurate as we think: we often underrate or overrate ourselves.

Case: Principal Kevin

Through coaching, Kevin became aware that he was more cognitive about his feelings than he wanted to be. He went through the coaching process with deep reflection on himself. He discovered that despite his open heart and kindness, he hid his emotions from himself and others. He focused more on emotional energy than in the past, which has led him to feel more engaged with and connected to his staff and others. His daily reflections are helping him touch his feelings more often. As one of the two people in charge of the Gray Fellows, he regularly visits the Kripalu Center for Yoga and Health—and twice a year brings the Fellows with him. Principals, including Kevin, get dedicated time to reflect on themselves in the safety of caring colleagues. This is the kind of training Principal Kevin and the Fellows want and need to replenish themselves.

5. *I understand my triggers and how to manage them.*
   We all get triggered and need to acquire ways to handle those triggers. What sets us off during the day? Are there particular phrases used by others, such as "Look—I know you are feeling angry"? Are there particular individuals (we all know them) who are just a mismatch for us personality-wise? Are there particular interactions (shaming or blaming) or behaviors (such as interrupting over and over) that bring us from zero to ten in a second? When you keep track of your emotional patterns over time and begin to pay closer attention to what shifts you into the red on the Mood Meter immediately, or what starts your heart racing, you can identify triggers. And when you can do that, you can choose and use a helpful regulation strategy to manage those moments—such as positive reframing ("she's just started this job—she'll get there"), using self-talk ("this feeling, too, shall pass"), taking deep belly breaths and reciting a calming mantra, walking away, feeling gratitude for another opportunity to learn about yourself, or sending a text to ask for a call with a colleague—just to name a few.

Case: Assistant Principal Mariela
Assistant Principal Mariela shared a laundry list of unhealthy regulation strategies that she used repeatedly during the pandemic: oversleeping, overeating, and venting. As she continued in coaching, she slowly but surely replaced some of these unhealthy and unhelpful habits with exercise and journaling. Today during her session, Mariela feels a lot better about herself, and while she still feels that she has a long way to go, she is proud of her new healthy

habits. She is even considering starting a weekly exercise class at her school. She is already talking about applying for a principalship in the next year or so.

6. *I've learned how to help myself when stressful situations arise and name my feelings.*
   Coaching allows us to build muscle by working with our emotion skills. Using a nuanced and expanded feelings vocabulary will allow you to build accurate mental models of a wider range of specific emotions. Having and using more differentiated, nuanced feeling words allows you to "name it to tame it"; when you understand your emotion, you can address it and regulate it with helpful and effective strategies. Being under stress is not the best time to build your vocabulary, but if you make a daily and weekly effort to learn and use more feeling words regularly to name particular emotions, those words will show up when you are under stress. Consider what you might do to manage being disappointed rather than angry. Consider how much more accurately and authentically you can communicate with others with an expanded feelings vocabulary.

Case: Calvin and Principal John
Calvin reported, "Last week I visited Principal John's school at the end of the day as we decided to play a game of tennis after work. I got there in time to make his staff meeting. I sat quietly in the back of the room so as not to disturb the meeting. Ten minutes into the meeting, I heard John say, 'No way, we are not going to spend more time and money on SEL this year. We have to raise those reading scores.' He was practically screaming at one of his more dedicated staff members. This was not the John that I knew. The meeting ended shortly after his outburst, and staff quietly left the room. I waited until we were in the car to ask, 'What was going on in there, John? I'm not used to seeing you so angry, and about SEL, no less.' 'I don't know what's gotten into me lately,' he responded, downtrodden. 'I'm just exhausted. Between the job, pressures at

home, and taking classes toward my doctorate at night I'm short-tempered and irritable a lot of the time. You know I love the SEL work, but our kids did poorly on the practice tests this week in reading and I don't know how else to help.'"

Although Calvin was John's boss, he was also John's friend and colleague. "John," Calvin said, "you need to learn some strategies for reducing your stress. How about I give you a coach to help you sort things out and help you come up with some positive strategies?" "You know," John said, "I think I will take you up on that, Cal, before I alienate my whole staff, and my wife and kids!"

7. *My leadership style has shifted, and I now support others and kindly encourage their best performance.*

Too often we get locked into one leadership style when we know that different approaches work well with different people. The concept of a leader as coach is essential to the building of trusting relationships based on honest dialogue, not fear. Using a coaching mindset—encouraging all feelings and ideas, holding space for others' emotions, empathic listening, showing curiosity with genuine questioning, and reminding others of their strengths and past successes—can go a long way to scaffold your learners' experience and growth.

Case: Principal Diane

Principal Diane shared how she changed her leadership style from being more top-down to more participatory, empathic, and supportive. When she first started her principalship, she thought that she had to be the person who was in control of everything. A self-proclaimed workaholic, she had her hands on almost everything. A few years ago, she began studying with the Gray Fellows initiative, learning strategies for being present, empathic, and compassionate with her followers. She now uses her breath to slow herself down and not take over everything, to encourage others to develop their own skills. When she went through the coaching experience, she worked on shifting her leadership style and released her true caring nature. She let go of the reins, and the result was a happier principal and staff.

8. *I have gained confidence in my abilities to create a supportive work environment.*
Establishing a positive climate depends on the culture that we build. A culture that breeds dishonesty, distrust, and an individual instead of collective spirit will exhibit a climate of negativity. The key is creating psychological safety—encouraging all voices to be included, shifting to a climate of all learning rather than a focus on performance, elevating the importance of cooperation and collaboration, and encouraging challenging voices without fear of retribution. In such an environment, people are willing to speak, to innovate and create, and to support others to do the same. A culture that is psychologically safe breeds good feelings, trust, and productivity.

Case: Principal Javier
Principal Javier leads a top-performing K–8 school that consistently receives awards and numerous accolades for students' achievement. He holds very high expectations for his teachers and at times pushes them further than they feel able to go. He made a conscious decision not to let go of his expectations but to allow teachers more space to build community, acquire social and emotional skills, and focus on their well-being. This year, he has provided his teachers with ongoing professional development in adult social and emotional learning and programmatic curriculum using the Responsive Classroom and RULER approaches with students. A very private person, Javier admits that he is working on his own emotional expression and regulation of his emotions. His stern facial expressions still sneak out whenever he sees pedagogy that is less than perfect. In his coaching sessions, he thinks about his values and reviews his ESCI data to help him improve his self-awareness and emotion regulation. This doesn't come easily to him, but his willingness to incorporate his

emotional self into his leadership is witnessed by school members. Slowly, he is starting to be seen as more approachable, and others are beginning to trust him more. The positive feedback he is getting is very validating and inspires him to continue the work.

9. *I am building more positive relationships.*

Being aware of where your bridges need to be built will help you to lean into those areas and focus on them. Coaching allows leaders to take a look at their relationships; for some, this is the first time they have done so. They explore to whom they want to move closer and from whom they need a bit more distance. How can they bring more energy and positivity to some interactions in the service of more collaborative, psychologically safe, and productive environments? When the leader at the top makes building relationships central to his or her goals, the message becomes clear: working collaboratively matters.

This message resounds clearly to the principals, then to the students and their families. Teams work collaboratively with a clear focus in building psychologically safe environments. The school culture mirrors this work, and everyone takes a part in making the climate respectful and caring. This positive culture has been a hallmark of Fran Rabinowitz's work throughout her career.

Case: Fran Rabinowitz—Executive Director of the Connecticut Association of Public School Superintendents (CAPSS)

Fran Rabinowitz is one of the most loving, generous, and brilliant superintendents we know. During the pandemic, Fran knew that increasing communication with her group of supervisors would not only give people more support during a challenging time but also give people the opportunity to be more engaged with others and build more positive relationships. During this time of uncertainty and unpredictability, Fran found that these supportive relationships added to her own well-being, building and encouraging a positive outlook. Like many of us, she knows that relationships are everything, and during the COVID years, she heard feedback about the need for more frequent communication: more connection with like-minded people adds positivity to everyone's well-being. Years earlier, as superintendent of schools in Bridgeport, Connecticut, she had trained and coached her leaders in emotional intelligence. Bridgeport became a leader in EI work because of her leadership and the use of the RULER approach. Now as the executive director of CAPSS, she continues her quest to help superintendents and their constituents build positive, caring compassionate relationships as the foundation of leading, teaching, and learning.

10. *I am setting goals for myself to work on unwanted behaviors and responses.*

Setting short-term goals for changing what is difficult to change— accompanied by targeted self-talk ("I can do most anything for two hours")—can help encourage you to get moving on a writing project you are putting off, conduct meetings with difficult parents ("I am learning from them; I am learning my own reactions"), or set limits ("I won't smoke today" or "I will grab my colleague and go for a walk during break—and *not* light up"). Having a coach to support your work helps us stick to our plans.

Case: Principal Dawn

Principal Dawn is having trouble sleeping at night. As a deeply dedicated leader, she can't help but to check her phone looking for the next requirement she will have to fulfill or the next person she has to check in with by tomorrow. She checks Twitter constantly to be sure that she doesn't miss any important messages from the central office. The emotion regulation strategies that she is learning help her calm down, reframe, and relieve some of the anxiety. She is setting small goals, such as not looking at the clock when she feels compelled to do so. Instead, she listens to music and does a mindfulness exercise. She said that it isn't easy to change this behavior, but she is working on it and is determined to reduce her anxiety and balance her life more. Her coach points out her 5.0 achievement score and her 5.0 empathy score, and they discuss how these strengths drive her to achieve and put others first. Dawn acknowledges this tendency, and the two discuss small steps that she can take to start shifting the negative patterns that are affecting her sleep.

11. *I am using strategies such as visualization, breathing, reframing, self-talk, and distractions to work with my negative self-talk and stress.*

Make a list of regulation strategies. Use the How We Feel app. Take a week or two and go through each strategy—gratitude, kindness strategies, meditating, movement strategies, social strategies—and see what feels right for you or, even better, what feels right for you in a given situation. Throughout coaching, we encourage both coach and client to have a toolbox of strategies to call on in the moment of stress—such as yoga, meditation, tai chi—that are long-term well-being strategies. It's important for us to notice the behaviors that certain emotions seem to encourage. Talking through decisions first with your coach and identifying the feelings that come up for you when certain decisions are made can enhance your ability to know when the timing is better to make certain decisions and when to delay others. Upbeat and positive emotions lead you to high energy and pleasant feelings. Low energy and unpleasant emotions lead you to sadness or even fatigue. Talk to yourself about it. This process requires reflective time, so take time every day to close your eyes, breathe, and reflect on decisions made and decisions to be made.

Case: Superintendent Dara

Dara felt stuck. Recently she told her coach, Migdalia, that she was tired of being constantly triggered at work. People whom Dara used to count on in the district office were letting her down consistently. They just seemed to be worn out, she told us, maybe even melancholy in the past months. Dara said she was beginning to feel that way, too. "How many times can I be angry and disappointed before just turning my emotions off?" she asked. One of her building principals noticed her shift in mood and suggested that she use one of the many apps out there to learn some new skills and emotion strategies and bring them into her daily practice. She told Coach Migdalia, "I hate that people are noticing my moods. I have to find a way to handle my emotions better." Determined, Dara downloaded the new app she had heard about in her RULER schools—How We Feel—and started using it daily. After tracking her emotions, noticing patterns, and watching the videos to learn more about emotional intelligence, she told her coach that she wanted to practice a new strategy every week. At night she used the Calm app, which helped her wind down for sleep. By her third session with Coach Migdalia, Dara was practicing gratitude and kindness strategies and had registered for a yoga class! She shared, "I am thinking about how my emotions and feelings factor into my decisions."

12. *I learned that I can be too empathic.*

Most of us in education are trained to pay attention to others first, to consider their needs, to be servant leaders. We often leave ourselves outside the circle of people we give empathy and compassion to, leading to burnout and fatigue. When we always put everyone ahead of ourselves, we may find ourselves resentful of the very people for whom we felt empathy. Ponder this. Maybe the issue is not about being too empathic, but more about poor management of time and priorities. Coaching and paying more regular attention to how we feel can help us set healthy boundaries, which are critical in any relationship. Principal Suzanne began to consider this as she reviewed her competency data with her coach.

Case: Principal Suzanne

Principal Suzanne shared her thoughts with Coach Sonia: "I am quick to empathize and often give time I do not have. I often struggle with being stuck in the empathy trap—spending too much time in others' shoes and forgetting what I am feeling. When I finally take time for me, some crisis comes up at home, and I need to be there for my children or my husband. As it is, I'm rarely home in time for dinner. My family is tired of eating takeout. I have to pull back somewhere. I find myself getting sick a lot and am always tired."

Coach Sonia paraphrased Suzanne's words and then asked her to look at her ESCI data again. Coach Sonia said, "Yes, you scored very high in your empathy competency, but I would like you to notice your emotional self-control score. What do you see here?" Suzanne replied, "I scored myself higher than others rated me." She continued defensively, "But that's because I am always controlling my emotions. I know that." Coach Sonia responded, "Yes, we have been talking about that. But tell me what happens when you are in the middle of completing a critical report that is due tomorrow and a colleague calls you on the phone to ask for your help with one of her mandates? What happens for you?" Suzanne said, "Well, I stop what I am doing and talk with her." "And how does that serve you?" Sonia asked. Suzanne replied, "It doesn't. Now I have to stay late to finish the report." Coach Sonia continued with this line of questioning, helping Suzanne see where her priorities lay and what she could do to change this behavior. Sonia then shifted her questions to go deeper: "Tell me what your home life might look like if you were able to be home early most days?" Suzanne reflected as a few tears fell onto her cheek. "I'd be happier and healthier," she replied, wiping away the tears. Over the next month, Suzanne practiced ways to be assertive about her own needs while she still shows others that she cares.

We hope that these cases give you some insight into the kind of work that is being done with school leaders in New York City and how the benefits show up in their everyday lives. The more in touch with their feelings leaders are, the better decisions they will make for others, while considering their own needs as well. These testimonials and snapshots fill our hearts as we watch and listen to the better choices school leaders are making for themselves as a result of their reflective self-work.

GUIDELINES AND RECOMMENDATIONS
FOR LEADERSHIP DEVELOPMENT

In this section, we offer a few guidelines to help you seek greater well-being and human connection for yourselves, your staff, and for the parents and young people you serve.

These guidelines are not all-inclusive but will hopefully give you some food for thought. These guidelines are presented sequentially but can be used more fluidly based on the school leader's readiness level and the complexity of the school or district.

Guideline 1: Create a Safe Learning Environment

No one learns without feeling safe emotionally, psychologically, and physically. Work on creating and maintaining psychologically and physically safe spaces for reflection and deep conversations for all community members.

Guideline 2: Build a Personal and Collective Vision

Build individual visions that look to the future and lead you to positive outcomes you may have thought impossible. Share your vision with your community and make it a collective vision that sparks the imagination and desire of everyone.

Guideline 3: Set Goals Based on Vision

Move toward your vision by setting short-term goals and action steps. Keep yourself accountable, and as you reach each goal on your journey, reflect and reassess until you reach your long-term goal of realizing your vision.

Guideline 4: Recognize and Live Social and Emotional Skills and Competencies

Check in with your emotions regularly and honor them all. Remember that the information you glean from emotions can be used wisely in the service of your goals. Be attuned and present with self and others.

Guideline 5: Seek a Coach, Mentor, or Spiritual Guide as a Tool for the Reflective Process

Choose to work with a positive other—a coach, a mentor, or a spiritual guide to hold the mirror up for you and create the opportunity for self-reflection. Never stop listening and asking questions on the road to discovering and deepening your "why."

Guideline 6: Build Resilient and Generative Teams

Effective peer learning communities are inclusive and empowered by the synergy of common passions, aspirations, and practical problems. A sense of belonging and trust is important to develop in these like-minded teams and is achieved through creating psychologically safe spaces. The positive group synergy, along with psychological safety, motivates school leaders to share and learn from one another together.

Guideline 7: Cultivate Relationships and Build Trust

Above all, be trustworthy. Show up as you really are. A caring, sincere leader will gain loyal followers.

We shared this chapter with you so that you could peek into the coaching process and learn about some of the growing edges of school leaders who, like you, are being asked to build their own resilience. Coaching provides that psychologically safe place where these leaders work through mindsets and behaviors that hold them back from being their ideal best selves. Anything is possible with vision and commitment.

In the following chapter, you will hear the stories of leaders who have infused this work into their schools and districts—lessons learned to affirm, inspire, and motivate you!

CHAPTER NINE

Emotionally Intelligent Leadership: Thinking Systemically

The biggest issues of our time are calling all of us to develop a whole-systems understanding of the world—to acknowledge that the whole is more than the sum of its parts—and to listen, deeply and consistently, with all of our senses, in order to strategize a more sustainable and equitable future.

—ELIZABETH A. SOLOMON

No matter where we are in our lives, no matter the path we took, we didn't get here alone, even though each of our paths is unique. For *all* of us in leadership, someone—or some ones—paved the way. There were people before us carving out the role, defining the protocols, and thinking about the whole school community and schools as systems. People before us have been thinking about the educational needs of school leaders and training for specific practices. Our process of creating STAR Factor included thinkers, big ideas, and practitioners who shared their experiences with us. This book is built on all of the work done by those who came before us, those who mentored us, and those who were passionate about creating opportunities both to help school leaders grow and to let the public know about what they do every day for children and families. It's time to allow their voices to be heard.

Both of us have been immersed in the field of emotional intelligence and SEL and feel strongly that the missing piece is the adult development that we explore throughout this book. We have focused heavily on leaders' behaviors and mindsets that ensure the successful implementation of SEL programs or approaches for students. We have provided insights into the processes and kinds of professional development that support school leaders through their own self-reflection on their leadership. We've talked about training and coaching that help in transforming yourself and those you lead. We spent some time thinking about what well-being means for each of us and why we need more time taking care of ourselves and modeling this self-care for others. We explored what it means to be self-aware and how being self-aware is the first step toward better self-management, how empathy is at the heart of trust and building relationships, and how authenticity allows relationships to grow and needed change to happen.

This final chapter focuses on thinking about how leadership drives the systems in schools. In this book, our focus has been on emotionally intelligent leadership to support culturally responsive academic social and emotional learning for students. We talked about the need for change, the vision that drives it, the steps to take, and the outcomes we hope to see. Effective implementation requires intensive strategizing by the leader and team members who design and carry out the plan. This vision and the steps to achieve it become a living document memorialized in each year's consolidated plan and at every level of curriculum and instruction across the grades. And it doesn't stop there. The integration of this new initiative needs to be visible in every part of the system—budget planning, hiring, scheduling, schoolwide activities, parent education and leadership, student leadership, and extracurricular activities. In this way, your *why*, as Simon Sinek says, sits at the center of everything that you do.[1]

This is not easy in a school or small district, and it's even more challenging in a large city such as New York, with 1,700 schools and more than 1.5 million students. Bringing SEL to scale has been the focus of CASEL for many years now. We learned a lot from CASEL's Collaborative Districts Initiative, which studied and scaled high-quality, evidence-based SEL in eight of the country's largest and most complex school systems. Its goal was to create a comprehensive shift in how superintendents and entire school districts approach education. For a decade, these school districts *co-learned* with CASEL leaders about sustaining SEL. And they found that when SEL is implemented across systems, it becomes foundational to the culture, family and community partnerships, and student outcomes. The findings of this initiative can be read in the report *2011–2021: 10 Years of Social and Emotional Learning in U.S. School Districts.*[2]

The report confirms that effective, sustainable implementation requires the following:

1. Leaders model, cultivate, and elevate a shared vision of SEL.
2. Core district priorities connect SEL to all departments and individuals, so everyone is invested.
3. Schools have resources and pathways to guide SEL implementation, as well as room to innovate and customize SEL for their communities.
4. SEL informs and shapes adult learning and staff culture and climate.
5. Students' families and communities are cocreators of the SEL vision, plans, and practices.
6. External and internal communities of practice strengthen implementation.

When the entire district is on board, from the superintendent on down, a statement is made: *We believe in SEL, and we are all going to make it happen.*

While we have learned a lot about how SEL has served children and families, little has been written about the role of school leaders in this process—what they do, how they do it, and what they learned along the way. How does the leader—superintendent, principal, assistant principal—develop his or her emotional intelligence, the social and emotional competencies that are needed as a person and a leader?

IN THE PAGES AHEAD . . .

This chapter tells some of the stories of dedicated, emotionally intelligent school leaders who are committed to the social and emotional development of adults and children in the leaders' districts and schools. We asked these leaders to share their thoughts, their feelings, and their processes. In most cases, they supported and led the change from the top by stewarding the work, while someone else took the lead in doing the groundwork. We learned from years of research and our own experience that when leaders, superintendents, principals, or CEOs say they believe in something, they make sure it happens; this includes their direct participation in training and team meetings and coaching. We also know that SEL is a game changer. It transforms people, their mindsets, and behaviors, and then it changes the environment—the culture and climate of our organizations. Why? SEL develops our inner and outer selves, and the culture slowly shifts. Relationships grow—among adults, between adults and students, and ultimately among students. These connections get stronger, healthier, more empathic, and more caring. Emotions are discussed and encouraged in the classroom and schoolwide context. Conflicts are better managed, and everyone is working on being their best selves. Communication improves as everyone listens better and acquires better expressive language to get their needs met as well as to meet others' needs. Conversations become more meaningful. Mindsets that *emotion matters* and SEL strategies are infused into every part of the system. Parents learn from their youngsters and see a positive difference in their ability to communicate, express, and manage their emotions. Leaders create circles, not only for students to share their personal experiences but also for parents to come together to support one another in building their children's skills. They learn together, plan together, test ideas together, and reflect and build their emotional intelligence skills together.[3] Violence dissipates as young people model their new skills and become leaders of the school, replacing their more negative role models. Staff meetings become places to share not only thoughts but feelings, too. Differences don't divide us; instead, curiosity and kindness bring us closer. Individuals transform, and as they do, so does the system.

Our thinking about implementation and practice has been informed and enriched by consulting with and reading the luminaries in the field of systems thinking and by our learning from practice in our own and other organizations over the years. We have learned from Peter Senge about systems: how they work, what a true learning organization is, and what it takes to lead that organization.

Senge shares:

> Systems change is inherently an "inner" and "outer" process. It involves deep shifts in mental models, relationships, and taken-for-granted ways of operating. It involves shifts in organizational roles and formal structures, metrics and performance management, and goals and policies. Because of this, we believe that the development of self is foundational. This inner work—which involves developing awareness, compassion, understanding, and wisdom— also extends to teams, networks, organizations, and ultimately to the larger systems within which we work.[4]

THINK ABOUT IT

After reading Peter Senge's quote, what resonates with you about change in your own district and school?

Otto Scharmer, known for his development of Theory U, a future-oriented change management method, is a senior lecturer at the Massachusetts Institute of Technology (MIT) Sloan School of Management.[5] Scharmer asks us to consider how essential our self-awareness is in accomplishing the changes that we desire. He adds that "we cannot change a system unless we address consciousness and make a system see and sense itself."[6] So, as individuals and organizational leaders, we must invest in deep learning individually and collectively to transform the education systems where we work.

One of our early teachers was James Comer, the Maurice Falk Professor of Child Psychiatry at the Yale University School of Medicine's Child Study Center in New Haven and a world-renowned psychiatrist. He taught us about the critical need for social and emotional learning and the impact it would have on the school community and system. Comer's School Development Program, also known as the Comer Process or Comer Model, aims to improve the educational experiences for poor and low-income minority young people by building strong relationships with parents, educators, and children, thereby creating a positive school climate for learning.[7] Comer's strong belief in the relationship between families and schools gave us one of the first SEL approaches designed to build relationships between the home and the school staff with the purpose of improving the climate and culture of the schools in low-income communities. He encouraged us to persevere with our work, and to be cautiously optimistic—but realistic about meeting with others' resistance to change.

From Peter Senge, to Otto Scharmer, to James Comer, their teachings have expanded our thinking about systemic SEL. We recognized some time ago that adult development is a critical aspect of implementing and sustaining schoolwide SEL. So, when we talk about infusing SEL into a school, we are most often talking about system change. To fully transform a district or school, every part of the system must be touched. Think about all the parts of a school that are affected by deepening our ability to use our emotions wisely.

I (Janet) remember this process well during the 1990s, when as assistant principal, I led this change process in my middle school of 1,700 beautiful, rambunctious middle school students in Southern California. I watched it unfold on every level of the school and eventually, because of our superintendent's commitment, throughout the entire district. We started to implement SEL at one middle school with 1,700 students. Within three years, SEL was in most K–12 schools, meaning that 25,000 students were acquiring the desired SEL skills. These were exciting times! What we didn't know then but do now was that to sustain SEL, we needed all the leaders trained and on board. They weren't. So, when Rene Townsend, our caring, smart emotionally intelligent superintendent, left the district a decade later, SEL disappeared with her.

Implementation of any innovation can be taxing and take longer than desired, but using effective approaches can make the difference for sustainability. This chapter tells the stories of how *star leaders*— superintendents, central office leaders, principals, and a union president—embraced emotional intelligence, both personally and professionally, to ensure that SEL grows in their organizations. As you read through each story, note the strategies these leaders used to develop themselves and the people they lead.

STORIES FROM THE FIELD

We offer these stories as examples of the successes and challenges that leaders have discovered along the way, for themselves and others, and to provide examples to learn from. Each person's efforts express noteworthy examples of dedication and a strong belief in the possibilities of transformation that could unfold; the work always starts with us. Eventually, all adults model and develop everyone in the community who is open to change. Remember the Mahatma Gandhi quote so many of us had hanging on our walls, "Be the change you wish to see in the world"? As leaders, we need to inspire, encourage, support, and trust our teachers. Small steps are more adaptable than larger ones. Changing mindsets through professional development, presentations, courses, and so on comes first. Visual representations of how students respond to the strategies give encouragement and hope to everyone—including photos, YouTube videos, family videos, teachers' and parents' reports, and so on. The practice of learning strategies in the classroom follows, with coach support. Shared conversations by teachers expose emotion skills and competencies selected for development. Students feel the difference in teachers' behaviors; the strategies become real. As teachers find ways to manage their emotions better, so do the students. The goal is a new paradigm in schools in which students take responsibility for their social, emotional, and academic well-being, supported by their teachers who are doing the same.

But don't get us wrong—this shift we are hoping for does not come easily. For some adults, being vulnerable by showing their feelings is a frightening prospect. Others would rather stay in emotional labor, not allowing themselves to express their emotions, rather than violate contextual rules or feel the discomfort of expressing certain emotions to specific people.

We are blessed to know and to have trained hundreds of school leaders. The stories from the field we chose to share shine a light on their work. This chapter resounds with the principle that *leaders matter*, as do their personal and professional development, the relationships they build, their knowledge, and their ability to think systemically and for the long run, not a quick fix.

These stories are not meant to be read in one sitting. Read each one separately. Think about it. Share it with a colleague. Use it as a reading to open a dialogue at a meeting or a class. Our first story, told by Bonnie Brown, represents the beginning of learning about emotional intelligence in New York City schools. How did former superintendent Bonnie Brown make inroads in her self-contained special education district, District 75, which served twenty-three thousand students with physical, cognitive, and psychological challenges? Dr. Deidre Farmbry addresses the difficulties she faced and the steps that she took when she assumed the superintendency in a system where Black and Brown students were underperforming, there were no Black and Brown leaders, all administrators were White, and a pervasive racist attitude existed throughout the district and the community.

This story is followed by former chancellor Carmen Fariña's account of her thoughts and actions while shifting the culture of school leaders of New York City schools through training and coaching of district superintendents and central office personnel. Next is an interview with Dolores Esposito, the executive superintendent selected by Chancellor Fariña to lead leadership pipeline work as part of the Principal Supervisors Initiative through the Wallace Foundation. Then we hear from the former president of the school leaders' union in New York City, Mark Cannizzaro, who recently began an initiative to develop a cadre of leaders to coach in EI-based coaching. This work is being continued under the leadership of President Henry Rubio, through the Executive Leadership Institute, the professional development arm of the organization.

Onward to the state of Washington to hear from central office administrator Laurie Morrison, who shares the strategies that she used to create a coaching culture in her school district. Finally, we hear from David Adams, CEO of Urban Assembly High Schools and CASEL board member, who helps us think about the responsibility of the top school leader in supporting middle managers. In all these stories, we hear how these leaders held the container for others to grow as they lived their values authentically, shifted their own and others' mental models, and used their emotional intelligence to lead.

Bonnie Brown, Former Superintendent, New York City's District 75

During the years I was superintendent, 2006–2010, the district was serving over 23,000 students in self-contained buildings, cluster sites in district school buildings, hospitals, and on home instruction. The largest group of students (11,000+) were dealing with emotional issues, and there were also over 6,600 students with autism spectrum disorders. My own education journey spanned thirty-five years in this district working with a wide range of students with varying challenges. As such, my goal as superintendent was two-pronged—to support the students who would be in the district until they aged out at twenty-one years of age due to their overwhelming needs for educational/clinical/medical support and, concomitantly, create a plan for those that had the capacity to eventually return to mainstream education settings in their home schools. It was apparent to me that the students who had emotional issues would have to learn to self-regulate their behavior by developing tools and strategies before they could ever hope to transition to a less restrictive setting.

Over the years I had been trained in many methods of what was then called "behavior management." Many programs had been implemented that provided schoolwide intervention frameworks, like PBIS (Positive Behavior Interventions and Supports), or others that trained staff on how to intervene with students in distress, like Therapeutic Crisis Intervention Without Physical Restraint, Life Space Crisis Intervention (LSCI), Children in Crisis training, and so on. What was clear to me was that these programs were all attempts at intervention after an untoward incident and were not focused on prevention or how to avoid future incidents. Various vendors would approach me with the newest and glitziest programs in a box to "manage" student behavior, but they were not evidence-based, offered no compelling data, and put the burden of regulating student behavior on the shoulders of teachers and clinicians instead of focusing on teaching students to self-manage their own behaviors and build regulation skills.

One day at the end of the school year in 2008, Janet and Robin invited me to a think tank meeting at Columbia University to discuss yet another new concept—social-emotional learning. Being a skeptic, I went expecting another vendor presentation and then a hard sell. Instead, I was introduced to a Yale professor named Marc Brackett. I was also introduced to the work of CASEL, the Collaborative for Academic, Social, and Emotional Learning, based in the US that was committed to the process of supporting people in "acquiring the knowledge, skills and attitudes to develop healthy identities, manage emotions, improve relationships, feel and show empathy, and make responsible and caring decisions."

LIKE-MINDED COLLEAGUES

Finally, I had found people who understood the forgotten concept that you were meant to close the barn door before the cow gets out! Here were people who were not looking for the silver bullet to "fix" youngsters who were broken but were finding ways to avoid the damage proactively. The mindset was changing from intervention to a model of prevention and moving away from punitive consequences and de-escalation of behaviors to a focus on identifying feelings, labeling them, understanding their antecedents, looking at how they are being expressed, and then regulating them successfully. Thus, I became acquainted with RULER, a program created by Marc Brackett, Robin Stern, and their team at Yale, that began with the idea that emotions matter and then taught skills in how to recognize, understand, label, express, and regulate them.

I was drawn to RULER not just because of specific skill training and adult involvement but also because RULER developers believed that SEL could be taught even to those on the spectrum with necessary adaptations. Thus began a collaboration that has lasted fourteen years and is still ongoing.

I also connected with Dr. Janet Patti from the Hunter College educational leadership program (ADSUP, or Administration Supervision), and we met to discuss her leadership coaching offerings through her work with Dr. Robin Stern and their coaching program, STAR Factor. Since I am a strong believer that leaders and parents should practice what they preach and be appropriate role models for their children, I knew that I had to start at the top with school leaders and focus their thinking on their leadership skills.

THE PLAN

As superintendent, I supervised fifty-eight school organizations that were housed in 350 sites throughout the five boroughs. Many of my school leaders were principals with multiple assistant principals and were considered leaders of "cluster schools" that geographically were in different buildings. In such an unwieldy situation, how does one begin a new initiative and hope for implementation with both fidelity and sustainability? I decided upon an application process that focused on leadership and staff stability, alignment of RULER with existing programs such as PBIS or LSCI, long-term goals and objectives, and past success in train-the-trainer type professional development. I received many applications but chose six schools to begin the pilot.

I decided that each one of the principals in the pilot schools would be coached in emotional intelligence. Thus, while staff and students were being trained in the anchor tools and strategies of the RULER approach, school leaders were honing their own EI competencies.

For the next two school years, I added schools to the RULER pilot in intervals as well as adding school leaders in these schools to the STAR Factor coaching model. In the schools where I began the leadership coaching, in year 2 we added coaching of the assistant principals. My goal was to improve the climate and culture in those schools by building strong teams highlighting inspirational leadership, delegation of responsibility, empathy, achievement orientation, positive outlook, and the ability to manage conflict. In some instances, where a particular school might have experienced interpersonal difficulties amongst leaders, I added group coaching as an option for the leaders to strengthen their skills collectively. In order to demonstrate my commitment to this type of professional development for school leaders, I added SEL goals and objectives to my district's Comprehensive Education Plan. I also mandated that all the schools involved in the pilot add goals in their own School Comprehensive Education Plan to support the work in EI and SEL.

THE OUTCOMES

We were able to document less attrition of school leaders to surrounding suburban school districts as well as an increase in the number of intermediate supervisors who were applying for the principalship. On an organizational level, we saw a decrease in the number of grievances on the part of the staff, and higher levels of teacher participation in after-school and extracurricular activities, and as superintendent, I witnessed a shift in performance planning objectives of my school leaders. After coaching, their personal objectives were more focused and clearer, and their expectations for staff were increasingly realistic and supportive. In short, I saw the desired shift in school climate and leader retention that I had hoped to see.

As for students in the schools implementing the RULER program, I was able to collect data to see several shifts, including a decrease in student suspensions, fewer incidents reported involving student aggressions both verbal and physical, improved student attendance, and an improvement in the four-year graduation rate. At the same time, the number of students with emotional challenges who were able to return to less restrictive learning environments had increased. In my own mind, I thought this was a no-brainer—*win-win!*

I retired from the New York City Department of Education in 2010 and since then have been working in the field of social-emotional learning and leadership development at the Yale Center for Emotional Intelligence as a trainer and coach. The work in SEL changed my schools, my district, myself, and my own relationships.

Lessons learned from Bonnie

- Creating an application process stirred interest.
- Individual principal conversations about RULER implementation enhanced engagement.

- Research-based university-connected programs held promise for future evaluation and learning.
- Individual meetings with other superintendents bringing the work to their districts created a new learning community.
- It is important to articulate the vision to all stakeholders and ask for buy-in.
- EI and SEL were included in all district language and spoken language.
- The superintendent personally participates in the coaching process.
- Top management are in tune with individual schools' leadership needs.
- Include team development work when necessary to strengthen the team and scale the work.

THINK ABOUT IT

Take a moment: Can you think of a time in your own career when you finally found like-minded people? How did these colleagues influence your work?

Deidre Farmbry, CASEL SEL Consultant

The following story is from Deidre Farmbry, EdD, currently a senior consultant at CASEL, who guides superintendents with implementation processes across the country.[8] Deidre has sat in every administrative and supervisory seat throughout her career. Her story resonates with so many of us who are working hard to create inclusive schools, giving us insight into the internal self-talk of the leader as we find out about the actions she takes. Dr. Farmbry has also been extremely valuable in consulting on this book to advise us of our blinders as White women.

> *"Am I lost?" asked the traveler.*
> *"No," said the guide, "just on a circuitous route to finding a stronger you!"*

After serving for three successful years as a principal of a high school with a 99 percent Black student population, I became a regional superintendent in a blue-collar, predominantly White section of the city, characterized by schools that were becoming increasingly minority each year, to the outrage of many community residents who disliked the fact that "those kids" were invading their neighborhood. When I was appointed to be the leader of the nine schools in this section of town, I was greeted with a high degree of suspicion regarding my intentions and my allegiance. One neighborhood rebel made sure that there was some veiled reference to me in the community newspapers for several weeks after my appointment, by writing articles for the gossip section questioning, "Why in the world is the principal of that school coming to lead here?" It became clear to me that at this stage of my journey, my leadership transition plan had to focus on developing an understanding of the context in which I was now being asked to lead, with a special emphasis on analyzing the overt hostility I was experiencing. Dealing with personal attacks on my integrity was a new challenge, so here I was, once again, *lost*.

I found strength while traveling down this unfamiliar path from a spiritual guide, the Serenity Prayer: "God grant me the serenity to accept the things I cannot change, the courage to change the things I can, and the wisdom to know the difference." While the words helped me get a handle on the scope of need versus my personal capacity to address the needs of ignorant people with provincial mindsets, I continued to feel the intense pressure of the Black community urging me to act and the White community daring me to do so. The leadership challenge for me in facing such polarized pressure was to arm myself with evidence for any hunch I felt that significant numbers of students were not being served well in the schools in this part of town, and then to use the evidence to build a coalition willing to support me in implementing changes contrary to the way "things have always been done here."

And proof was not hard to find. I remember returning to my office after my first visit to the neighborhood high school and commenting that the school was still predominantly White. After my second visit to the same site the next day, I returned commenting that the school I had seen that day was predominantly Black. My two successive visits to the school highlighted the reality that the impression one gained was highly dependent upon which program was being viewed. Stark racial segregation was the norm inside the building, even though this particular school was listed as a site of the school district's desegregation plan and was highly coveted by minority students beyond the community. In essence, the system of rostering students to the school's small learning communities resulted in the formation of racially segregated programs with noticeable differences in terms of academic rigor and access to opportunities afforded at the school. When I informed the principal's predominantly White cabinet of my two distinct snapshots of the school, I was asked, "So do you think we have a problem here?" For a fleeting moment, I began questioning my own perspective, thinking that perhaps I was lost! Then, it hit me that the leaders of the school were the ones who were truly lost in their understanding of the inequities the school was perpetrating by virtue of how the organization was structured. From the tone with which the question was asked, I knew that the cabinet was trying to disarm me, because in making visible an aspect that was apparently invisible to them, I was making them vulnerable to the tension-laden fallout when raw racial realities are exposed. In the name of exercising responsible and responsive leadership, I was intent on unraveling the protective cocoon the leadership team had spun to their benefit and the benefit of some children. Yes, the journey through the terrain of race relations and educational inequity got tougher, yet I came to view this road, not as a detour, but as a road I most definitely was destined to travel!

Having learned the value of "wise guides" on my previous detour, I took a similar route in securing appropriate resources to help me face this challenge. I hired a young, White female who had just moved into this community to fill a vacancy in a key position on my leadership team. She assisted me with the bridge building that needed to be done by possessing the insider's eyes and ears at community meetings, sometimes accompanying me and at other times going as my representative. I retained the services of a no-nonsense, "in-your-face" consultant on race relations who happened to be Black. She conducted cross-constituent workshops and was able to unearth deeply seeded beliefs hampering the capacity of the nine schools in my region to serve all students equitably. I purchased for all my principals Beverly Daniel Tatum's book *Why Are All the Black Kids Sitting Together in the Cafeteria?* and dedicated a portion of time at my principals' meetings to reading and interpreting the book, focusing on its application to the school sites. Finally, I arranged for community meetings to be held in the housing project where some of the bussed students resided, as a way of breaking down feelings of alienation that had disenfranchised many Black parents, fortifying the school's choice to render them invisible and insignificant.

What I gained by being a leader in this section of the city, once I clarified who was really lost—an awareness that boosted my confidence to exercise a different dimension of positional authority— was an understanding of the power of schools to be the locus of change for community issues, and the responsibility of leaders to coach their constituents out of destructive comfort zones. However, I realized that this journey had to begin not with a focus on academics, but a focus on attitudes. I had to enhance my own capacity to navigate this road, so I read books pertaining more to sociology than education, for I needed material relative to identity formation and how communities develop and protect themselves from the encroachment of "others." Here, the others looked like me, so I felt compelled to develop a leadership agenda for change based on a moral imperative predicated on my belief that separate is unequal. Even though a major landmark court decision provided the nation with a judicial basis for eradicating inequities, too many communities lack leaders willing to face the consequences of conscientious leadership. I could not be one of those leaders who turned a blind eye to the bold contrasts I witnessed. So, on this journey, I developed the internal fortitude to use my position of leadership to steer a community in need of guidance in the right direction.

Lessons learned from Deidre
- Identify the barriers.
- Reframe your purpose when necessary.
- Lead with a moral imperative agenda.
- Remain courageous and depersonalize attacks.
- Study and learn more about identity and equality.

THINK ABOUT IT

Take a moment: Reflect on how the issues of race have been up front and center in your leadership.

Former Chancellor of New York City Schools Carmen Fariña and Executive Superintendent for Leadership Dolores Esposito
In 2006, the New York City Deputy Chancellor, Carmen Fariña, reached out to us and asked us to train her local instructional superintendents (LISs) in emotional intelligence leadership. We did. She told us:

We inherited a system very much like the old top-down systems. Our senior leaders had been beaten down and worn out, and our principals too. Parents were ignored. We believed that we could build a community and organically they could shift the culture. My executive director of professional development, Laura Kotch, knew that we could change this climate so that it wasn't all about mandates. There are times when you need mandates, but it isn't the way to get people to change.

Unfortunately, soon after, the New York City Department of Education went through a complete restructuring. In this process, Carmen left her position of deputy chancellor, the LIS position was phased out, and so was our emotional intelligence work! When Carmen returned as chancellor in 2014, she wanted to make a change in the system and once again pursued our EI leadership work as part of her leadership development plan, supported by her partnership with the Wallace Foundation's Principal Supervisors Initiative (PSI). Carmen understood that leadership matters, and our coaching and training work was included as a component of leadership development for superintendents sponsored by her partnership with the Wallace Foundation. She hired Dolores to lead the PSI.

Carmen told us:

> The work gave us a common language that helped even the playing field. We selected and sent superintendents for coaching and training in New York City with Dr. Patti from Hunter College and Dr. Stern and Dr. Brackett at Yale. Working with the universities helped give the initiatives clout; the work was research-based. The training was right for us—it was organized. It had a structure with rules, easy to follow. The work sold itself, person by person—no memos, no mandates. Mandating kills any program. The superintendents were the first group trained. We listened to each person's individual needs and brought them into the conversation.

Chancellor Fariña also realized that EI work isn't for everyone. Many of her cabinet members who were more instrumental in their way of being, more linear, wouldn't buy in—so she and Dolores concentrated on those who did want to participate. She said: "As chancellor, I remained quiet. My silence was effective. Dolores was perfect for leading the initiative."

She spoke about how she led by example:

When I greeted folks, I asked them how they were feeling about x, y, or z. When I gave constructive feedback, I always started on a positive note. We had to change the paradigm. We were shifting how we make strong leaders. Everyone loved the privacy and deep learning; but they were stressed out. We brought parents into the conversation from the districts that had a developed parent component. Parent coordinators wanted training so they could prepare other parents. The superintendents who did this early on got more buy-in.

Dolores explained:

In 2014, when Carmen was the chancellor, I was hired as the executive superintendent of leadership, a central office citywide role to manage and oversee the Principal Supervisor Initiative, intended to reimagine leadership at the central and district level, in collaboration with the Wallace Foundation. In this role, during my second year of leading and managing the professional development for superintendents, I engaged Chancellor Fariña to consider emotional intelligence–based leadership training and coaching that would give leaders the tools to lead with this missing component of leadership development. In the past, we emphasized instructional and organizational leadership practices that were important, but these essential, adaptive leadership skills were missing.

We wanted to deepen the practices that were introduced in 2004 to some of us and offer them to all senior leaders, as a lever for systemic improvement. Focusing on the Professional Standards for Educational Leaders, PSEL, particularly standard 3, allowed us to better align professional development practices and include emotional intelligence–based training, coaching, and development more strategically. Emphasizing this aspect of adult development was a way to improve culture, psychological safety, and culturally responsive practices that support the academic and social-emotional well-being of every child.

Leaders who participated in our training sessions over the next three years demonstrated more self-awareness, empathy, and agency to better cultivate supportive learning environments for all, as they kept students at the center, as part of Chancellor Fariña's Framework for Great Schools. They were also able to demonstrate other key leadership practices such as effective team-building skills and developing more positive relationships with key constituents such as union leaders, parents, elected officials, and community organizations. We formed a variety of focus groups for superintendents, assistant superintendents, and central office leaders from different departments to guide planning, galvanize resources, and implement strategies.

In 2017, members of my team, along with the superintendent focus group, began an EI leadership pilot called Equity, Excellence, and Empathy, E3, that aligned with the chancellor's vision and priorities. We began with eight districts and grew to nineteen districts citywide. It was in this phase that we expanded the training to superintendent teams and principals and shared best SEL practices using Yale University's RULER approach as foundational. We trained and coached forty-three out of forty-six superintendents who then offered this same opportunity to their principals, resulting in over 350 principals trained by STAR Factor citywide in that year. Additionally, we also expanded SEL training to over 350 schools using the RULER approach citywide in 2019. Even though Chancellor Fariña retired in 2018, the work continued to evolve citywide under different chancellors who also cared about SEL for every child. We used an inquiry model—learn, practice, reflect, and share. The system is now more advanced with better tools and resources to help school communities to implement SEL for all students.

Dolores spoke enthusiastically about this work:

Emotions are contagious. It's what I believe, how I lead, and my way of being. I try to listen to, include, and engage others—to be mindful of the key constituents that we work with and to be mindful of every member of the system and their levels at each part of the system and be deliberate. In a large urban environment such as New York City, unless the chancellor believes in and promotes this work at all levels of the organization, it will not move forward. At the district level, the superintendent needs to champion the work, and at the school level, the principal, and the school leadership team, must incorporate this learning into the mission and vision of the school. Furthermore, to promote systemic change, we need to be aware of the mental models that exist to help navigate through the system to expand the emotional intelligence work in a systemic way.

Former Chancellor Fariña said: "Education is about being human, connecting with others, and being a good person. We planted seeds which are still blossoming."

Lessons learned from Carmen

- Appoint a high-level professional to lead who believes in and models the EI leadership work.
- Empower superintendents to lead the system.
- Articulate the vision for building a supportive environment and emotional intelligence.
- Provide leadership training and coaching to all stakeholders.
- Meet individually with all stakeholders, superintendents, and principals.
- Visit schools and all departments to articulate the vision and engage all stakeholders in every citywide initiative.

Lessons learned from Dolores

- Garner the chancellor's support to convey purpose and hope for the future.
- Use effective communication skills to convey purpose and alignment to organizational values.
- Build relationships with all key stakeholders, including but not limited to universities, the Wallace Foundation, unions, parents, and the community.

- Engage key stakeholders and provide opportunities for meaningful input.
- Begin with superintendents and senior leaders who have influence, decision-making ability, and genuine care.
- Invite leaders to join as a pilot using a team approach.
- Start small with focus groups that believe and commit to the learning.
- Model learning as a habit of practice. Dolores continued developing her skills as a coach and meta-coach through STAR Factor and Daniel Goleman's coach training. Be guided by this maxim: Do what you have to do, so you can do what you want to do.[9]
- Practice patience, perseverance, and humility.
- Develop and train select focus groups of leaders that include practitioners and representatives of key stakeholders at all levels of the system.
- Strive for authenticity, ownership, and a systemic approach to develop leaders using the PSEL standards to develop the whole leader.
- Celebrate early wins along the way.

THINK ABOUT IT

Take a moment: Reflect on the steps that Carmen and Dolores took to move their agenda forward. What would be your key strategies in your school or district?

Mark Cannizzaro, Council of School Administrators President, 2012–2022

Mark Cannizzaro worked as a school leader for seventeen years before he accepted the role of president of the Council of Supervisors and Administrators (CSA) of the largest school system in the United States, New York City, where he served for the past ten years. Mark retired this year but not before he was able to usher in the professional development of adults as internal coaches trained in emotional intelligence leadership so that CSA could be a force for change.

Challenges for leaders today. We asked Mark what he sees as the major hurdles that school leaders face today. He said:

> Honestly, it is the constant immediate demands on their time. People are asking for things and needing things that have nothing to do with education, and they want you to stop what you're doing and immediately respond to those things. Second, the number of responsibilities has grown tremendously, and the immediacy of everything becomes an urgent matter and takes school leaders away from the day-to-day job of educating children.
>
> When I visit schools, you can see what I'm talking about immediately. In simple conversation, we hear the frustration of principals about the demands on their time. This job has always been challenging and time-consuming, but it's now become a 24-7 job. School leaders are telling us that the job is affecting their personal relationships with their families; it's affecting not only their emotional health but their physical health. Most do not even take a break to eat lunch.
>
> There are fewer and fewer people interested in taking school leadership positions, which means, obviously, a smaller talent pool to choose from, which is beginning to have a negative effect on the system. In my eyes, it's still the most rewarding job you can ever have. I often romanticize my time as a principal, and I tell people it's the hardest job I've ever had in my life, including the one I have now, but it's also the best job I've ever had in my life, including the one I have now.

WHY BRING EI LEADERSHIP AND SEL TO SCHOOLS?

It's about survival—being able to reflect. Social-emotional learning is about stepping out of the immediacy of the situation and stepping back a little bit. We all falter from time to time. I liken the work to remembering that you're on a diet, because I have a goal and my goal is to lose weight. If the goal is not constantly top of mind you tend to go off it a little bit, like exercise, for example. When you go through an emotional stressor you remind yourself that you have the skills to step back and tell yourself that this, too, will pass. If you're maintaining, it helps you remember your goal, so I then choose to handle the situation intellectually, so when it sneaks up on you, you'll be ready. Some days are better than others, but I like it because it keeps me in that frame of mind.

WHAT SKILLS ARE THE MOST IMPORTANT FOR PRINCIPALS TO LEARN?

Emotion regulation is key. I think that every living being in this world can probably remember a time or several times when they've reacted to a high-stress situation emotionally and didn't accomplish the goal that they would have liked to accomplish because of their reaction. In this business, whether you're working with children who are still developing or parents who have no greater love than the love of their child, you need to know a lot about regulating other people's emotions. At the same time, the all-important work of regulating yourself goes side by side with "other" regulation. If you're not regulating yourself, you can have a very difficult time regulating others.

ESSENTIAL SKILLS FOR TODAY'S LEADERS

The three top skills leaders need to learn are emotion-regulation, reflection, and knowledge (a schema to make sense to people). And no matter how calm you may be today, tomorrow can turn you around completely. You need to articulate and validate people—understand where they're coming from. As I mentioned earlier, there's no greater love than the love a parent has for the child. That child might be driving your teachers bonkers, but remember that there is someone at home who loves that child more than any-thing in the world. You have to understand where they're coming from, stand in their shoes; have empathy.

HOPEFUL OUTCOMES

We have already begun to sense the changes resulting from our work in small doses. We notice that when people are socially and emotionally aware they can articulate better their frustration and the problems or limitations that they're dealing with. Before this, people were bottling everything up inside and not responding to the mandates, with "I can't do all of this!" or "Much of this isn't going to move the agenda forward anyway." I think the pandemic has exacerbated some of the school leaders' agency, and their self-talk is saying, "I'm going to finally push back." And they are doing this in a much more intelligent way; they are not lashing out. As a union, those are the type of things we've been trying to tell people for a long time. Don't get me wrong, this is still an ongoing battle, trying to get people to understand that your own health, the health of your family, and the type of relationships you build must always come first. I'll see a principal at a meeting and hear, "Everything's great—my school is great." And then when I visit the school and talk privately, the truth comes out: "I'm exhausted. . . . I gained twenty pounds from my poor eating habits due to the late hours I'm keeping."

MESSAGES FOR SCHOOL LEADERS

Spend some time working on social-emotional learning and social-emotional intelligence. It gives you a much better toolbox to be able to articulate what it is that you need in order to be successful. It empowers you to articulate what you're doing intentionally and why you're doing it and how it's best for the kids and best for the school without sounding combative. There's a point of diminishing returns, and you're able to articulate that a lot better when you're socially and emotionally aware. That's the key. It's an ongoing process. It's about building relationships and building trust; it's about self-reflection; it's about validating other people. It's about so many little pieces that create the transformational leadership experience, and it happens over time. Sometimes I believe it begins to happen when you're not even aware of it.

It's being authentic. I think it is what allows you to lead and guide others in a differentiated way by understanding where they're coming from. Recognizing that the conversation I had with one person may be a very different conversation than with another. It's really about your self-awareness, and that helps you understand other people's level of self-awareness and build from there. It's the kind of work that prepares school leaders for the hard work they do every day.

Lessons learned from Mark

- Listen regularly to school leaders.
- Reduce excess mandates.
- Self-reflection and self-awareness are essential.
- Be authentic.
- Leaders fear pushback from top management.
- Provide professional development and space.
- Hire a director for overseeing adult coaching.
- Take concrete actions to build psychological safety so people can engage in new initiatives without fear of speaking up.

THINK ABOUT IT

How might you pursue strong partnerships that will support your values and beliefs?

Laurie Morrison, Former Central Office Administrator,
Highline School District, Seattle

Laurie was the executive director of instructional leadership at Highline School District in Seattle, Washington, at the time of this interview.
She shared her experience with the transformative work in emotional
intelligence that she and her colleague, Kimberly, began a few years ago
with principals:

> It was such a great experience. It's probably the highlight of our
> careers in Highline, and, you know, we were super lucky in that a
> couple of things were happening at the same time. So, we were doing
> the RULER approach in our elementary schools for about two years.
> The middle and high school started to get a little more interested
> later. Kimberly and I were doing a lot of talking about SEL at the
> adult level, and we had a superintendent who was right there with us.
>
> So, we created a kickoff event for all school and district admin-
> istrators, where we partnered with Marc Brackett, who did SEL for
> adults, and an introduction to the RULER approach for all our schools.
>
> Our superintendent called all administrators to a meeting to dis-
> cuss the issues around equity for all: every team, every school, every
> central office team, her cabinet, and the school board. She told us that
> we were to create a charter for adults that focuses on their leadership
> work. Simultaneously, the board with the superintendent created an
> equity policy, which said that equity was now a focus of teaching and
> learning. But few leaders knew what that meant. We had a diverse
> student population and staff. Administrators were mostly White.
>
> So, when we came out of that Leadership Institute, we started to
> combine social-emotional learning in service of leading for equity.
> To have deep conversations around equity, you must be able to
> explore your blind spots. You can't do the equity work without
> doing the social and emotional work to create the safety to look at
> and share parts of ourselves.

We didn't have the capacity to do the coaching one-on-one, so we did it as a group. We administered the ESCI. Then we brought administrators together and went over the general interpretation of their data. They got their reports, and I used mine as an example. After this session, the group continued to come together to make sense of their ESCI because we already had created the conditions for our learning. We were now a professional learning network using the charter as our first point of reference.

THE IMPACT

There was no longer this element of competition. We were a true collaborative. There was safety in being courageous and vulnerable with one another. Out of this collaboration, a group of eight principals emerged that met periodically to talk about their goal-setting, sparked by our conversations about development. At the same time, Kimberly and I were working with them individually, which was part of our job responsibility. We manifested a stance for our position as principal supervisors, assuring that we were not there to evaluate them but rather to reflect with them, coach them. We were school leaders' supervisors there as a resource for their chosen area of leadership growth. And so that was the culture that we were building, and it just worked with our network of principals; it was all of them! We asked ourselves, "How do we get them to push back on each other? How do they become in charge of their own learning?" So out of that push came our leaders, setting up their own learning plans.

Rather than an evaluative structure, leaders were creating what they wanted to learn about, their unique self-exploration. They asked Kimberly and me to provide and interpret the ESCI and to give them feedback. They also began asking us and each other questions like, "How are you going to know you're better at it? How do you know that we are asking the right questions? Where in the data are certain behaviors visible?"

That continued over the course of six years, and they still do it. It's remarkable, but the principals said, "We're not letting these things go. We want to still pay attention to our inner work." After two years of a pandemic, a new superintendent has come on board. I hope the work is going to stay.

Our principals are special people who are willing to take this deep dive. Only a few principals resisted it. One principal would sit back with her arms crossed.

Now she has the warmest heart—I mean just the diamond in the rough. She had been a principal for twenty years, she said, "I've got five more years in me. I'm just kind of gone." But she saw the power of the work transforming her peers' school cultures not just for students, but for adults.

WHAT TRANSFORMATION LOOKS LIKE

The district's adult culture changed so much. If we were going to have conversations around race, we had to create, see, and make courageous spaces. Many don't know how to lead for equity, but when they entered through the meeting room door, the right conditions existed for addressing it. The staff was with them. My job was to support and supervise school leaders.

Sometimes I'm a direct supervisor of the school or of the school leader, but probably 80 percent of the time I'm going to be alongside the leader, figuring it out together in a coaching role.

It's great! They make plans in small groups with input from each other. They take the ESCI by the time they're a second-year leader as an opportunity to get feedback.

We want our leaders to be well and whole, and we want them to be around for a long time. I was the lead facilitator for our Aspiring Administrators Academy, and the theme over the last five years that I've done it has been emotionally intelligent leadership. Every month we would meet, and no matter what we were talking about, it fits within that frame.

I really believe that once people, especially people who are a little more resistant or more logical and sequential, understand the brain research behind emotional intelligence in leadership, it serves as a hook to draw them into the conversations.

Our school leaders were hungry for the work. The charge of the school district, leading for equity, was their challenge.

I had an authentic and safe relationship with each principal. They couldn't just perform for me. I told them, "Let's be real in our work, honest about what your SEL growth edge is so that we can focus there." It was a special time in Highline.

SUCCESS WAS CONTAGIOUS

Another adult move that we made was to take ourselves out of the equation, so that the facilitation, collaboration, and peer-to-peer work weren't dependent on us. I think that one thing that has really withstood the test of time over the last six years is that the leaders are so committed to working with one another, and they don't need me. The group dynamic forced that to happen, because I couldn't do one-on-one coaching. Instead, I helped create the conditions and the venue for leaders to learn from one another. I realized that when they get together, they need to talk about their stuff, that's what they need. And it wasn't like I could teach or do what we do with coaching in between. They wanted to get to the nitty-gritty and share information. Lessons learned! Success!

THINK ABOUT IT

Take a moment: What can you take from Laurie's story to inform your own leadership practice?

David Adams, CEO of Urban Assembly Schools

David Adams, the Black male CEO of the Urban Assembly network of high schools in New York City, has been very active in promoting national SEL for many years, as a teacher, site coordinator, district coordinator, and researcher of SEL. He oversees the implementation of SEL in twenty-eight New York City high schools as well as schools across the country. He also sits on the board of directors of CASEL, the Collaborative for Academic, Social, and Emotional Learning. We asked David for his view of how the SEL work is moving forward in New York City. From where he sits, he sees it as developing. His focus has been on moving student SEL forward in all city schools using the DESSA, an assessment of students' social and emotional skills.[10] He hopes to create a common language among the 1,700 schools and to use this instrument for assessing and then teaching to the specific SEL skills needed by each child. In our interview with David, he shared his thoughts about how to move change and provide support for principals and superintendents:

> SEL implementation is about communication and it's about clarity. Being able to assess and then create support around those assessments will help move our work forward. We want SEL in all 1,700 schools. We are working with schools to translate the DESSA assessment into insight, so that young people can understand their strengths and challenges.
>
> Nothing moved the work forward on a large scale until this. This is positive, important work for young people, and I think that as a leader you must have faith in yourself and faith in your people to move change forward. Then people start to believe in you, too.

We discussed his vision for the Urban Assembly schools. David shared:

> The Urban Assembly is an organization that solves problems. We have a system. We solve *how* problems, not *what* problems. We don't focus on what should be happening, we focus on how to

develop systems to solve the how. We translate the what into the how in schools and identify it as scalable with generalizable problem sets. Together we develop solutions for these problem sets. Our mission and purpose in the world, and what we're contributing to the educational space, is the focus on how we implement, not what we implement. Our relationships with our schools are very important. We watch what is working and what is not and come up with a good solution.

I feel that we spend too much time in education telling leaders, "You should be doing this. You should be doing that, and don't you know this is wrong?" Who's helping folks figure out how to operationalize all they manage? I would never go to a principal and say, "You should build an advisory." I'll go to a principal and say, "How might we organize time for direct instruction of SEL in your school?"

They keep problem-solving and come up with all these great solutions that I would never know because I'm not the principal. I don't know the school; I don't understand the schedule. Why would I even pursue that? What I can do, though, is say, "Well, here are some solutions that other people have shared, including principals, or assistant principals." Another question I might ask is, "How might we ensure that staff have opportunities to develop their SEL skills?" And a principal might say, "I wonder if we take five minutes at the beginning of Class X?" And I might say, "Let's start with three minutes here." A teacher question I might ask is, "How might we integrate some of these concepts into our instructional core?"

LEADERSHIP LESSONS

What matters is that we honor the experience of our administrators and our teachers. I think we honor our educators when we come to them with problem sets and then work with them on solutions to implement and study the results.

One of the underestimated concepts of leadership is that you must see the folks that you're asking to follow you and give them the things that they need to follow. And everybody needs something different. And in helping others you must work on changes in yourself. You need to be able to find the things that people need inside of you. You need to lift them up.

But if you do a really good job, then they're giving you what you need to lead. It becomes this circle of trust and investment, and that's what moves the work forward. It's that circle: I see you, you see me, and we see our mission and move forward. Everybody is meant to be in the growth process. I feel very sustained by the relationships that bring us toward our mission and to have an opportunity to contribute to improving public education. And that's such a wonderful mission to get up and do each day. And the bonds we form, those spaces in which we are focused on a common understanding of what we want to do together, are strong.

David explains that for leaders to do this they have to have well-being:

But how do we do it? I mean I feel nurtured through high-quality relationships. I feel nurtured in spaces where I'm learning what my folks need from me and working to grow into the leader that they deserve. And they are responding to that leadership and then giving me the motivation to continue to push through. I feel very sustained by the relationships that bring us toward our mission.

So, the more we can help school leaders with the development of individual school systems, the more the collective will come forward, and it will be more of a relationship-oriented school, which then is going to nurture everything else nicely.

The most important piece of leadership is understanding how your support systems are going to operate so that you have the energy to take care of your folks. And I think when we understand the role of bonds and the role of vulnerability in and sitting in those bonds, then we can do anything. There's nothing that would stop us from accomplishing the most challenging of situations because we care about each other, and we care about what we're trying to accomplish. Systems ground us so that we have time to solve big problems. Struggles happen when you can't see beyond yourself—can't make space for another, and aren't self-aware.

Lessons learned from David

- Focus on *how* we implement, not *what* we implement.
- Obtain chancellor support for the implementation of citywide assessment using the DESSA.
- Give complete agency to school principals to develop plans.
- Work on developing one's own self-awareness.
- Promote leader well-being.
- Build bonds of caring with school leaders.
- Engage in collaborative problem-solving with schools.

THINK ABOUT IT

Take a moment: Think about the relationships that you have with your staff and supervisees.

Do you believe that they feel cared for by you and your team? How could you show caring, compassion, and support them even more?

As we reflect on these leaders' stories, let's remember your story, written before you began this book. How would it look to you now? Take some time to write it. What has changed and what has remained the same? What would you want people to take away from your story?

As we close this chapter, we ask you to relish in the knowledge that by reading this book, you have taken the first step toward approaching your emotionally intelligent leadership; if you have already embraced EI, we trust that this reading has allowed you to deepen your commitment to the work and to feel a sense of belonging with a community of leaders who also anchor their practice in EI. Remember that you, school leaders, are the knot that holds it all together. Nurture yourself. Take time for yourself, your families, your friends, and both your personal and professional selves. You've earned it.

A special thank you to Bonnie Brown, Dr. Deidre Farmbry, former chancellor Carmen Fariña, Dolores Esposito, former CSA president Mark Cannizzaro, Dr. Laurie Morrison, and David Adams for their contributions to this chapter. And thank you for reading our book.

We would love to hear your stories of how your emotional intelligence is showing up in your lives and in your schools. Please send them to us at connect@starfactorcoaching.com.

Afterword

In the late 1990s, my uncle Marvin and I set out together to bring social and emotional learning to schools. Marvin was a middle school teacher in New York who had remarkable success with his students. He had figured out the missing link in a child's journey toward personal, social, and academic success: the ability to use their emotions wisely. Marvin knew that if we grew up learning emotion skills, we would be better learners, decision-makers, friends, parents, colleagues, and partners; better able to deal with life's challenges; and better equipped to have well-being and achieve our goals and dreams. I knew firsthand, from a young age, that his ideas worked, because they made it possible for me to navigate my childhood trauma, including sexual abuse and extreme bullying.

But Uncle Marvin and I failed. We were only prepared to help teachers deliver lessons to children. We weren't ready for the many teachers who were resistant to the ideas. "Teaching kids about the feeling of despair makes me sad," one said. "I'm not prepared to hear what these kids might share," said another.

So Marvin and I went back to the drawing board. We saw that we would never reach children until we first enlisted teachers who understood the importance of emotion skills. And soon after that, we realized that only if there was commitment from the school leader could an entire school be transformed. It was at that point in my career that I met Janet and Robin who quickly became close colleagues and collaborators. Janet and Robin were pioneers in supporting educational leaders in learning and applying the skills of emotional intelligence to their personal and professional lives.

What I learned from them—as you have also learned, now that you've read this book—is that emotions are one of the most powerful forces within a leader. Through compelling stories, poignant case studies, and a comprehensive review of the research literature, Janet and Robin showed us that a school leader's emotional intelligence influences everything: from management style to navigating complex relationships to school climate to crisis intervention to SEL innovation. It's a leader's emotional intelligence that determines the ability to motivate, inspire, show compassion (and have self-compassion), have difficult conversations, and deliver constructive feedback, and lead a successful school—especially through uncertain and stressful times.

Yet many school leaders will go through their careers trying hard to pretend otherwise. As we read in this book, expressing our true feelings can leave us vulnerable and exposed. It can make us say or do things we regret. Many of us learned early on from the people who taught us and raised us to hide or bury our true feelings—even from ourselves. And these mindsets about emotions get passed along to others. Everyone in a school community is learning by watching and listening to their leader—their role model.

When we deny ourselves "permission to feel," many unwanted outcomes arise. We lose the ability to perceive what we're feeling. And when that happens, we're unable to understand what's happening in our lives that's causing us to feel the way we do. As a result, we can't express our emotions clearly, especially in ways the people around us would understand. And this makes it impossible for us to do anything productive about our feelings: to use them wisely and learn how to make them work for us as leaders, not against us.

Only a few naturally insightful among us can claim to have the mindsets, skills, and strategies discussed in this book without consciously pursuing them, practicing them, and refining them. I had to learn them (and am continuously learning them). The concepts in this book are ripe for school leaders of all ages, genders, backgrounds, and personality types—introverted or extroverted, stress-prone, or happy-go-lucky.

We often think of leadership as being driven by charisma, intelligence, experience, and the desire for measurable results. All those things are in the mix, of course. But as we've learned from this book, emotional intelligence is one of the most powerful skills a school leader can develop. Now's the time to create an emotion revolution in our nation's schools. This book shows school leaders how.

Marc A. Brackett
Professor, Yale Child Study Center;
Founding Director, Yale Center for
Emotional Intelligence; Author,
Permission to Feel
June 3, 2023, New Haven,
Connecticut

Course Description: Leadership to Enhance Human Resources

The following course description is for a first-semester master's degree course taught by Janet at Hunter College of the City of New York. It is provided as a tool for those of you who wish to weave emotional intelligence knowledge, skills, and dispositions into your courses or professional development.

Effective management of personnel requires exemplary leadership ability. This course allows the prospective leader to examine the essential competencies of self-awareness, social awareness, self-management, and relationship management to foster the leadership of positive and productive school culture and climate through the development of the human resources and structures needed to support student achievement. The course prepares the school leader to develop intrapersonal and interpersonal skill sets that build positive, trust-based relationships. Aspiring leaders learn how to create a reflective learning organization in which social, emotional, and cognitive development becomes a conscious effort on the part of the adults who work with young people.

A major tenet of this course is that school leaders need to be intentional about their own personal and professional development. They do so by developing their social and emotional intelligences. They self-reflect and seek feedback from others. School leaders employ and model effective leadership skills, including empathic listening, assertive language, and emotion regulation, to aid them with conflict management and negotiation and other stressful difficult situations. They build a dynamic culture and climate grounded in social and emotional intelligence.

Equity is at the heart of the school leader's intentions. School leaders develop an equity lens and learn how to integrate this into their school's culture. This course lends itself to transformational and authentic leadership that builds true collaboration for learning.

Throughout the course, aspiring leaders experience and apply these essential leadership competencies and skills, as they work with their colleagues to develop their own social and emotional intelligence leadership behaviors.

Anchored in adult development, social and emotional intelligence, intentional change, and systems theory, aspiring leaders learn critical skills of how to motivate others, facilitate group processes, have difficult conversations, give and receive feedback , and promote a safe and caring culture and climate that encourages shared vision, collegial inquiry, collaboration, and trust.

COURSE FORMAT

This is a four-credit hybrid course to be conducted as fifteen sessions.

CLINICAL APPLICATIONS

Thirty hours of field-based clinical applications are required for this course. These clinical hours are met by documentation of (a) team meetings to accomplish site-based objectives; (b) the SEL-based school climate walk and analysis; (c) meetings with school and community-based leaders to enhance acquired skills; (d) applications of emotional and social competencies in field settings as documented by assessment tools and written reflections; and (e) application of any course-related learning or strategies acquired within the school setting.

REQUIRED AND RECOMMENDED READINGS/ ASSESSMENTS

Brackett, M. (2019). *Permission to feel: Unlocking the power of emotions to help our kids, ourselves, and our society thrive.* Celadon Books.

Patti, J., & Tobin, J. (2006). *Smart school leaders: Leading with emotional intelligence.* Kendall Hunt Publishers.

Ury, W., & Fisher, R. (1981). *Getting to yes.* Penguin Books. (Purchase latest edition.)

Lantieri, L., & Patti, J. (1996). *Waging peace in our schools.* Beacon Press. (Chapters 3 and 4 are available in Course Materials on Blackboard.)

Required readings are in Course Materials on Blackboard.

ONLINE ASSESSMENTS:

1. Thomas-Kilmann Conflict Mode Instrument (TKI)
2. The Leadership Practices Inventory, self
3. Emotional and Social Competency Inventory (ESCI), self

The Collaborative for Academic, Social, and Emotional Learning (CASEL), http://www.casel.org (exploration of this website and access to documents throughout the semester are required).

Additional articles will be read throughout the class and will be provided on Blackboard.

COURSE OBJECTIVES

Students who attend this introductory course will enhance their knowledge, skills, and abilities as future leaders to improve student achievement by creating a culture and climate of learning. Specific skills include the ability to do the following:

1. Effectively use communication as a tool for opening dialogue and building relationships among school personnel.
2. Increase motivation and job performance among staff members.
3. Identify and develop one's self-awareness regarding leadership strengths and challenges and ability to manage self-behaviors.
4. Increase social awareness and ability to effectively manage the behaviors of others.
5. Utilize appropriate leadership styles based on context with a focus on distributive and facilitative, authentic, and transformational leadership.
6. Promote equity, make ethical decisions, and engage in dialogue with diverse groups with the goal of promoting learning for all students.
7. Acquire skills in promoting social justice practices that create culture and influence climate.
8. Acquire knowledge and skill in systems thinking.
9. Demonstrate the ability to work productively in teams and engage teams in team performance.
10. Develop a personal vision and a professional vision that drives schoolwide culture and climate with an SEL lens.
11. Identify social and emotional practices in schools that develop students' prosocial skills and create a positive learning environment.
12. Be prepared to lead SEL implementation in schools.
13. Practice and acquire skills in enhancing emotional intelligence.

COURSE EVALUATION

Rubrics to guide this grading process will be available on the Blackboard site.

- Personal, Professional Leadership Assignment 1 = 45%.
- SEL Implementation Assignment 2 = 50%.
- Teamwork and Online Participation are embedded in all assignments. An extra 5% is given for visible participation.

If you would like to receive the full course outline with all assignments, please contact us at connect@starfactorcoaching.com.

The Twelve Emotional and Social Competencies of the Emotional and Social Competency Inventory (ESCI)

Emotional self-awareness: Recognizing one's emotions and their effects.

Emotional self-control: Keeping disruptive emotions and impulses in check.

Adaptability: Flexibility in handling change.

Achievement orientation: Striving to improve or meet a standard of excellence.

Positive outlook: Persistence in pursuing goals despite obstacles and setbacks.

Empathy: Sensing others' feelings and perspectives and taking an active interest in their concerns.

Organizational awareness: Reading a group's emotional currents and power relationships.

Coach and mentor: Sensing others' development needs and bolstering their abilities.

Inspirational leadership: Inspiring and guiding individuals and groups.

Influence: Wielding effective tactics for persuasion.

Conflict management: Negotiating and resolving disagreements.

Teamwork: Working with others toward shared goals. Creating group
   synergy in pursuing collective goals.

Source: Korn Ferry, "Emotional and Social Competency Inventory (ESCI)," https://
www.kornferry.com/capabilities/leadership-professional-development/training
-certification/esci-emotional-and-social-competency-inventory.

Emotion Regulation Strategies

Positive Self-Management Strategies in the Moment

The Strategy	The Situation	Your Thoughts (the Leader)	The Intervening Moment—Pause and Mental Shift	Your Strategy in Action
Breathing Be mindful that the most effective short-term strategy to calm the body and the mind is breathing. Taking three to five deep breaths physiologically and mentally calms the body down immediately.	A teacher who had applied for the AP position did not get it due to seniority. She set up a meeting with the principal to discuss this. Rather than attend the meeting, she handed the principal her letter of resignation, effective immediately. The principal screamed at her and told her to get out.	*She really pissed me off! After all I have done for her, she leaves me like this?* *Damn, I wish I could have told her how I feel—angry and hurt. Instead, I got triggered and acted foolishly.*	You take five deep belly breaths and think: *Let me take some breaths and compose myself.*	You call her room to set up a second meeting and apologize for your reaction. Together, you make an appointment for the next day.
Belly breaths, or diaphragmatic breathing, can be used to relax by breathing fully into your diaphragm while lying down. Place your hands on your abdomen and your upper chest to feel the movement of the inhalation and exhalation. Breathe in through your nose,				

Positive Self-Management Strategies in the Moment

The Strategy	The Situation	Your Thoughts (the Leader)	The Intervening Moment—Pause and Mental Shift	Your Strategy in Action
and exhale through pursed lips. Deep, slow breathing exercises can help us calm down when we are feeling anxious, stressed, or overwhelmed.				
Cognitive Reappraisal By *cognitive reappraisal*, we mean telling a different story about what happened. We may experience an event or situation that brings up negative thoughts and we change them to more positive possibilities. To do so, we need to work with our internal dialogue, our self-talk.	Principal Sue observes a teacher for the third time. When Sue first worked with this teacher, she thought the teacher would never make it, but today, Sue sees improvement based on the previous feedback. Principal Sue reappraises her thinking and decides to work with the teacher some more.	As you enter the classroom, you feel that apathetic feeling taking over: *What a waste of time. This teacher will never make it.*	You remember your work in emotional intelligence leadership and tell yourself, "It's been two weeks since I last saw her, and I'm hopeful that she has had time to practice her strategies."	After fifteen minutes in her classroom, you feel your body relax and notice the smile on your face. Today, you see the improvement based on your previous feedback. You further reappraise your thinking and decide to work with her some more.

(continued)

Positive Self-Management Strategies in the Moment

The Strategy	The Situation	Your Thoughts (the Leader)	The Intervening Moment—Pause and Mental Shift	Your Strategy in Action
Positive Self-Talk This is our internal dialogue. Our self-talk reveals our subconscious thoughts, beliefs, questions, and ideas. Self-talk can be both affirming or hurtful; it can encourage us or make us feel hopeless. The more we are in touch with it, the better we can evaluate whether the messages being received are helpful or not. As a self-management strategy, positive self-talk can shift the way you handle a situation as you see the problem in a new or different light.	Superintendent Yako, at a meeting with her principals, was sharing the latest thinking in math instruction with her principals. She had made it clear that all schools would need to adapt to the new curriculum as it was completely in line with the updated math standards. She could see that several principals were unhappy just by looking at their faces. Three of them verbally said so.	*How dare they take such a stance. Most of them have the lowest scores in the district. They should be thankful that there is a new approach that will help improve their scores.*	You pause and mentally put yourself in their shoes, remembering what it was like for you when you were a principal.	You sit back in your chair and mentally turn your scowl into a slight smile. You say "Let me take a step back. Tell me, what are your concerns about this new approach? What are your thoughts on how to move this approach forward?"

Positive Self-Management Strategies in the Moment

The Strategy	The Situation	Your Thoughts (the Leader)	The Intervening Moment—Pause and Mental Shift	Your Strategy in Action
Distraction Distraction is a temporary strategy to get your mind off the present issue by doing something that will help you shift to a positive mood.	Assistant Principal Lashawn was angry and hurt because Principal Karlene overpowered her in the presentation they had jointly prepared for the staff.	*I can't believe that Principal Karlene did it again. She tells me that she wants me to take the lead, and then she takes it, and I can't get a word in edgewise.*	You understand that you are too angry to deal with the principal right now and plan to talk with her tomorrow.	Rather than confront her now, you distract yourself by visiting a third-grade classroom to watch the expert teacher interact with her children.
Seek Social Support When stressed, angry, sad, or needing affirmation, have your go-to people you know will listen. As humans, we need connection to others. One of the top reasons for depression is loneliness, an absence of soul connections.	The chapter leader just left Principal Dan's office after proposing a plan that Dan does not approve of. Dan is angry and disappointed because he feels that he probably knows more about the background than the chapter leader.	*I hate this guy sometimes! I'm not going to let him stop me. I'll find a way to move him off of this direction.*	You wait a minute to cool down. After some time, you decide to get another opinion on the proposed plan.	You call your assistant principal, who is at another site, to share what happened, let off some steam, and strategize. You conclude that the chapter leader is more logical and that you are more emotional. Thank goodness the AP was available.

Positive Self-Management Strategies over Time

The Strategy	The Practice	The Commitment
Mindfulness	*Mindfulness is focusing on your awareness by sensing and feeling in the moment, without interpretation or judgment. It involves working with the breath. Breathing exercises don't have to take a lot of time out of your day. It's really just about setting aside some time to pay attention to your breathing, being present.*	Many of the practices that follow are mindful. Build small practices into your daily routines and increase them as you become more seasoned.
Meditation	Sitting meditation is the most basic form of meditation. A sitting meditation can be either guided, which means that you follow along with a meditation guide, or unguided. To practice a sitting meditation, sit comfortably upright in your chair, cross-legged on the floor, or even lying down. Close your eyes and focus on taking deep breaths in and out. Whether your meditation is guided or not, do not attach yourself to the thoughts that naturally come up during your practice. Simply be aware of them, label them as thoughts, and allow them to pass through you. The point of meditation is not to immediately erase our internal chatter; instead, it allows us to become witnesses of it, so that we can separate ourselves from our thoughts.	If you are a beginner, you may find it difficult to sit for long periods of time. Start with five minutes and breathe through the active thoughts that pass through your mind. Do not hold on to them. See them and let them go.

Positive Self-Management Strategies over Time

The Strategy	The Practice	The Commitment
Reflective Inquiry *Inquiry* work supports self-awareness. It helps us identify personal and professional stressors by looking inward, allowing us to be more proactive in regulating our emotions	Meditations: body scan, visualization, loving-kindness, sitting meditation, walking meditation. Learn more at https://www.mindful.org/how-to-meditate/. *Daily personal check-ins* are a form of inquiry that is good to use to begin a workday, meeting, or before an important event. Take a few minutes to sit in stillness by practicing a mindful meditation. During your time in stillness, quietly reflect on how you are feeling today, without judgment. Just notice what comes up as you breathe in and out. *Journaling.* Immediately following your meditation, take a few minutes to journal what came up for you. This type of check-in can be practiced with others as well. Following your journaling, you could take a few minutes and share with a colleague what came up for you.	Committing to a form of inquiry work will surely increase one's self-awareness. Self-awareness is the anchor of emotional intelligence. It supports development in self-management, social awareness, and management of our relationships. Instead of ruminating on an event, take some time to purposely reflect on the situation. Write what happened in a journal and write what you should have done differently. Once you complete this exercise, let go of the event and start fresh the next day.

(continued)

Positive Self-Management Strategies over Time

The Strategy	The Practice	The Commitment
	Ongoing personal check-ins. Make time to briefly check in with yourself throughout the day. Ask yourself, "How am I feeling?" This allows you to gauge your emotions as well as your energy levels. If you notice you are low energy, consider rescheduling important meetings.	
Coaching Coaching creates a safe space where you can explore with a trained coach the parts of yourself that may be impeding your performance or your inner or outer development in areas that concern you.	Coaching is increasingly becoming a must for all leaders. It provides comfort and support to all systems leaders. Share your personal and professional concerns in a safe place.	There are many different forms of coaching. We propose coaching designed to work through difficult situations by working with your emotions.

Purposeful Work Strategies to Support Self-Regulation

The Strategy	The Practice	The Commitment
Reflect on your purpose.	Continuously reflect on your purpose. Ensure that your position aligns to your purpose. If you noticed a misalignment with your intended professional vision and the position you are currently holding, consider alternatives. Craft your career to align to your goals, whether that means adjusting your current position's goals or seeking a new position.	It is helpful to take time every few months to reflect on your life—professional and personal—and ask yourself whether you are living your own truth. It's too easy to get caught up in the daily routines and stray away from your purpose.
Plan ahead.	Planning can help alleviate stress later during the week by organizing your schedule, being mindful of any scheduling conflicts, rescheduling things that may limit your ability to balance your responsibilities and personal life. Also, planning ahead by designating upcoming deadlines helps with better time management, further alleviating stress. Develop an organizational system that works for you. This has to be developed over time by you. What works for me may not work for you. Always leave time before and after meetings for planning and reflection.	The time commitment varies with these practices. But the more you practice planning ahead, the less stress you will encounter.

(continued)

Purposeful Work Strategies to Support Self-Regulation

The Strategy	The Practice	The Commitment
Prioritize a balanced personal and professional schedule.	Schedule breaks and time for self-care. We often must remind ourselves that we have a life outside of our jobs. We must be intentional with prioritizing our self-care. Make it a point every day to take a lunch break. Schedule the time to exercise, practice mindfulness strategies, spend time with loved ones, and engage in your hobbies. Using a planner may be helpful as a way to support committing yourself to these moments of self-care.	Start by taking thirty minutes a week to review your schedule for the week. Carve out thirty minutes to an hour a week to read with curiosity or learn something new.
Set clear boundaries.	Distance yourself from situations that may hinder your energy or self-regulation. Say no when you know that the request involves self-sacrifice. Reflection and self-awareness help us identify our triggers. Using this self-awareness, we should be mindful of what to limit in both our personal and professional lives.	This is daily work and should be part of your active repertoire.
Cultivate a positive mindset.	Be deliberate about shifting to positive thoughts when you find yourself blue. Establish positive affirmations that you can call on when feeling down.	Use your self-talk to shift from a negative to a positive mindset. The more positive we are, the kinder we will be to ourselves and others.

Notes

CHAPTER 1

1. Mendemu Showry and K. V. L. Manasa, "Self-Awareness: Key to Effective Leadership," *IUP Journal of Soft Skills* 8, no. 1 (March 2014): 15–26.
2. "New Surgeon General Advisory Raises Alarm about the Devastating Impact of the Epidemic of Loneliness and Isolation in the United States," U.S. Department of Health and Human Services, May 3, 2023, https://www.hhs.gov/about/news/2023/05/03/new-surgeon-general-advisory-raises-alarm-about-devastating-impact-epidemic-loneliness-isolation-united-states.html.
3. Julie K. Yamamoto, Mary E. Gardiner, and Penny L. Tenuto, "Emotion in Leadership: Secondary School Administrators' Perceptions of Critical Incidents," *Educational Management Administration & Leadership* 42, no. 2 (2014): 165–183.
4. Stephanie Levin and Kathryn Bradley, "Understanding and Addressing Principal Turnover: A Review of the Research," Learning Policy Institute, March 19, 2019, https://learningpolicyinstitute.org/product/nassp-understanding-addressing-principal-turnover-review-research-report.
5. Julie Yamamoto, Mary Gardiner, and P. I. Tenuto, "Emotion in Leadership: Secondary School Administrators' Perceptions of Critical Incidents," *Educational Management Administration and Leadership*, February 2013.
6. Emily T. Sullivan, "Principals Are on the Brink of a Breakdown," *EdSurge*, July 6, 2022, https://www.edsurge.com/news/2022-07-06-principals-are-on-the-brink-of-a-breakdown.
7. National Association of Secondary School Principals (NASSP), "NASSP Survey of Principals and Students Reveals the Extent of Challenges Facing Schools,"

September 6, 2022, https://www.nassp.org/2022/09/06/nassp-survey-of -principals-and-students-reveals-the-extent-of-challenges-facing-schools/.

8. Adam Ehrman and Lauren Wolff, "Stress, Stressors, Superintendents, and School Boards," Illinois Association of School Boards, March/April 2019.

9. Principal Kevin interview by Janet Patti, November 2022; "Beating the Odds 2016: Top High Schools for Low Income Students," *Newsweek*, August 11, 2016.

10. Ishwar V. Basavaraddi, "Yoga: Its Origin, History, and Development," Ministry of External Affairs, Government of India, April 15, 2015, http://www.yogamdniy.nic .in/WriteReadData/LINKS/File577a4a83f0b-996b-4119-842d-60790971e651 .pdf; "The Hindu Roots of Yoga and the Take-Back Yoga Campaign," Hindu American Foundation, https://www.hinduamerican.org/projects/hindu-roots -of-yoga?gclid=Cj0KCQjwjo2JBhCRARIsAFG667VTRtqvTbDqFX5Ga7YX8TT9 pgDCxEP1AyFMxxhSLkPWrmsglt0-NzIaAldNEALw_wcB; "Wellness Practices from Around the World," SCL Health, https://www.sclhealth.org/blog/2018/11 /wellness-practices-from-around-the-world/; Mary Koithan and Cynthia Farrell, "Indigenous Native American Healing Traditions," *Journal for Nurse Practitioners* 6, no. 6 (2010): 477–478; Edward Shizha and John Charema, "Health and Wellness in Southern Africa: Incorporating Indigenous and Western Healing Practices," *International Journal of Psychology and Counselling* 4, no. 5 (May 2012), https://www .researchgate.net/publication/266232670_Health_and_wellness_in_Southern _Africa_Incorporating_indigenous_and_western_healing_practices; Funlayo E. Wood, "Sacred Healing and Wholeness in Africa and the Americas," *Journal of Africana Religions* 1, no. 3 (2013): 376–429.

11. Global Wellness Institute, "History of Wellness," https://globalwellnessinstitute .org/what-is-wellness/history-of-wellness/.

12. Bill Hettler, "The Past of Wellness," *The History and Future of Health Promotion and Wellness*, September 25, 1998, https://hettler.com/History/hettler.htm.

13. Courtney E. Ackerman, "What Is Positive Psychology and Why Is It Important?" *Theory and Books*, April 20, 2018, https://positivepsychology.com/what-is -positive-psychology-definition/.

In the 1960s and '70s, Seligman had developed the theory of learned help-lessness, in which people see most problems coming from their lack of con-trol. He began to shift people's behaviors by focusing on the positives, using inspiration and optimism as powerful tools for improving maladies such as depression.

14. Joaquín Selva, "The History and Origins of Mindfulness," *Theory and Books*, positivepsychology.com, March 13, 2017, https://positivepsychology.com/history -of-mindfulness/.

15. Ausiàs Cebolla et al., "Contemplative Positive Psychology: Introducing Mindful-ness into Positive Psychology," *Psychologist Papers* 38, no. 1 (March 2017): 12–18.

16. "Well-Being Concepts," Centers for Disease Control and Prevention, https://www .cdc.gov/hrqol/wellbeing.htm.

17. John F. Helliwell et al., eds., *World Happiness Report 2023* (11th ed.), Sustainable Development Solutions Network, 2023.

18. Marnie Hunter, "The World's Happiest Countries," *CNN*, March 20, 2023, https://www.cnn.com/travel/article/world-happiest-countries-2023-wellness/index.html.

19. John F. Helliwell, Richard Layard, and Jeffrey D. Sachs, "The Happiness Agenda: The Next 10 Years," chapter 1 in *World Happiness Report 2023*, edited by Helliwell et al., https://worldhappiness.report/ed/2023/the-happiness-agenda-the-next-10-year/#:~:text=Citation%3A,Development%20Solutions%20Network.

20. Interview with James Floman, research associate of the Yale Child Study Center, December 12, 2022.

21. Stephanie Levin and Kathryn Bradley, "Understanding and Addressing Principal Turnover: A Review of the Research," Learning Policy Institute, March 19, 2019, https://learningpolicyinstitute.org/product/nassp-understanding-addressing-principal-turnover-review-research-report; National Association of Secondary School Principals, "September 2020," *NASSP News*, September 2020, https://www.nassp.org/publication/principal-leadership/volume-21-2020-2021/principal-leadership-september-2020/nassp-news-september-2020/.

22. Melissa Kay Diliberti and Heather L. Schwartz, *Educator Turnover Has Markedly Increased, but Districts Have Taken Actions to Boost Teacher Ranks: Selected Findings from the Sixth American School District Panel Survey* (Santa Monica, CA: RAND, 2023), https://www.rand.org/pubs/research_reports/RRA956-14.html.

23. Mayo Clinic Staff, "Job Burnout and How to Spot It," https://www.mayoclinic.org/healthy-lifestyle/adult-health/in-depth/burnout/art-20046642#:~:text=Job%20burnout%20is%20a%20special,as%20depression%2C%20are%20behind%20burnout.

24. Gunnar Aronsson et al., "A Systematic Review Including Meta-Analysis of Work Environment and Burnout Symptoms," *BMC Public Health* 17, no. 1 (2017): 1–13.

25. Kathryn S. Whitaker, "Exploring Causes of Principal Burnout," *Journal of Educational Administration* 34, no. 1 (1996): 60–71.

26. Richard D. Sorenson, "Stress Management in Education: Warning Signs and Coping Mechanisms," *Management in Education* 21, no. 3 (2007): 10–13.

27. Caryn M. Wells, "Principals Responding to Constant Pressure: Finding a Source of Stress Management," *NASSP Bulletin* 97, no. 4 (2013): 338.

28. Meena Srinivasan, interview by Janet Patti, October 19, 2022. See Transformative Education Leadership, "Inner Personal Development in Service of Outer Systemic Transformation," https://www.teleadership.org/.

29. Sagger Mawri, "Beware High Levels of Cortisol, the Stress Hormone," Premier Health, August 23, 2022, https://www.premierhealth.com/your-health/articles/women-wisdom-wellness-/beware-high-levels-of-cortisol-the-stress-hormone.

30. Christina Maslach and Michael P. Leiter, *The Truth About Burnout: How Organizations Cause Personal Stress and What to Do About It* (Hoboken, NJ: John Wiley & Sons, 2008).

31. Christina Maslach and Michael P. Leiter, "Early Predictors of Job Burnout and Engagement," *Journal of Applied Psychology* 93, no. 3 (2008): 498.

32. Peter DeWitt, "We Should Be Concerned About the Mental Health of Principals," *Education Week,* August 22,2020, https://www.edweek.org/leadership /opinion-we-should-be-concerned-about-the-mental-health-of-principals /2020/08.

33. "Single Mother Statistics That Will Shock You," *The Life of a Single Mom,* https:// thelifeofasinglemom.com/single-mother-statistics-parent/.

34. Maven, "Parents at the Best Workplaces: The Largest-Ever Study of Working Parents," Great Place to Work, 2020, https://www.mavenclinic.com/lp/parents -at-the-best-workplaces-2020, cited in "8 Marks of the Best Employers for Working Parents," From Day One: A Forum on Corporate Values, December 14, 2020, https://www.fromdayone.co/2020/12/14/8-marks-of-the-best-employers-for -working-parents/.

35. Kaila Simms, "Curbing Workplace Burnout in Young Mothers of Color," Great Place to Work, January 2, 2022, https://www.greatplacetowork.com/resources /blog/curbing-workplace-burnout-in-young-mothers-of-color.

36. Anna Lucente Sterling, "What Burnout Looks Like for People of Color," *Spectrum News,* April 23, 2021, https://www.ny1.com/nyc/all-boroughs/news/2021/04/23 /what-burnout-looks-like-for-people-of-color.

37. A. Lees and David Barnard, *Highly Effective Headteachers: An Analysis of a Sample of Diagnostic Data from The Leadership Programme for Serving Headteachers,* report prepared for Hay/McBer, 1999.

38. Jeremy Sutton, "Martin Seligman's Positive Psychology Theory," *Theory and Books,* positivepsychology.com, 2016, https://positivepsychology.com/positive -psychology-theory/.

39. Peter Gibbon, "Martin Seligman and the Rise of Positive Psychology," *Humanities* 41, no 3 (Summer 2020): https://www.neh.gov/article/martin-seligman-and-rise -positive-psychology.

40. Margaret L. Kern et al., "A Multidimensional Approach to Measuring Well-Being in Students: Application of the PERMA Framework," *Journal of Positive Psychology* 10, no. 3 (2015): 262–271.

41. Jim Harter, "The Loneliest Employees," *Workplace,* Gallup, November 15, 2021, https://www.gallup.com/workplace/357386/loneliest-employees.aspx ?utm_source=twitter&utm_medium=o_social&utm_campaign=workplace _articles&utm_term=gallup&utm_content=cb03bd78-87a1-490e-9df2 -82d085e66d50.

42. Principal Dawn, interview by Janet Patti, September 15, 2022.

43. James Densley, David Riedman, and Jillian Peterson, "School Shootings Are Already at a Record in 2022—with Months Still to Go," *The 74,* October 29, 2022, https:// www.the74million.org/contributor/698865/; "School Shootings This Year: How

Many and Where," *Education Week*, updated June 15, 2023, https://www.edweek
.org/leadership/school-shootings-this-year-how-many-and-where/2023/01.
44. Aaron Kupchik et al., "Analysis: School Shootings Are Too Common, but Schools
are Still Relatively Safe," *The74*, June 6, 2022, https://www.the74million.org/article
/analysis-school-shootings-are-too-common-but-schools-are-still-relatively-safe/.
45. The US Department of Homeland Security defines a hazmat suit as "an overall
garment worn to protect people from hazardous materials or substances, including chemicals, biological agents, or radioactive materials." HAZWOPER/OSHA
Training LLC, "Hazmat Suits: Level of Protection," 2023, https://hazwoper-osha
.com/blog-post/hazmat-suits-levels-of-protection.
46. Jerry Patterson, *The Anguish of Leadership* (Arlington, VA: America Association
of School Administrators, 2000), 36.
47. Patterson, *Anguish of Leadership*, 50.

CHAPTER 2

1. "Building Your Resilience," American Psychological Association, February 1,
2020, https://www.apa.org/topics/resilience/building-your-resilience.
2. Robin Stern and Courtney E. Martin, *Project Rebirth: Survival and the Strength of
the Human Spirit from 9/11 Survivors* (Boston: Dutton, 2011).
3. Interview with Principal Brooke Jackson, September 1, 2022.
4. Interview with Principal Brooke Jackson, August 10, 2021.
5. David Robson, "Interoception: The Hidden Sense That Shapes Wellbeing,"
August 15, 2021, *Guardian*, https://www.theguardian.com/science/2021/aug/15
/the-hidden-sense-shaping-your-wellbeing-interoception.
6. Richard J. Davidson, "Mindfulness-Based Cognitive Therapy and the Prevention
of Depressive Relapse: Measures, Mechanisms, and Mediators," *JAMA Psychiatry*
73, no. 6 (2016): 547–548.
7. "Building Your Resilience," American Psychological Association.
8. Richard Boyatzis and Annie McKee, "Intentional Change," *Journal of
Organizational Excellence*, Summer 2006, https://www.doi.org/10.1002/joe.20100.
9. Denisa R. Superville, "Principals Need Social-Emotional Support, Too," September 14, 2021, *EducationWeek*, https://www.edweek.org/leadership/principals
-need-social-emotional-support-too/2021/09.
10. Paulo N. Lopes et al., "Emotion Regulation Abilities and the Quality of Social
Interaction," *Emotion* 5, no. 1 (2005): 113; John D. Mayer, Richard D. Roberts,
and Sigal Barsade, "Human Abilities: Emotional Intelligence," *Annual Review of
Psychology* 59 (2008): 507–536; John D. Mayer and Peter Salovey, eds., *Emotional
Development and Emotional Intelligence* (Basic Books, 1997).
11. Marc A. Brackett, Susan E. Rivers, and Peter Salovey, "Emotional Intelligence:
Implications for Personal, Social, Academic, and Workplace Success," *Social and
Personality Psychology Compass* 5, no. 1 (2011): 88–103.

12. Jubin Abutalebi et al., "Bilingualism Tunes the Anterior Cingulate Cortex for Conflict Monitoring," *Cerebral Cortex* 22, no. 9 (September 2012): 2076–2086, https://www.doi.org/10.1093/cercor/bhr287.
13. Interview with Principal Brooke Jackson, July 22, 2022.

CHAPTER 3

1. "Daniel Goleman," Key Step Media, https://www.keystepmedia.com/authors /daniel-goleman/.
2. Daniel Goleman, *Leadership: The Power of Emotional Intelligence* (Northampton, MA: More Than Sound, 2011).
3. Richard E. Boyatzis, "Managerial and Leadership Competencies: A Behavioral Approach to Emotional, Social and Cognitive Intelligence," *Vision* 15, no. 2 (2011): 91–100; Marc A. Brackett, Susan E. Rivers, and Peter Salovey, "Emotional Intelligence: Implications for Personal, Social, Academic, and Workplace Success," *Social and Personality Psychology Compass* 5, no. 1 (2011): 88–103.
4. Bruce J. Avolio and William L. Gardner, "Authentic Leadership Development: Getting to the Root of Positive Forms of Leadership," *Leadership Quarterly* 16, no. 3 (2005): 315–338.
5. Kenneth Leithwood et al., *How Leadership Influences Student Learning: Review of Research* (New York: Wallace Foundation, 2004); Pninit Russo-Netzer and Anat Shoshani, "Becoming Teacher Leaders in Israel: A Meaning-Making Model," *Cambridge Journal of Education* 49, no. 3 (2019): 369–389; Cheng Yong Tan, "Examining School Leadership Effects on Student Achievement: The Role of Contextual Challenges and Constraints," *Cambridge Journal of Education* 48, no. 1 (2018): 21–45.
6. Paul T. Hackett and J. William Hortman, "The Relationship of Emotional Competencies to Transformational Leadership: Using a Corporate Model to Assess the Dispositions of Educational Leaders," *Journal of Educational Research & Policy Studies* 8, no. 1 (2008): 92–111; Leithwood et al., *How Leadership Influences Student Learning: Review of Research*.
7. Julia Mahfouz, Mark T. Greenberg, and Amanda Rodriguez, *Principals' Social and Emotional Competence: A Key Factor for Creating Caring Schools* (University Park: Pennsylvania State University, College of Health and Human Development, 2020).
8. Raquel Gómez-Leal et al., "The Relationship Between Emotional Intelligence and Leadership in School Leaders: A Systematic Review," *Cambridge Journal of Education* 52, no. 1 (2022): 1–21.
9. Janet Patti et al., "Developing Socially, Emotionally, and Cognitively Competent School Leaders and Learning Communities," in *Handbook of Social and Emotional Learning: Research and Practice*, edited by J. A. Durlak, C. E. Domitrovich, R. P. Weissberg, and T. P. Gullotta (New York: Guilford Press, 2015), 438–452.
10. Boyatzis, "Managerial and Leadership Competencies."

11. Megan Happ et al., "How We Feel App: Helping Emotions Work for Us, Not Against Us," Yale School of Medicine, Center for Emotional Intelligence, December 2, 2022, https://medicine.yale.edu/news-article/the-how-we-feel-app-helping -emotions-work-for-us-not-against-us/.

12. Tashsa Eurich, "What Self Awareness Is and How to Cultivate It," *Harvard Business Review*, January 4, 2018.

13. Mendemu Showry and K. V. L. Manasa, "Self-Awareness: Key to Effective Leadership," *IUP Journal of Soft Skills* 8, no. 1 (March 2014): 15–26.

14. John D. Mayer, *MSCEIT: Mayer-Salovey-Caruso Emotional Intelligence Test* (Toronto: Multi-Health Systems, 2002).

15. Tasha Eurich, *Insight: The Power of Self-Awareness in a Self-Deluded World* (London: Pan Macmillan, 2017).

16. Nir Eyal, "Here Are the 4 Simple Introspection Steps That Will Boost Self Awareness," *Nir and Far*, https://www.nirandfar.com/introspection.

17. Anthony M. Grant, John Franklin, and Peter Langford, "The Self-Reflection and Insight Scale: A New Measure of Private Self-Consciousness," *Social Behavior and Personality: An International Journal* 30, no. 8 (2002): 821–835.

18. Audrey M. Beauvais, Azize Atli Özbaş, and Kathleen Wheeler, "End-Of-Life Psychodrama: Influencing Nursing Students' Communication Skills, Attitudes, Emotional Intelligence and Self-Reflection," *Journal of Psychiatric Nursing* 10, no. 2 (2019); Fen-Fang Chen, Shu-Yueh Chen, and Hsiang-Chu Pai, "Self-Reflection and Critical Thinking: The Influence of Professional Qualifications on Registered Nurses," *Contemporary Nurse* 55, no. 1 (2019): 59–70; Rick Harrington and Donald A. Loffredo, "Insight, Rumination, and Self-Reflection as Predictors of Well-Being," *Journal of Psychology* 145, no. 1 (2010): 39–57; Rick Harrington, Donald A. Loffredo, and Catherine A. Perz, "Dispositional Mindfulness as a Positive Predictor of Psychological Well-Being and the Role of the Private Self-Consciousness Insight Factor," *Personality and Individual Differences* 71 (2014): 15–18; Lu Liu and Jian Liu, "The Ability and Characteristics of Self-Reflection and Insight in Schizophrenia and Depression Patients," *Chinese Journal of Behavioral Medicine and Brain Science* (2018): 31–34; Jennifer A. Lyke, "Insight, but Not Self-Reflection, Is Related to Subjective Well-Being," *Personality and Individual Differences* 46, no. 1 (2009): 66–70; Joseph Selwyn and Anthony M. Grant, "Self-Regulation and Solution-Focused Thinking Mediate the Relationship Between Self-Insight and Subjective Well-Being Within a Goal-Focused Context: An Exploratory Study," *Cogent Psychology* 6, no. 1 (2019): 1695413, https://doi.org/10.1080 /23311908.2019.1695413.

19. "About Us," Transformative Educational Leadership, https://www.teleadership .org/about.

20. TEL brings together a racially and culturally diverse group (at least 50 percent leaders of color) who are dedicated to creating a more compassionate and

interdependent world. Ultimately, TEL is a beloved community of awakened educational leaders who receive the support and skills necessary to create transformative change in the communities they serve.

21. Interview with Meena Srinivasan, March 11, 2023.

22. James W. Pennebaker and Joshua M. Smyth, *Opening Up by Writing: How Expressive Writing Improves Health and Eases Emotional Pain*, 3rd ed. (New York: Guilford Press, 2016).

23. Amy Morin, "How to Know if Zen Meditation Is Right for You: Benefits, Uses, and Access to the Unconscious," *Very Well Mind*, April 17, 2023, https://www.verywellmind.com/what-is-zen-meditation-4586721.

24. Sonja Matejko, "What's the Background of Mindfulness?," *PsychCentral*, June 13, 2022, https://psychcentral.com/lib/a-brief-history-of-mindfulness-in-the-usa-and-its-impact-on-our-lives#1.

25. Ellen Langer, *Mindfulness* (Boston: Lifelong Books, an imprint of Da Capo Press, 2014); Jerome Anthony Lewis, Zachery M. Himmelberger, and Dean Elmore, "I Can See Myself Helping: The Effect of Self-Awareness on Prosocial Behaviour," *International Journal of Psychology* 56, no. 5 (October 2021): 710–715, https://doi.org/10.1002/ijop.12733.

26. Center for Healthy Minds, University of Wisconsin–Madison (website), https://centerhealthyminds.org/.

27. Valerie Brown and Kirsten Olson, *The Mindful Leader* (Thousand Oaks, CA: Corwin, 2015). Valerie is a practicing follower of Vietnamese master Thich Nhat Hanh and follows the teachings of the Dharma. "Students of Thich Nhat Hanh and Practicing the Plum Village Tradition," http://orderofinterbeing.org/. Kirsten Olson is an alumni of the Harvard Graduate School of Education and an author of numerous books and articles; she works with transformational leadership in schools.

28. Mind & Life Institute (website), https://www.mindandlife.org/.

29. Michelle Kinder, "Why Mindfulness Belongs in the Classroom," *Mindful*, January 25, 2017, https://www.mindful.org/why-mindfulness-belongs-in-the-classroom/.

30. Dr. Froner has brought mindfulness into his 9–12 school. He and his colleague, Dr. Noah Angeles, have received funds from the Gray Foundation to bring mindfulness and deep reflection to New York City principals. Gray Fellows study with Kevin and Noah during a year and a half. They practice mindfulness and receive coaching in emotional intelligence leadership. Dr. Kevin Froner, interview by Janet Patti, September 2022.

31. CRASEL, or Culturally Responsive Affirmative and Social and Emotional Leadership, Harlem Renaissance Education Pipeline, Inc., https://www.hrepinc.org/about-us.

32. *Mapping Police Violence*, Campaign Zero, updated March 31, 2023, https://mappingpoliceviolence.org.

33. Adam Gabbatt, "Homicides Rise Across US Cities Amid Pandemic and Economic Crisis," *Guardian*, August 12, 2020, https://www.theguardian.com/us-news/2020/aug/12/us-stats-latest-pandemic-economic-crisis.

34. Hannah Schoenbaum, "Report Says at Least 32 Transgender People Were Killed in the U.S. in 2022," *PBS NewsHour*, November 16, 2022, https://www.pbs.org/newshour/nation/report-says-at-least-32-transgender-people-were-killed-in-the-u-s-in-2022.

35. Thomas S. Sugrue, "2020 Is Not 1968: To Understand Today's Protests, You Must Look Further Back," *National Geographic*, June 11, 2020, https://www.nationalgeographic.com/history/article/2020-not-1968.

36. Jordan Bell, Karen Zaino, and Yolanda Sealey-Ruiz, "Diggin' in the Racial Literacy Crates," *Equity & Excellence in Education* (2022): 1–14. In 2004, the architect of the concept of racial literacy, Harvard professor Lani Guinier, implored a shift from racial liberalism to racial literacy. She critiqued racial liberalism as an inactive, deficit approach to racial equality that subjugates Black people to the position of victims and does not activate the required anti-racist stance that White people must take against their own racist ideals and actions.

CHAPTER 4

1. Aristotle, *Nicomachean Ethics*, 2.1108b.

2. Snezhana Djambazova-Popordanoska, "Implications of Emotion Regulation on Young Children's Emotional Wellbeing and Educational Achievement," *Educational Review* 68, no. 4 (2016): 497–515; Pablo Fernández-Berrocal and Natalio Extremera, "Ability, Emotional Intelligence, Depression, and Well-Being," *Emotion Review* 8, no. 4 (2016): 311–315; Chris Kyriacou, "Teacher Stress: Directions for Future Research." *Educational Review* 53 (2001): 1–27; John D. Mayer, David Caruso, and Peter Salovey. "The Emotional Intelligence Skill Model: Principles and Updates," *Emotion Review* 8, no. 4 (2016): 290–300.

3. Amy C. Edmondson, "Psychological Safety," https://amycedmondson.com/psychological-safety/.

4. Andrea L. Bell, "What Is Self-Regulation and Why Is It So Important?," *Good Therapy*, September 28, 2016, https://www.goodtherapy.org/blog/what-is-self-regulation-why-is-it-so-important-0928165.

5. Daniel Goleman et al., *Emotional Self-Awareness: A Primer* (Northampton, MA: More Than Sound, 2017).

6. Daniel Goleman, *Emotional Intelligence* (New York: Random House, 2006 [1995]).

7. Kerry J. Ressler, "Amygdala Activity, Fear, and Anxiety: Modulation by Stress," *Biological Psychiatry* 67, no. 12 (2010): 1117–1119.

8. Goleman et al., *Emotional Self-Awareness*.
9. "Mental Illness," National Institute of Mental Health, https://www.nimh.nih.gov /health/statistics/mental-illness.
10. "Mental Illness," National Institute of Mental Health.
11. "Our History," CASEL, https://casel.org/about-us/our-history/#founding.
12. "Our History," CASEL.
13. RULER, Yale University (website), https://www.rulerapproach.org/; "The Responsive Classroom Approach," Responsive Classroom, https://www.responsiveclassroom .org/about/; PATHS Program LLC (website), https://pathsprogram.com; "Social Decision Making," Rutgers University Behavioral Health Care, https://ubhc.rutgers .edu/education/social-decision-making/overview.xml.

CHAPTER 5

1. Dr. Vivek Murthy, "The Devastating Impact of the Epidemic of Loneliness and Isolation in the United States," US Department of Health and Human Services, May 3, 2023, https://www.hhs.gov/about/news/2023/05/03/new-surgeon -general-advisory-raises-alarm-about-devastating-impact-epidemic-loneliness -isolation-united-states.html.
2. Peter Senge et al., "Introduction to Compassionate Systems Framework in Schools," Abdul Latif Jameel World Education Lab, Massachusetts Institute of Technology, Center for Systems Awareness, March 2019, https://jwel.mit.edu /assets/document/introduction-compassionate-systems-framework-schools.
3. CASEL, "Advancing Social and Emotional Learning," www.casel.org.
4. Raquel Gómez-Leal et al., "The Relationship Between Emotional Intelligence and Leadership in School Leaders: A Systematic Review," *Cambridge Journal of Education* 52, no. 1 (2022): 1–21.
5. Deidre Farmbry's letter to the editor was written based on her experiences in the Philadelphia schools.
6. Dan Goleman, "A Sixth Sense for Reading Your Company," *Insights: This Week in Leadership,* Korn Ferry, https://www.kornferry.com/insights/this-week-in -leadership/organizational-awareness-leadership#:~:text=Organizational%20 Awareness%20means%20having%20the,and%20dynamics%20within%20 the%20organization.
7. Gómez-Leal et al., "The Relationship Between Emotional Intelligence and Leadership"; Prakash Singh and Christopher Malizo Dali, "The Value of Empathy as an Instructional Leadership Competency for School Principals," Supplement, *Education as Change* 17, no. S1 (2013): S65–S78.
8. Robin Stern and Diana Divecha, "The Empathy Trap," *Psychology Today*, May 4, 2015, https://www.psychologytoday.com/us/articles/201505/the-empathy-trap.
9. "About Dr. Thomas Gordon," Gordon Training International, https://www .gordontraining.com/thomas-gordon/about-dr-thomas-gordon-1918-2002/.

10. Judith E. Glaser, *Conversational Intelligence: How Great Leaders Build Trust and Get Extraordinary Results* (New York: Routledge, 2014), 80.
11. Glaser, *Conversational Intelligence*, 80.
12. Judith E. Glaser and Ross Tartell, "Conversational Intelligence at Work," *OD Practitioner* 46, no. 3 (2014): 62–67.
13. Glaser, *Conversational Intelligence*, 69–70.
14. Glaser, *Conversational Intelligence*, 69–70.
15. Glaser, *Conversational Intelligence*, 69–70.
16. Mehmet Durnali, Sait Akbaşli, and Okan Diş. "School Administrators' Communication Skills as a Predictor of Organizational Silence," *i.e.: Inquiry in Education* 11, no. 2 (2019): 16.
17. Helen Riess, "Culture of Empathy Builder," Center for Building a Culture of Empathy, http://cultureofempathy.com/references/Experts/Others/Helen-Riess .htm; Helen Reiss, "The Science of Empathy," *Journal of Patient Experience* 4, no. 2 (2017): 74–77.

CHAPTER 6

1. Ann-Marie Nienaber et al., "A Qualitative Meta-analysis of Trust in Supervisor-Subordinate Relationships," *Journal of Managerial Psychology* 30, no. 5 (July 2015): 507–534.
2. Raquel Gómez-Leal et al., "The Relationship Between Emotional Intelligence and Leadership in School Leaders: A Systematic Review," *Cambridge Journal of Education* 52, no. 1 (2022): 1–21.
3. See appendix B for a list of the leadership competencies in the Emotional and Social Competency Inventory.
4. Jung Choi, "The Relationship Between Leadership Styles and Empowerment of Nursing Students," *Journal of Korean Academy of Nursing Administration* 12, no. 2 (2006): 196–203; Anthony Songer, Paul Chinowsky, and Colleen Butler, "Emotional Intelligence and Leadership Behavior in Construction Executives," *Proceedings of the 2nd Specialty Conference on Leadership and Management in Construction* (2006): 248–258.
5. Julie A. Wilson and Ann L. Cunliffe, "The Development and Disruption of Relationships Between Leaders and Organizational Members and the Importance of Trust," *Leadership* 18, no. 3 (2022): 359–382.
6. Editorial Team of LEAD, "10 Brené Brown Quotes to Inspire Success and Happiness at Work," *Indeed*, August 9, 2016, https://www.indeed.com/lead/10-brene -brown-quotes.
7. Megan Tschannen-Moran and Wayne K. Hoy, "A Multidisciplinary Analysis of the Nature, Meaning, and Measurement of Trust," *Review of Educational Research* 70, no. 4 (2000): 556; Megan Tschannen-Moran, "What's Trust Got to Do with It? The Role of Faculty and Principal Trust in Fostering Student Achievement"

(paper presented at the annual meeting of the University Council for Educational Administration, Kansas City, Missouri, November 2004).

8. This description of leadership is from the Future Leaders Institute. Spencer believed that men were products of their environment. Newspaperport, "The Great Man Theory of Leadership," Future Leadership Institute, August 19, 2014, https://fli.institute/2014/08/19/the-great-man-theory-of-leadership/.

9. See Judy B. Roesener, "Ways Women Lead," *Harvard Business Review*, November–December 1990: "[Women] are succeeding because of—not in spite of—certain characteristics generally considered to be "feminine" and inappropriate in leaders . . . women encourage participation, share power and information, enhance other people's self-worth, and get others excited about their work. All these things reflect their belief that allowing employees to contribute and to feel powerful and important is a win-win situation—good for the employees and the organization."

10. Paul Hersey and Kenneth H. Blanchard, "Situational Leadership," in *The Leader's Companion: Insights on Leadership Through the Ages*, edited by J. Thomas Wren (New York: Free Press, 1995), 207–211; Paul Hersey and Kenneth H. Blanchard, "Leadership Style: Attitudes and Behaviors," *Training & Development Journal* 36, no. 5 (1982): 50–52.

11. James R. Bailey, "The Best Managers Are Leaders—and Vice Versa," *Harvard Business Review*, September 22, 2022, https://hbr.org/2022/09/the-best-managers -are-leaders-and-vice-versa.

12. Ralph Nader, "Acceptance Statement of Ralph Nader for the Association of State Green Parties Nomination for President of the United States," Denver, CO, June 25, 2000, https://www.4president.org//speeches/nader2000acceptance .htm.

13. Kim Parker and Juliana Menasce Horowitz, "Majority of Workers Who Quit a Job in 2021 Cite Low Pay, No Opportunities for Advancement, Feel Disrespected," Pew Research Center, March 9, 2022, https://www.pewresearch.org/fact-tank/2022/03 /09/majority-of-workers-who-quit-a-job-in-2021-cite-low-pay-no-opportunities -for-advancement-feeling-disrespected/.

14. David Colker, "Warren Bennis Dies at 89; USC Professor Was Expert on Leadership," *Los Angeles Times*, August 2, 2014, https://www.latimes.com/local /obituaries/la-me-warren-bennis-20140803-story.html.

15. Songer et al., "Emotional Intelligence and Leadership Behavior."

16. Bernard M. Bass, "Leadership: Good, Better, Best," *Organizational Dynamics* 13, no. 3 (1985): 26–40.

17. Ralph M. Stogdill, *Handbook of Leadership: A Survey of Theory and Research* (New York: Free Press, 1974).

18. Raymond B. Cattell, "The Description of Personality: I—Foundations of Trait Measurement," *Psychological Review* 50, no. 6 (1943): 559.

19. Rensis Likert, *The Human Organization: Its Management and Values* (New York: McGraw-Hill, 1967); Gary Yukl, "Toward a Behavioral Theory of Leadership," *Organizational Behavior and Human Performance* 6, no. 4 (1971): 414–440.

20. Mehmet Bellibaş et al., "Does School Leadership Matter for Teachers' Classroom Practice? The Influence of Instructional Leadership and Distributed Leadership on Instructional Quality," *School Effectiveness & School Improvement* 32, no. 3 (2021): 387–412, https://www.doi.org/10.1080/09243453.2020.1858119.

21. Please refer to appendix B.

22. Izhak Berkovich and Ori Eyal, "Educational Leaders and Emotions: An International Review of Empirical Evidence 1992–2012," *Review of Educational Research* 85, no. 1 (2015): 129–167; Shane Connelly and Janaki Gooty, "Leading with Emotion: An Overview of the Special Issue on Leadership and Emotions," *Leadership Quarterly* 26, no. 4 (2015): 485–488; Janet B. Kellett, Ronald H. Humphrey, and Randall G. Sleeth, "Empathy and Complex Task Performance: Two Routes to Leadership," *Leadership Quarterly* 13, no. 5 (2002): 523–544; Rashimah Rajah, Zhaoli Song, and Richard D. Arvey, "Emotionality and Leadership: Taking Stock of the Past Decade of Research," *Leadership Quarterly* 22, no. 6 (2011): 1107–1119.

23. Howard M. Weiss and Russell Cropanzano, "Affective Events Theory," *Research in Organizational Behavior* 18, no. 1 (1996): 1–74.

24. Kenneth Thomas and Ralph Kilmann, "Thomas-Kilmann Conflict Mode," *TKI Profile and Interpretive Report* 1, no. 11 (2008).

CHAPTER 7

1. Kenneth Leithwood, Jingping Sun, and Randall Schumacker, "How School Leadership Influences Student Learning: A Test of 'The Four Paths Model,'" *Educational Administration Quarterly* 56, no. 4 (2020): 570–599.

2. Kenneth Leithwood et al., *How Leadership Influences Student Learning: Review of Research* (New York: Wallace Foundation, 2004); Jason A. Grissom, Anna J. Egalite, and Constance A. Lindsay, *How Principals Affect Students and Schools* (New York: Wallace Foundation, 2021).

3. Marc Brackett, *Permission to Feel: Unlocking The Power of Emotions to Help Our Kids, Ourselves, and Our Society Thrive* (New York: Celadon Books, an imprint of Macmillan, 2019).

4. Terry R. Bacon, *The Elements of Power: Lessons on Leadership and Influence* (New York: AMACOM Books, 2011).

5. Bacon, *Elements of Power.*

6. Bryan Robinson, "Remote Work Is Here To Stay and Will Increase into 2023, Experts Say," *Forbes*, February 1, 2022, https://www.forbes.com/sites/bryanrobinson/2022/02/01/remote-work-is-here-to-stay-and-will-increase-into-2023-experts-say/?sh=215aa9da20a6.

7. New York City Department of Education, "A School Without Walls," https://aschoolwithoutwalls.org/.

8. Vanessa Urch Druskat and Steven B. Wolff, "Building the Emotional Intelligence of Groups," *Harvard Business Review*, March 2021, https://hbr.org/2001/03/building-the-emotional-intelligence-of-groups.

9. "Team Emotional Intelligence Survey Accreditation," EI World, https://www.eiworld.org/courses/team-emotional-intelligence-survey-accreditation/.

10. Urch Druskat and Wolff, "Building the Emotional Intelligence of Groups."

11. Urch Druskat and Wolff, "Building the Emotional Intelligence of Groups."

12. Jon Blistein, "BTS Announce Hiatus as They Open Up About Recent Struggles: 'We've Lost Our Direction,'" *Rolling Stone*, June 14, 2022, https://www.rollingstone.com/music/music-news/bts-hiatus-announcement-1367882/.

13. Jasmine Washington and Leah Campano, "Here's What Each BTS Member Plans to Do During Their Hiatus," *Seventeen*, updated June 15, 2023, https://www.seventeen.com/celebrity/music/g40310892/bts-hiatus-plans/bout.

14. Ann Silvers, "Brene Brown Vulnerability Definitions and Quotes with Images," *Ann Silvers, MA*, https://annsilvers.com/blogs/news/brene-brown-vulnerability-definition-and-quotes.

15. Patrick Lencioni, *The Five Dysfunctions of a Team* (San Francisco: Jossey-Bass, 2002), 187–190.

16. Patrick M. Lencioni, *The Ideal Team Player: How to Recognize and Cultivate the Three Essential Virtues* (John Wiley & Sons, 2016), 157–158.

17. Allison Holzer, *Dare to Inspire* (Boston: Lifelong Books, an imprint of Da Capo Press, 2019), 261–262.

18. Allison Holzer, *Dare to Inspire*, 24.

19. Mike Pegg, "M is for Robert Muller: His Work on Building a Better World," *Positive Encourager*, June 25, 2022, https://www.thepositiveencourager.global/robert-mullers-work-to-build-a-positive-planet.

CHAPTER 8

1. Courtney Martin was a twenty-five-year-old budding writer at the time. Together we wrote our first manual: Janet Patti, Robin Stern, Courtney Martin, and Marc Brackett, *The STAR Factor Emotional Literacy Coaching Manual* (New York: STAR Factor, 2005). Courtney is an American feminist, author, speaker, social and political activist, and author of four books. Her most recent book is *Learning in Public: Lessons for a Racially Divided America from My Daughter's School* (New York: Little, Brown, 2021).

2. Consortium for Research in Emotional Intelligence in Organizations (website), https://www.eiconsortium.org/.

3. Lee Mitgang, *Perspectives—The Making of the Principal: Five Lessons in Leadership Training* (New York: Wallace Foundation, 2012).

4. Mónica Byrne-Jiménez and Margaret Terry Orr, "Thinking in Three Dimensions: Leadership for Capacity Building, Sustainability, and Succession," *Journal of Cases in Educational Leadership* 15, no. 3 (2012): 33–46.

5. Howard Gardner, *Multiple Intelligences: The Theory in Practice, A Reader* (New York: Basic Books, 1993).

6. Christie Brungardt, "The Intersection Between Soft Skill Development and Leadership Education," *Journal of Leadership Education* 10, no. 1 (Winter 2011): 1–22.

CHAPTER 9

Epigraph: Elizabeth A. Solomon, "Organizational Awareness: Systems Thinking with Emotional Intelligence," *New Realm*, May 12, 2021, https://newrealmcoaching .com/blog-1/organizational-awareness-systems-thinking-with-emotional -intelligence.

1. Simon Sinek, "How Great Leaders Inspire Action," filmed September 16, 2009, in Newcastle, Washington, TED video, 17:48, https://www.ted.com/talks/simon _sinek_how_great_leaders_inspire_action?language=en.

2. CASEL, *10 Years of Social and Emotional Learning in U.S. School Districts: Elements for Long-Term Sustainability of SEL*, CASEL, November 2021, https://casel.org/cdi -ten-year-report/?view=true.

3. Maurice J. Elias, PhD, Rutgers Social-Emotional and Character Development Lab (www.secdlab.org), is coauthor of *Emotionally Intelligent Parenting: How to Raise a Self-Disciplined, Responsible Socially Skilled Child* (New York: Three Rivers Press, 1999).

4. "What Is Systems Change?," Academy for Systems Change, https://Academy forchange.org/about-the-academy/.

5. Scharmer is also the cofounder of the Presencing Institute. He chairs the MIT IDEAS program for cross-sector innovation. Scharmer is the author or coauthor of several relevant books that add to our conversation about self-awareness.

6. Otto Scharmer, "COVID, Climate, and Consciousness: How to Reimagine Our Civilization" (presentation at the 2020 Integral European Conference, May 27–31, 2020), https://integraleuropeanconference.com/2020/07/29/community-voting -announcing-best-keynote-and-presentations/.

7. "Comer School Development Program," Child Study Center, Yale School of Medicine, https://medicine.yale.edu/childstudy/services/community-and-schools -programs/comer/.

8. The story that follows is part of a trilogy of leadership stories written about three different positions Deidre held during her leadership journeys. Her story of her encounter with outright discrimination in her role as district superintendent speaks to the reality that systemic racism is at the heart of racism's persistence at schools even now—until a brave leader commits to fighting the good fight so that all children thrive.

9. Jason Esposito, principal, Berner Middle School, Massapequa School District.
10. The DESSA (Devereux Student Strengths Assessment) is a tool designed to measure the social and emotional competencies of students in grades K–12. "The Leading Social and Emotional Assessment for K–12," Aperture Education, https://apertureed.com/dessa/.

Acknowledgments

We feel deeply blessed by many people—our teachers, mentors, colleagues, friends, and families, who always inspire us with conversations, support, and collaboration.

We are so grateful to have been guided by our wonderful editor, Shannon Davis, at Harvard Education Press, and her team, Michael Higgins and Anne Noonan, who have worked very hard alongside us in making this book a reality.

We give our deepest gratitude to our colleague, Katie Francis, for her belief in the transformative power of our work and the importance of getting it out there. Thank you for your many hours, days, and weeks of researching, reading, and editing and for the careful and thoughtful feedback you gave us. This book could never have become a reality without you.

Thank you to Dr. Deidre Farmbry, for reading this book in its entirety with a lens toward equity that allowed us to confront our own biases as we wrote. This was a great gift. Deidre, we thank you also for your contribution of stories that give light to the struggles that we face in education due to racial, economic, and social class differences.

A huge thank-you to Courtney Martin who, as a young writer at the time we wrote the first STAR Factor coaching manual, was the power behind getting it done and out there. STAR Factor coaching would not exist today had you not recorded our discussions.

We are grateful to all our teachers and mentors, who came before us and inspired us to set our life course in bringing emotional intelligence to school leaders—from Peter Salovey and John Mayer's writing of the first academic paper and Dan Goleman's early popular book *Emotional Intelligence*, which made the work come alive to us; to Richard Boyatzis and Cary Cherniss, who were always there to answer our questions and provide feedback on our work and their belief in the need for it in education; and to the Consortium for Research in Emotional Intelligence members whose research and insights continue to teach us today; to Peter Senge for deepening our understanding of systems thinking; to our CASEL family and teachers, most especially Linda Lantieri, always our mentor and friend; Maurice Elias, who never said no when we needed his wisdom; and Eileen Rockefeller Growald and Tim Shriver, whose dreams and undying support and leadership made SEL a reality in the US. We are grateful to Shelly Berman, Norris Haynes, Mark Greenberg, Mary Utne O'Brien, David Slyter, the late Joe Zins, and the man whose research and leadership made SEL possible in classrooms around the world, the late Roger Weissberg; to Jonathan Cohen, who brought us together in one of the early institutes at Colombia University; to Allison Holzer, who gave us coaching mentorship and inspiration; to our friend and colleague, professor, and author Marc Brackett, who collaborated with us to bring this work to New York City and who, along with Robin and others, developed the RULER exercises contained in our model; and to David Osher, for all you do to help us learn about what works in the field and for recommending that we write this book.

We are so grateful to all of our colleagues in educational leadership who early on taught us through their stories and support what is possible in education leadership: Jennifer Allen, Bonnie Brown, Mary Butz, Dawn DeCosta, Larry Dieringer, Arthur Foresta, Larrie Hall, Brooke Jackson, Vince Jewel, Marcia Knoll, Laura Kotch, Tony Picciano, Fran Rabinowitz, Rene Townsend, Craig Richards, and many others who crossed our paths.

We extend deep gratitude to the hundreds of aspiring school leaders who studied education leadership at Hunter College with Janet for more than twenty-three years, many of whom now hold leadership positions in New York City schools and beyond. You taught her about the many challenges of teachers that school leaders encounter, the realities of what young people are facing in schools and communities today, and the hopes and fears that you feel as you decide to move from the rank of a teacher to assistant principal, to principal, or to a district-level position.

Deepest gratitude to all of Robin's patients and all students at Columbia Teachers College for sharing your stories, your dreams, and your challenges with her—you have all been her most important teachers. Teaching and learning is always a two-way street. We thank you.

Our heartfelt thanks to the former principals and supporters who helped to frame this work in its initial stage of development because they believed in the power of this work, several who continue to coach for us today: Miriam Klein, Fran Levy, the late Frank Llandro, the late Stuart Sears, Migdalia Torres, and Mark Weiss—and to Bonnie Brown, who intuitively took a chance on us, bringing this work to her principals and their teams before we had built our credibility.

Thank you to all the New York City superintendents who believed in the work and brought us into your districts to embed emotional intelligence into the district's culture and climate: former District 20 superintendent Karina Constantino, District 21 superintendent Isabel Di Mola, former District 31 superintendent Anthony Lodico, former District 2 superintendent Bonnie LaBoy, District 25 superintendent Danielle Di Mango, District 10 superintendent Maribel Hulla, former District 19 superintendent Karen Watts and Deputy Janice Ross, District 26 superintendent Danielle Giunta, former District 27 superintendent Mary Barton, and to those of you who may have moved on to other positions or retirement.

Deepest thanks to our core group of coaches, who always provide insight to us and create a safe place for reflection for hundreds of New York City school leaders: Steve Appea, Ellen Bergmann, Jann Coles, Diane Da Procida-Sesin, Karla Jackson, Carmen Jimenez, Laurie Kelly, Fran Levy, Sonia Menendez, Phyllis Miller, Laurie Morrison, Elena Rovalino, Jane Sandbank, Philip Santise, Sharon Shapses, Migdalia Torres, Mark Weiss, and Jackie Young

Our heartfelt gratitude to everyone at the Yale Center for Emotional Intelligence, who supported our vision of embedding RULER tools into our leadership coaching. And especially to research scientist James Floman: your commitment to excellence in research continues to help us develop our theory of change-plans for future studies. Thank you, James.

We are grateful for our partnership with the Council of Administrators and Supervisors (CAS), who have embarked on the journey of bringing STAR Factor–trained coaches to New York City. Thank you, former president Mark Cannizzaro and seated president Henry Rubio, and Executive Director Eloise Messineo of the Executive Leadership Institute, the professional development arm of CAS, for your deep wisdom about the role of emotional intelligence in school leadership. And thank you to all the talented principals and supervisors who became coaches after completing their year-long training.

Our thanks to Dr. Kevin Froner and Dr. Noah Angeles, whose vision and perseverance brought our work into the powerful Gray Fellows program for school leaders. You now have your own coaches to provide a safe container for principals' reflection in New York City. Our thanks also to former Hunter College president Jennifer Raab, who supported Kevin and Noah in bringing wellness and coaching work to New York City principals. Thank you, Gray Fellows, for all of your coaches, especially Marisol Fejoo, Alexandra Hernandez, Emaralix Lopez, Katiana Louissant, and Jeneca Parker. Special thanks to Diane Da Procida-Sesin, who helped us beyond what at times seemed humanly possible with STAR Factor trainings and duties that Janet could never have completed while writing this book.

Since the first STAR Factor coaching training, hundreds of dedicated educators have gone through our training and coaching. Others have committed to becoming coaches in their own institutions. We thank you for your belief in us.

But none of the work in New York City would have happened without the insight and vision of former chancellor Carmen Fariña and the systems knowledge and tenacity of Dolores Esposito. Your influence and inspiration have brought this work to New York City districts and schools, where it is fast becoming a part of the culture of everyday life. Thank you.

We both want to thank our wonderful parents, who loved us, cared for us, believed in each of us, and supported our development: Theresa and Bob Chumenti, Candy and Donald Patti, and Roz and Dave Stern. They would be so happy and proud that we are serving children by training people who coach school leaders and teachers.

And of course, always, our personal and deepest gratitude to our families. Janet is grateful to her daughter, Roxana; her husband, Barry; and her sister, Carol, who also coaches; and to Gloria, Casey, and families who continue to inspire her. Robin is grateful to her children, Scott and Melissa; her husband, Mel; and of course Lena; and to her brother and family, Eric, Jacqui, Justin, Chelsea, Daniel, and Julia. Your love and generosity of spirit made it possible for us to dedicate our time to writing surrounded by your loving support, understanding, and wisdom, even when we missed some meals along the way! We are forever yours.

To all of you who have left footprints in our hearts, we are forever grateful.

About the Authors

JANET PATTI, EdD, is professor emeritus of the Hunter College School of Education, where her teaching and research were concentrated on educational leadership, with a concentration on emotional intelligence. Previously, she worked as a bilingual teacher, school counselor, and administrator in New York City and San Diego. She has consulted nationally and internationally, offering training and university presentations. Dr. Patti has written numerous articles and chapters and coauthored two books, *Waging Peace in Our Schools* and *Smart School Leaders*.

Her interest in emotionally intelligent leadership led her to explore the world of coaching as a viable tool for supporting school leaders. She is the cocreator, with Robin Stern, of the STAR Factor coaching model, which is widely used for the professional development of school leaders today.

Janet is a founding member of the Leadership Team of the Collaborative for Academic Social and Emotional Learning (CASEL) and is well regarded for her expertise in the implementation of school-based academic, social, and emotional learning. She is an active member of the Consortium for Research on Emotional Intelligence in Organizations, the International Society for Emotional Intelligence, the Association of

Coaching, and the Institute of Coaching at McLean Hospital, an affiliate of Harvard Medical School.

Currently, she is the chief executive officer of STAR Factor of NYC Inc., a leadership development and coaching organization grounded in the latest science and practice of emotional intelligence. STAR Factor Coaching has been working with leaders, schools, and organizations for more than two decades in New York City and abroad and to date has coached more than five hundred principals and nearly fifty superintendents.

ROBIN STERN, PhD, is the cofounder and senior advisor to the director for the Yale Center for Emotional Intelligence. She is the codeveloper of RULER (an acronym for the five key emotion skills of recognizing, understanding, labeling, expressing, and regulating emotions), an evidence-based approach to social and emotional learning that has been adopted by more than 4,500 schools across the US and in twenty-seven other countries. She is cocreator, with Janet Patti, of the STAR Factor coaching model, a coaching model anchored in emotional intelligence, to support school leaders in their personal and professional development.

Robin is a licensed psychoanalyst with thirty years of experience treating individuals, couples, and families. As a clinician she has been deeply interested in the role of emotions in both leading people to tolerate psychological abuse and the skillful use of emotional intelligence to heal from those relationships. She is a leading authority on gaslighting and the author of *The Gaslight Effect* (translated into 18 languages) and *The Gaslight Effect Recovery Guide*, and she is the host of *The Gaslight Effect Podcast*.

Robin is a cofounder with Marc Brackett, Andrea Hoban, and Matt Kursch, of Oji Life Lab, a digital EI learning system for businesses. Robin regularly consults with hospitals and companies on the application of emotional intelligence in management and leadership, working with individuals and groups. She is a member of the Consortium for Research on Emotional Intelligence, serves on the advisory board for organizations including Crisis Text Line, Think Equal, The Meeting House, and the International Society for Emotional Intelligence.

Most recently, with Marc Brackett, Zorana Pringle at Yale and Pinterest cofounder Ben Silbermann, Robin cocreated How We Feel, a free award-winning app designed to teach emotion skills and enhance well-being. Robin's work is featured in popular media outlets including *Psychology Today, Medium.com, Better.net, The Hill, Time,* and *Harvard Business Review.*

Robin and Janet are committed to helping people in their personal and professional lives to achieve their fullest potential and enhance their well-being and inner spirit through reflection in action and the building of emotional intelligence tools.

Index